Accessing the Classics

Accessing the Classics

Great Reads for Adults, Teens, and English Language Learners

La Vergne Rosow

LIBRARIES

U N L I M I T E D

A Member of the Greenwood Publishing Group

Westport, Connecticut • London

Library of Congress Cataloging-in-Publication Data

Rosow, La Vergne.
  Accessing the classics : great reads for adults, teens, and English language learners /
  by La Vergne Rosow.
       p. cm.
  Includes bibliographical references and index.
  ISBN 1-56308-891-6 (pbk. : alk. paper)
  1. Best books. 2. Best books—United States. 3. Canon (Literature) 4. Readers
for new literates—Bibliography. 5. Reading—Remedial teaching. 6. English
language—Study and teaching—Foreign speakers. I. Title.
Z1035.R825 2006
011'.73—dc22   2005030838

British Library Cataloguing in Publication Data is available.

Library of Congress Catalog Card Number: 2005 030838
ISBN: 1-56308-891-6

First published in 2006

Libraries Unlimited, 88 Post Road West, Westport, CT 06881
A Member of the Greenwood Publishing Group, Inc.
www.lu.com

Printed in the United States of America

The paper used in this book complies with the
Permanent Paper Standard issued by the National
Information Standards Organization (Z39.48-1984).

10 9 8 7 6 5 4 3 2 1

Dedicated to my father
who shared his love of Shakespeare with me
when he was a graduate student
and I was four.

Contents

Acknowledgments

First I wish to remember the ongoing encouragement of Robert Rosow, a pillar of tenacity. Next I wish to acknowledge Barbara Ittner for her determination to find one book among the annotations. And I thank the many teachers and librarians who have given me clues to the classics over the years, and especially to the librarians of the Beaumont, Huntington Beach, Burbank, Los Angeles, and Fountain Valley Libraries. For treks into dark and illuminating stacks, I thank Davis Dutton and his crew, Randy McDonald, Patty and Ren Tanner, and all the gifted folks at Camelot Books; they epitomize the spirit and the power of the independent bookseller. Thanks to colleagues Ellen Davis, Jackie Stark, Rod Moore, and Bill Wallis for opening their personal literature collections. I also want to thank my adult, teen, and preteen students, who showed me how little difference there was among them. Thanks, too, to Michelle Klein-Hass for making computerese make sense, and to David Rose for help with many details.

Introduction

We have all heard proclamations about the literacy crisis in America. In recent years, these proclamations have grown louder. District, state, and national literacy reports tell us that across the land readers are having more and more trouble understanding texts, writers are traumatized by communication challenges, and speakers have difficulty making themselves understood.

The 2004 National Endowment for the Arts (NEA) Survey *Reading at Risk: A Survey of Literary Reading in America*, based on responses from 17,000 adults over 20 years of polling, has delivered some very troubling outcomes (Bradshaw and Nichols 2004). According to NEA Chair Dana Gioia, there has been a steady decline in the reading of literature over the last 20 years, more so among young readers than older members of society. The report also shows that literature reading is reflected in education; "only 14 percent of adults with a grade school education read literature in 2004. By contrast, more than five times as many respondents with a graduate school education—74 percent—read literary works." People who read good books think differently from those who don't, and that thinking is reflected in communication skills. Gioia says, "print culture affords irreplaceable forms of focused attention and contemplation that make complex communications and insights possible. To lose such intellectual capability—and the many sorts of human continuity it allows—would constitute a vast cultural impoverishment." Quality of life and lifestyle are also affected by a person's literary reading habits. "Literary readers are much more likely to be involved in cultural, sports and volunteer activities than are non-readers. For example, literary readers are nearly three times as likely to attend a performing arts event, almost four times as likely to visit an art museum, more than two-and-a-half times as likely to do volunteer or charity work, and over one-and-a-half times as likely to attend or participate in sports activities. People who read more books tend to have the highest level of participation in other activities." Aside from personal benefits, the reading of literature by its citizens has an impact on society in ways that cannot be seen at first blush. In the preface to the report, Gioia points out that, "Reading is not a timeless, universal capability. Advanced literacy is a specific intellectual skill and social habit that depends on a great many educational, cultural, and economic factors. As more Americans lose this capability, our nation becomes less informed, active, and independent-minded. These are not

1

qualities that a free, innovative, or productive society can afford to lose." From the NEA findings, we may conclude that as the developing reader begins to identify books that will help with his or her communication skills, so will that reader be making a deliberate change that will improve society as a whole. What you read matters very much.

Seasoned teachers in institutions of higher learning from the public and private sector are complaining that the writing skills of the general student population are not at the level of students arriving ten or even five years ago. My own college and university students of 15 years ago were familiar with the works of Shakespeare and Aesop, albeit often in another language, albeit sometimes from oral traditions. Many of to-day's newcomers have neither a foundation of storytelling nor a history of reading for pleasure. Those skills must be taught before other learning makes sense. Every day in my reading and English as a second language classes, I rediscover a common element of the nonreader culture, a ten-dency to shy away from fiction, that "nonfunctional" literature they were taught early on had no value. My greatest challenge is to sell these adults and teens on the notion that it is okay to have a good time reading a good book. My greatest reward is when one of them comes back to in-form me that he or she has discovered that it is also beneficial. Weekly, I receive e-mails from would-be teachers, some of whom have dropped out of the traditional university programs for lack of language skills; I am at once relieved and dismayed. Relieved that their attitudes about language and literacy will not be passed on, dismayed that they have lost years of preparation time and are little prepared to face the kinds of read-ing that could make them intellectually whole. When I am able to follow up with telephone or person-to-person interviews, I grapple with how much to say when asked for recommendations. Would it be too shocking to suggest a peek at *Alice in Wonderland* or an afternoon just savoring Doré's illustrations of *Paradise Lost*?

High school teachers and middle school teachers also complain about their respective populations, claiming that each incoming class is less prepared. Playwright Ronnie Cohen, a full-time high school and part-time community college English teacher, is very concerned about the manipulation of terms in lieu of funding for every child. In collegial correspondence he writes "Hello. I was thinking, as many at the high school do, that Honors isn't Honors anymore. Some say that perhaps AP (advanced placement) classes are the new Honors classes, while Honors classes are pretty regular and regular classes tend towards the remedial, if that makes sense." Ever-changing academic terms may mask educa-tional shortcomings for a time, but they don't improve the conditions that lead to poor reading skills and limited reading habits.

Freelance writer Evelyn Lager teaches all levels of college English (including the officially separated and designated course in critical thinking) in college districts that serve both the elite, affluent students and the first generation college, financial aid recipients. To her, the problems are the same from one school to the next. In a 2004 letter she says, "Every semester new students delight and confound me by confiding their hope for a future of high achievement—and their expectation that the path to that future begins in our classroom. I'm confounded because each year they arrive less prepared with the basic skills they'll need to travel that path successfully. They are poorer at reading, writing, speaking, and reasoning. They are poorer in understanding how long and hard they'll need to work. Each semester I feel more painfully balanced on a razor's edge: Blunt truths risk discouraging worthy ambition, while diplomatic words endorse false certainty that self-esteem, unlike virtue, is a guarantor of rewards both material and educative."

Brian Alan Yablon, community college adjunct and English teacher at a math-science magnet middle school, has witnessed a downward spiral in both college and middle school student performance. He says, " Over the course of the last fifteen years, I have noticed a general lessening or deterioration in the level of skills for students entering middle and high schools. Compared to fifteen years ago, students generally do not read as fluently, do not comprehend as much of what they've read, and write rather poorly. To address the 'flat' SAT scores and poor language skills, schools/districts have instituted regimented, 'teacher-proof' systems such as Open Court and have infused the curriculum with Standards (which is this generation's swing of the educational pendulum). The problems and solutions, however, lie in a different arena: teacher preparation, parent participation, manageable classrooms (size, materials, facilities), and economic equity. These are complex issues. Because students watch TV or play videogames or cannot listen to their parents read stories—lack of time—skills have gone down" (informal discussion, 2004). Note that Open Court, rather than fostering spontaneous language use in the academic environment, scripts exactly what the teacher is supposed to say to the students. Chillingly, my education students at Los Angeles Valley College report that in their teacher interviews, while more seasoned teachers are frustrated by the restrictions placed on them by Open Court, the newer teachers are starting to appreciate not having to think about planning or even what to say to the children in their classes.

Skills have gone down. So has familiarity with the common base of literature that once gave us a foundation from which to speak. When someone refers to Hercules or The Boy Who Cried Wolf or even Peter Pan, many are at a loss as to the implications. An understanding of idiomatic expressions and literary references that once facilitated communication has also gone down. A person might once have wailed

"Tomorrow and tomorrow and tomorrow," rightfully expecting that a world of meaning had been delivered. No longer. The growing diversity in the American population complicates the issue. That's a given. Yet, even if it might be possible to lay the blame on the underprepared learners, their teachers, their parents, or their socioeconomic conditions, laying blame won't help. But that doesn't mean we, as educators, can't help.

Though the reasons for our problems are complex and political, the solutions are within reach, for anyone who can speak any language, at any age. That's what this book is about. It's underlying premise is that given proximity to the right books, an understanding of what causes literacy to develop, and motivation to effect change in their own lives, all readers can expect to get better at reading, writing, and speaking, and all readers can develop the sophisticated interest in classics that those fortunate children who grow up with them do: that sophisticated interest now categorized as critical thinking.

Today many schools spend a great deal of learning time and financial resources on improving test-taking strategies, strategies for taking tests that depend more on accurate circle-filling than on content. Some so-called reading tests completely overlook what the research suggests are good reader strategies and often employ contrived passages, short passages taken out of context, or just lists of words in isolation, thereby sending puzzling messages to teachers, students, and others who expect that what we test is what is we believe is important. The challenge is to help those who have received perhaps years of these misleading messages—but who don't understand they've been misled.

Some writing tests completely ignore what educators have known about the writing process for a very long time. They assign test takers irrelevant topics to respond to in fixed time frames that make revision—a critical cognitive approach to organization—impossible. That sends the message to many that only the first draft counts. That wrong message must be refuted.

Adults and teens who don't fully comprehend text, who lack writing skills, or who shrink from speaking situations, already know they have problems. They don't and never did need tests to tell them. What they do need is a great deal of quality *input*. Input is what goes into the brain. When we read or listen, we get input.

Research has shown again and again that we learn to read by reading. Frank Smith, in *Understanding Reading* (2004) and *Insult to Intelligence* (1986), spelled that out for us decades ago. And the more we read, the faster we read and the more we comprehend. But we need to read the right stuff.

We also learn to write by what we read. Steve Krashen has compiled countless studies that document that (see., e.g., Krashen 2004). Richard Allington and Donald Graves have confirmed the findings over and again (see, e.g., Allington 1991; Graves 2003). We know that what we read matters very much.

We also learn vocabulary and language skills from what we read. Richard Allington (1991), Jeff McQuillan (1998), and Lucy Tse (Krashen, Tse, and McQuillan 1998) have done numerous studies proving this. Readers can acquire thousands of words a year—just by reading for pleasure. That means writers and speakers (writing and speaking are *output* of what is already in the brain) will have more words to allow precise language to flow from the pen or roll off the tongue. Reading books with new words provides the input needed to write and speak more effectively.

So, reading a lot of the right stuff will, in and of itself, cause reading improvement, writing precision, and speaking confidence. All without drills and direct study.

However, simply telling students to read a lot so that they will be able to read, write, and speak well is not enough. Explaining that they will appreciate literary allusions, will be able to employ appropriate metaphors, and will sound at once clear and sophisticated when they become well-read is insufficient. Students—all humans—must enjoy reading before they will practice, before they *can* practice enough to make an impact on their reading, writing, or speaking.

The purpose of this book is to help those who work with readers, writers, and new language learners—reading specialists, classroom teachers, librarians, literacy volunteers, homeschoolers— support any reader, at any level, in the quest to improve reading comprehension and related language arts skills. This book presents carefully selected titles that engage readers and lead them to more complex writings, writings that have echoed in educated minds and among well-read speakers for eons. Through the books in this guide, readers can "hear" the voices of those who have struggled ahead of them, people who have prevailed in the quest for reading, writing, and speaking prowess. Many of the authors in this guide have in their autobiographies told their own stories about literacy failures and overcoming related obstacles. (Indeed, more than a few award-winning authors were unsuccessful in school.) At the start of each collection, a biographical summary reveals whether this writer was given an understanding of the classics as a birthright or whether, by some unseen hand, the writer was driven to read more and understand more than the pedestrians in whose midst he or she walked. We learn to write by what we read. So it was as these authors read. So it will be as our students read from the titles offered here.

> *When you read a classic you do not see in the*
> *book more than you did before. You see more in* you
> *than there was before.*
> —Clifton Fadiman, *Any Number Can Play*

Purpose, Scope, and Audience—Why This Book

Why classics? Every day there are newspaper ads, TV wisecracks, political comparisons, and sobering stories that employ one or two literary allusions requiring a connection between a classical literary scene and a contemporary situation. The classics contain a history of our spoken and written language. They provide the foundation for all subsequent literature: from tragic figures, who are destined to repeat the past mistakes of humanity, to comic buffoons, who mix metaphors in a way that makes them appear inept. The language user who is grounded in the classics is bound to both enjoy language-related activities and employ the literary techniques already worked out by past masters. The more we know of the classics, the better prepared we are to enjoy sophisticated contemporary literature and language—and to use it for our own purposes. Brazilian educator Paulo Freire strove to provide his students with the power of words, words that would give them the vision required to change their lives and times. People who have read the classics have more interesting, richer, fuller lives than those who have not. They comprehend the world in a different way. And that opens doors. Intellectually . . . spiritually . . . academically.

The titles annotated in this guide provide reading support for the underprepared teen or adult who cannot read English text well enough to satisfy his or her everyday needs, or who feels uncomfortable when faced with writing tasks, or who wants to improve his or her reading skills, or who lacks the words to speak clearly and effectively in public or private. Here is a path for the person who is struggling to learn independently or the one who wants to go on to the challenges of the GED, community college, or university.

The primary purpose of this book is to support and guide the reader, readers' advisor, librarian, teacher, homeschooler, tutor, parent, social worker, scout leader, community center head, book club leader, and others who want to foster language and literacy skills among teens and adults who are upgrading their reading and English language skills. The librarian may use this guide to help literacy volunteers, teachers, and self-help group leaders find appropriate readings. Appropriate readings offer readers high-interest, easy-to-comprehend books, thereby fostering the reading practice essential to all language arts skills, while introducing the classical names and titles that mark the line between the educated and the passive learner.

While many of the classics annotated in this guide offer easy-to-read passages in formats that foster pleasure for the uninitiated, the challenge is to keep pushing the reader (and helping the reader learn how to push himself or herself) to read a broader range of materials and to read more difficult texts. The broad reading helps develop background knowledge needed for general reading success. The deeper reading, as it is called, helps the reader experience and develop more sophisticated vocabulary and language in a single field. Both kinds of reading will assist the reader with lifelong literacy. The latter will be particularly helpful to the person who wants to attempt academic study. The independent reader has power. An informed, independent reader is the goal.

The focus of this book is on "classics"—that is, literature that has withstood the test of time. Some of these classics date back to early civilizations when stories were related orally; others were written in the modern era. Many of these works have been critically acclaimed, or are award winners; others only received recognition long after their original publication. Emphasis here is on novels, but nonfiction works, plays, poetry, short stories, and even picture books are also included, particularly when they lend support to understanding and accessing classic literature. As we read beautifully written messages, so do we learn how to write them and so do they become ours for verbal expression.

> *Life being very short, and the quiet hours of it few, we ought to waste none of them in reading valueless books.*
> —John Ruskin, *Sesame and Lilies*

Adult and Teen Readers—Identified

There are many obstacles for those who serve teen and adult readers. The diversity of the groups—cultural backgrounds, age, levels of reading sophistication and abilities, reading tastes, motivations, literacy habits, or attitudes—all can influence which book should be pulled from the shelf.

The adult and teen readers this book will help are those who are seeking simple but intellectually engaging reads and ways of moving up to more challenging texts. They are also expecting the books they read to help them learn something of value. These adult and teen readers may include

- those learning to read and those working to become better readers;

- readers who are successful in their day-to-day lives, but who, having decided to return to school, find their educational background, reading, and writing skills are no longer up to academic rigors;

- ESL learners, those who are learning how to speak, read, and write English as a second language (and sometimes as a third, forth, or fifth language); literacy in the first language varies widely; and

- those who may have once had a strong command of written and spoken English, but who have lost their ability to use language through stroke or head injury.

> *He knew everything about literature except how to enjoy it.*
> —Joseph Heller, *Catch 22*

Four Myths About Developing Readers

Myths about developmental level readers are so plentiful it would be impossible to list them all. Among the most damaging are these:

- **Developing readers can't read long books.** Although long books may well be intimidating to look at, and small print is hard on the eyes of anyone over 14, new readers may find fascinating reads within thick books. That can be facilitated by a caring tutor who reads aloud, by an audio recording, by focusing on selections within the book, or by leading up to the long book by reading many smaller ones on related topics that build both background knowledge and relevant vocabulary. Reading a long book is the *only way* to learn how a long text is organized.

- **Developing readers are not very intelligent**. Many bright children are confronted with anti-literacy environments during the time when they should be learning to love reading. Children who reach fourth grade without knowing how to read are destined to have some extremely unhappy school experiences. That, in turn, can create a downward spiral that fosters a fear of literacy-related activity, fear that can last a lifetime. Teens or adults who are in this situation are not less intelligent than they were before entering school. They just can't read and write well. Given the right books and nurturing, anyone who could speak a language, any language, by the age of five has enough brain power to do anything.

(Of course, the more they read, the more words they will know. And the more words they know, the higher their IQ scores will be.)

- **Developing readers are lazy**. Fear of books and writing can be misinterpreted as an unwillingness to work. While the nonreader may have developed all manner of literacy avoidance strategies, some of which seem antisocial, laziness is not a strategy.

- **Developing readers have no hope after the age of seven**. It is never too early to begin literacy exposure. It is never too late to start. When motivation is present, literacy and language development are possible.

The art of reading is to skip judiciously.
—Philip Gilbert Hamerton,
Intellectual Life

Motivating Readers

In my work with adults and teenagers from the United States and many other countries, I have discovered that the person's motivation has a lot to do with what reading material interests the individual and what topics will best serve that individual's needs. The reasons teen and adult readers want to improve may be clearly stated, may be vague, or may be related to affective issues too sensitive to be articulated. There are numerous reasons why a person wants to get better at reading in English. Here are some that my students have given:

- To read to a child

- To help a child become a reader

- To help a child with school work

- To create a literate home environment

- To make their children or grandchildren proud

- To make their parents or grandparents proud

- To impress a sweetheart

- To read to an elderly or visually impaired person

- To become a better writer

- To learn to write business letters

- To move ahead or change jobs

- To hone academic reading skills
- To build background knowledge
- To use English in school
- To use English in day-to-day life
- To use English when traveling
- To read for pleasure in English
- To read in English for information
- To participate in Internet activities
- To write letters to loved ones
- To translate from one language to another
- To communicate better with extended family members
- To communicate better in day-to-day transactions
- To gain independence
- To be able to talk about books with literate associates
- To sound more intelligent when speaking
- To regain the once held, now lost language of literature

Reading more good literature will address all of these issues and more.

Although the four groups of learners mentioned above have many similarities, they are not identical in terms of English language development.

The English-speaking teenager or adult who has grown up in an English-speaking community, but who cannot participate in the literacy activities of that community, may not have been exposed to the fundamental reasons why people read for pleasure. Such individuals have not had a chance to engage in the daily activities that explain why so many children learn to read and write almost automatically and very quickly. Their perceptions about what reading is and why people do it are limited to the *functional* literacy notions. For them, writing well often refers to good penmanship, not getting ideas from the head to the paper. Their perceptions about literacy may very likely be the same as those whose heritage language is not English and who do not read for pleasure. A person who only uses text for functional purposes—like identifying soft drink brands—is limited to what else there is to learn from the functional context (the soft drink package or the ads), regardless of the language used. Indeed, preliterate and low-literate adult perceptions about books and attitudes regarding writing are very much alike all over the world.

Likewise, avid readers and literate adults are very much alike all over the world. They know that reading for pleasure (in any language) expands vocabulary and increases background knowledge without effort. So, for those who are already literate in one or more languages and are simply working on improving their English, there is a great need for finding books to read that are both interesting and easy enough to read independently.

Those who have had language abilities but have lost them due to stroke or head injury may still "hear" the words in their heads but may not be able to call out the words they need. Or they may know the meaning but not be able to think of the right word as they speak or write—even though they once had a strong command of the language. For them, being read *to* and hearing books on tape may be both pleasurable and beneficial.

The "Suggestions for Use" section of this introduction gives more specific recommendations for identifying the reader's needs. New or improving readers and new or improving learners of English both need help finding good books. This book is designed to help their advisors guide them.

> *Read the best books first, or you may not have a*
> *chance to read them at all.*
> —Henry David Thoreau,
> *A Week on the Conrad and Merrimack Rivers*

Selection Criteria for Books Included Here

The books annotated in this volume are selected based on a number of criteria, some of which were essential, and others that were simply desirable. All of the titles share the following criteria:

- **Authentic literature**—These are books written to be enjoyed by readers from the general population. As they wrote, the authors focused on the story—not word lists or sentence length. They wrote in a way that told the story best—not directed by a formula. This applies to original works of literature and popular myths taken from an oral tradition and written down for posterity. There are also works so filled with archaic language that they cannot be read with ease by modern speakers of English and so have been retold to serve the needs of today's popular readers. *Note:* Beyond those just mentioned, there are some very well written retold tales; in such cases, they are so identified and a rationale is given. They, too, were written for general audiences.

- **Classics**—These books and stories have withstood the test of time.

- **Books**—Although magazines, online journals, and some newspapers contain well-written, well-edited stories, some of which have become classics, only books are annotated here, making access to the texts easy. *Note:* Some stories presented in book format here have also enjoyed publication in magazines or other periodicals.

- **Pleasure**—This author or her students have found these titles to be good reading. Although no attempt has been made to present a comprehensive presentation of all books categorized as classics, the ones that are here may be considered very good reads.

In addition, when selecting titles, the following qualities were considered:

- **Illustrations of merit**—Either enchanting or informing, the illustrations are a treat unto themselves and support comprehension or extend the information delivered by text. The captions accompanying drawings or photographs must be clear and informative, providing scaffolding for reading more solid text areas.

- **Good writing models**—Beautifully written prose at once shows the reader how fine writing sounds and how long texts are organized. Most, but not all, will have praiseworthy, if not award-winning, language—models for the reader's own writing.

- **Cultural literacy**—Some very good books should be read by everyone—whether they want to or not—because they have greatly influenced our language and culture.

- **Educational content**—These books upport academic study, building background knowledge for less supportive texts encountered later, or providing useful information that the reader can apply to life situations. They may extend understanding of other times, places, and people. They include the well-researched fiction or nonfiction book that provides the reader with clear notes for support, a useful bibliography, a clear chronology for quick reference, or an index that makes it easy to find things again. Such features in pleasure reading are a fine way of showing some features a research paper is supposed to have—thereby modeling the value of this perhaps seemingly redundant information.

- **Brevity**—The book is either a short book, a longer book with short chapters or passages, or a book of passages that do not rely on specific prior knowledge for comprehension—a book that can be opened anywhere and read.

- **Compelling novels and well-told tales**—These stories compel readers to keep on going and teach readers how a long piece of literature is organized.

- **Memorable characters that readers can identify with and learn from**—These characters may appear in modern references. Oliver Twist comes to mind. So does Tiny Tim. And Scrooge.

- **Promotes reading**—Some fiction writers have a recurring literacy theme, having characters solve problems by reading or based on things read. Some writers blatantly attribute their success to library access. Some writers attribute their survival to books.

- **Bilingual edition**—This may be a modern text in the language first written and a modern English language translation, an ancient or archaic text translated line for line or passage by passage, or an ancient text with modern interpretation.

- **Retellings and reinterpretations**—These may be reinterpretations of old tales using a new format (play to prose or vice versa); old tales using modern English; new tellings of popular folktales with updated language; or tales presented in a simpler format, such as a readers' theatre interpretation of a pivotal passage.

- **Visual clarity**—This is achieved either through large print, a clear font, white space (through generous leading between lines and wide margins), or the placement of a few lines of print per page.

- **Pleasant format and binding**—The size and weight are inviting, making it pleasant to look at or to hold. Lightweight hardbound editions can be very pleasant to carry about or read in bed. Pages feel nice, increasing the pleasure of the reading experience.

- **Affordability**—These are editions that may not be as desirable as others annotated in the same collection, but they are available at a cost that is favorable to a small budget. These are of particular interest to the person who has read an expensive library edition but wants to have a reference copy for his or her personal collection. It is also helpful to the person who is attempting to build a new library collection quickly.

- **Accessibility**—Editions selected for this collection came from sources that are accessible to the general public. Where out-of-print editions have been annotated, they are available on library shelves, can be found readily in used bookstores, or are available online. In the event that a hard-to-locate edition is mentioned, alternatives are suggested.

And finally, titles were considered in context, according to the following criteria:

- Books by authors of multiple titles—Because finding a favorite author is one good reader indicator, some authors are included because they offer readers a chance to find more books in the same style.

- Fit into a collection of authentic titles with similar vocabulary and sentence structure, thereby supporting broad reading practice.

- Fit into a collection of titles, either within a topic that fosters reading books with increasingly more difficult language, thereby scaffolding literacy and language development; or building background knowledge and related basic vocabulary so that longer books on the same topic become accessible.

- Fit into a collection of titles within a topic.

- Extend collection diversity—The books provide a broad range of cultural and ethnic perspectives, broadening the reader's understanding of unfamiliar lifestyles and value systems.

- Classic example—These books help to illustrate what makes exemplary books remain popular generation after generation.

New books are published all the time, and some become hard to find almost immediately. Also, the habits and preferences of developing readers can call for innovation. A reader who enjoys a particular writer's style or illustrator's work may be directed toward new titles by that person, for example. The readers' advisor (RA) may want to use these criteria to select other titles.

All books are divisible into two classes, the books of the hour, and the books of all time.
—John Ruskin,
Sesame and Lilies

Organization of This Book

The titles in this book are organized into five broad chronological chapters, moving from ancient literature through medieval and renaissance texts, to romantic and Victorian age literature, to books from the modern era. Within the chapters, titles are grouped around primary classic authors, alphabetically arranged. The exceptions to this format are the ancient myths and literature of the Middle Ages, which, because authorship is generally unknown, are arranged alphabetically under geographical headings in the first chapter and topical headings in the second. The abbreviations B.C.E (before the common era) and C.E. (of the common era) are used rather than B.C. and A.D.

Under each author, users will find titles categorized sequentially according to reading level. This approach is meant to give readers a chance to enter the texts at various points of proficiency and then build on that. Rather than an age or grade rating, this guide uses a process approach to accessing the literature. For reprinted titles, the reprint date appears first, with the original publication date in parentheses following it.

> *Most of the basic material a writer works with*
> *is acquired before the age of fifteen.*
> —Willa Cather, quoted in
> Rene Rapin, *Willa Cather*

Traditional Age Rating

Although age ratings may be useful in traditional educational settings, they do not serve the users of this guide well. Because of the need to provide scaffolding, a building up of abilities through increasingly more challenging texts, and because of the need to develop strong literate attitudes quickly that evolve over decades in literate homes, the books here tap into many categories for the needs of the developing older reader of English. Although a love of books is surely fostered by being read to in a loving person's lap, so too is it fostered by pictures that thrill the senses with colors and imagery. Part of this quick introduction to classics provides the visual delights enjoyed by the advantaged early reader.

For example, a biography targeted to young readers may skip some adult content about that person's life; but the reader may still expect to acquire a great deal of background knowledge and information, from both the text and the illustrations, that will support and lead to more challenging biographies. At the same time, that illustrated book is one the adult or teen can then read to younger members of the family, thereby passing on a well told tale and a culture of literacy. So, the titles here are not rated according to age, although, where extreme content or language is concerned, the annotations attempt to forewarn.

Instead of the traditional ratings, the approach we employ in this guide reflects a process, as follows:

START HERE!	This indicates a book that is easy to read, either because the pictures and words work together, there is very little text per page, there are very few pages, the author scaffolds information about challenging words, or the context supports the language effectively. This designation means that of all the books shown on this topic, this will be one the adult new reader or new learner of English will be able to navigate with the least amount of frustration. Or this may be a book that has such sensational pictures it is worth just looking at for the pleasure and information that will emerge from them.
NEXT READ	Titles that are slightly more challenging than the START HERE! books fall into this category. Readers who have successfully navigated titles in the START HERE! category, or readers with more proficiency, will want to read these books.
SUPPORT HERE	These books may have challenging text, but the text is supported by very short passages, large print, lots of helpful pictures, other books in the same section, or an audio recording. Some of the books in this category have internal support through detailed illustrations or sidebars that explain what is going on in more detail. The specific type of support available is mentioned in the annotation.

CHALLENGING READ	These are good books that are best if *read to* the adult new reader or English learner, but which he or she will eventually want to go back to for independent reading. These titles are more difficult than those in the previous categories, either because the print is smaller, the vocabulary is more sophisticated, the grammatical structures are more complex, or there is not much other reading material suggested to build the background knowledge of the reader. Still, these are good books that appeal to a broad range of readers. The new reader may access this text by listening to an audio recording of the book, watching a movie of the book, or reading the support books in the chapter first, preferably with a tutor or teacher providing support and guidance. Readers want to know about the availability of good books that offer more insights into their areas of interest. Like proficient readers, the new reader may be interested in a short, but highly relevant, passage in a CHALLENGING READ book; some passages are, therefore, identified.

It is understood that reading levels of any kind are just guides. They can never adjust to the vocabulary, background knowledge, schema, interests, or mood of the reader, all of which have a great deal to do with reading comprehension. This book identifies four reading categories based on surface elements of the texts presented. Like other reading levels, they are admittedly text-centered, not reader-centered. Although the levels are provided as a guide to help the reader identify the order in which the annotated books may be read, it is the *reader* who must make the decision about what book to start, what book to finish, and what book to cast aside. That's the power of reading.

> *Just get it down on paper, and then we'll see what to do with it.*
> —Max Perkins to Marcia Davenport

A Word About Preliterate and Low-Literate Teens and Adults

The titles annotated in this guide are appropriate for preliterate learners, those who cannot read or write their own names yet, those who do not understand the concept of the letters of the alphabet, and those who are in need of individualized help (preferably a tutor who can meet with them more than once a week). Though there are years of negative perceptions that need to be overcome, and usually the idea that they cannot read or cannot learn, any adult who can talk can also learn to read and write well.

However, giving the adult that first five years of make-up time—replacing the five years of bedtime stories, background building of cultural literacy, introductions to idiomatic expressions, practice reading the pictures in a book, read-alouds making the sound-symbol connections, and repeatedly discovering the fascinating times that come from books—all of this takes time. So, the tutor of the preliterate adult or teenager needs to stick with that student, not demanding independent learning until these elementary connections are made. Although some preliterate students move ahead at a rapid pace, what they need most is encouragement and support. Just as it does no good to demand that a new babe walk before the legs are solid, it does no good to demand that new readers practice reading before enough input has gone into their heads. Reading aloud to them helps. Talking about pictures helps. Writing down their stories helps. All of that provides literacy input. For more on this. see *In Forsaken Hands: How Theory Empowers Literacy Learners* (Rosow 1995).

> *Literature is strewn with the wreckage of men who have minded beyond reason the opinion of others.*
> —Virginia Woolf,
> *A Room of One's Own*

A Word About Text Avoidance and Vision

As alluded to above, there are many affective reasons why a mature person may avoid looking at text. There are also physical reasons. If adults or teens complain that text jumps around, gets blurry in places, makes them dizzy, or gives them headaches, they may have vision problems. It is one thing to recommend that people get an eye exam, and quite another to support them through it for the purpose of helping them read. Even those who wear glasses may have the above-mentioned complaints. Here are a few points to keep in mind:

- Reading text is different from sewing, jewelry-making, or other close-work tasks. It requires the person to scan whole pages of print while looking at one set of words. Therefore, when the reader goes to the ophthalmologist, he or she should take a book and be ready to show the doctor what distance the book should be for comfort.

- Cost may keep a person in glasses that don't work or out of glasses altogether. The Lions Club organization has a program designed to help people with vision problems.

- Making an appointment can be complicated for non-English speakers or those with limited communication skills. Helping the adult or teen make an appointment and remember to go can make all the difference in helping him or her read. Teachers may help students prepare a list of prospective questions ahead of time to become familiar with doctor–patient protocols, thereby reducing anxiety. Tutors sometimes accompany their students to the doctor.

- Experiments with print size can be rewarding. Showing readers books with various print sizes and asking them to evaluate what is easy on their eyes may prove to them that they can indeed see some print without difficulty. It will also help them understand the value of print examination before checking out a library book. And it fosters decision making.

> *I learn by going where I have to go.*
> —Theodore Roethke, *The Waking*

Rosow Approach to Reading

Reading is key to the good life in a literate society. Avid readers have access to worlds of enjoyment, detailed information, sophisticated writing skills, fulfilling leisure time, and power. Nonreaders don't.

You learn to write by what you read. Therefore, what you read matters very much. Though avid readers intuit this, it is a concept that others need to acquire—or need to be taught. It seems simple, but it flies in the face of the notions that make readers think they must finish every book they start or that nonfiction is more important than fiction. Advising a mature new reader requires a balance between what the reader wants and what he or she needs. One approach to helping the new reader become independent is to share the theoretical concepts behind recommendations. Here are some of the concepts I share when working with adult and teen learners:

• Your time is precious. How you spend your leisure reading time can make a world of difference in your quality of life.

• When you are relaxed and comfortable, you will comprehend more easily, learn more, read faster, and be able to read longer than when you are under stress or are distracted. So, whenever possible, find a comfortable, quiet, well-lit place to read.

• It is better to read things you can read quickly and easily than things that make you struggle through word-by-word. That means it is important to find books at the appropriate level in your topic of interest.

• Pictures help comprehension. When you have a book or story with pictures, it is usually worthwhile to study the pictures and read the captions before reading the book or story.

• Pictures give information. In illustrated historical novels, for example, readers may expect to learn about clothing, furniture, and architecture that is not even mentioned in the text.

• You learn to write by what you read. Reading teaches you everything about writing a final draft that a good writer knows. Spelling, punctuation, grammar, syntax, vocabulary, idioms, metaphors, organization, and writing style are all modeled in everything you read. That's why what you read matters very much. Don't waste your precious reading time on poorly written text.

• Context gives meaning—to words, to phrases, and to ideas. Context is everything around a new word: the sentence, the paragraph, the story, and the pictures. Context is everything around a phrase: the sentence, the paragraph, the story, and the pictures. Context is everything around a sentence: the paragraph, the story, and the pictures. Context is the environment that gives meaning to what is in the environment. It makes the difference between a fish in the ocean, a fish in a bowl, and a fish on a plate. Context uses everything the reader already knows to give meaning to a few words.

• When you learn words in context—that is, from the story that is around them—you automatically learn the meaning of the word as it is used there, and you learn how to use the word—at least in one way. Context gives meaning to words, phrases, and ideas.

• Meaning is key. It is essential to reading, and it is essential to words. Memorization from lists is not the best use of your time. Reading from authentic texts you enjoy is better.

- When you know a word, it gives you a whole world of meaning when you see it. The more words you know, the faster you can read. When you know a word by sight, you will not have to slow down to figure it out. But coming to know it from context—with meaning connected to it—as you read is very different from memorizing it from a meaningless, teacher-centered or publisher-centered list.

- Reader-generated lists are useful. Avid readers often read materials that have words they don't know, but that interest them. They may underline them (never in a library book) or write them on a Post-it™ stuck on the page for further attention. Some later put the words on a new words list or in a personal dictionary. This kind of list is unique and meaningful to one reader. It is reader-centered.

- The more you read, the more you know. Just reading 10 minutes a day can cause you to learn hundreds of words a year and will increase your reading speed. More is better.

- Avid readers have substantial vocabularies. It is possible to grow your vocabulary by 5,000 words a year just from pleasure reading. So, what you read matters.

- Interest is essential. Intelligent people cannot stand to be bored; a bored brain will shut down. That's why finding books that are interesting will help you read more.

- Background knowledge will increase your reading speed and your comprehension. That is why it is easier to read a book about something you know or that has characters with whom you are already familiar than it is to read something that is completely unfamiliar.

- Support strategies are sensible. When you change topic areas, you may need to find books with bigger print and more pictures to support your comprehension. Finding ways to support your reading is sensible. It is proactive. It is not cheating.

Too often preliterate and low-literate adults have been taught that good books are only for educational purposes. While this notion traditionally limits the reader to boring passages with short, choppy sentences, such as most encyclopedia entries, it is far better than no interest in text at all. With opportunities to advise the reader over time, the RA can help the adult or teen evolve into a reader who knows how to look for new information in well-written nonfiction and eventually from well-researched fiction.

*It was books that taught me the things that tor-
mented me most were the very things that connected
me with all the people who were alive, or who had
ever been alive.*

—James Baldwin, in the *New York Times*
(June 1, 1964)

Reading Changes Lives

Whether you are an educator, librarian, or parent, you are a change agent. Your power is great enough to change the world for the preliterate adult or teen and for the new speaker of English (who sometimes is also preliterate in the first language). Following the belief that it is never too late for literacy to begin, you can steer those readers into worlds of unimagined pleasure, pleasure that brings with it reading skills, writing abilities, and the speech patterns of the educated classes.

What the above-referenced would-be readers need is not more of what has not worked—for most have spent countless hours filling in blanks, memorizing lists of meaningless words, and reading uninteresting, unmemorable passages. Developmental reading passages should be memorable, highly memorable. To find pleasure in print, new readers need text that is at once consistently interesting and extremely easy to comprehend. For the experienced student—the teen who cannot read well and the adult who may have left school years before—memories of reading are not related to pleasure. Indeed, they are typically memories of harsh punishments and humiliation during reading sessions. Or such readers are unable to conjure any memories at all, having pushed the negative experiences far into the recesses of their minds. The challenge now is to provide an experience that is qualitatively different from so-called reading experiences of the past.

Both interest and need are vital to helping new readers and language learners find the right reads. Highly engaging, accessible books provide readers with the necessary to practice a lot. Practice is essential to improvement. Key to finding books that interest the reader is knowing the reader. Questions that will ferret out possible book topics are discussed elsewhere in this introduction.

The same principles apply to the literate new speaker of English, also referred to as an ESL (English as a Second Language) or EFL (English as a Foreign Language) student. For the language learner who is literate, however, there is no need to sell the idea of reading as language power. But most of the selections in this book will also suit their language development needs. Where a title is inappropriate, the annotation so indicates.

I never read a book before reviewing it; it prejudices a man so.
—Rev. Sydney Smith, in *The Smith of Smiths,*
by H. Pearson (ch. iii, p. 54)

Annotations

This book provides annotations of great reads—classics, with traditional partial plot summaries, ideas about how the books might be used, and where to find support for reaching the more difficult levels. Icons indicate the following:

 illustrated

 big print

 author pick

 student favorite

 affordable book (that is, under $9.99) Note that the cover price of the book could be mitigated by buying it at a Friends of the Library book sale, at an independent bookstore closeout, or through a super-chain discount.

The annotations also give suggestions for related books that provide both breadth among like levels of difficulty and depth into the text or topic, so that the reader can do the practice essential for success. Where applicable, there are also indicators of special features concerning the book, such as a list of further reading titles, a chronology, a list of characters, or a map.

The unit introductions and annotations include selling points that you might employ to help the reader decide whether this is a desirable book. For example, a book that supports research may appeal to a new reader who plans to take composition classes. The ancient myths from the first chapter, for example, provide the foundation for a research trail leading from the first threads of a story that has been carried into today's language. One such example is Narcissus, the lad who so admired his own reflection that he fell in love; today we have the word narcissism in our language. Another example is references to the Medusa, a name that, without familiarity with the story, fails to give the world of meaning that a teaming head of snakes represents. The physical history of the land of the Greeks is also reflected in the myths, allowing the reader to observe how literature informs about conditions seemingly unrelated to the story.

Likewise, potential history enthusiasts may find the classics a great source of clues. In the second chapter, for example, the tale of the Pied Piper may lead the reader into a study of the Crusades or may reveal how one event can inspire a literary effort, just as one creative work inspires another.

Additional titles by the same author are often listed. Having a favorite author is a sign of a good reader. Additional titles in a series are also indicated, allowing a reader who finds a level of comfort in a particular format a chance to read more of the same.

Physical attributes (or surface features) that support the reader or that may deter the reader are also indicated. Big print or a palm-sized edition might make all the difference in whether or not a book will suit a reader.

The teaching ideas that are incorporated within the annotations typically address homeschoolers, teachers, or tutors, but can generally be interpreted for most learning environments.

Seasoned learners, whether they are in school or are attempting to teach themselves independently, are fully capable of participating in their own learning. Unfortunately, those who have been exposed to traditional drill and practice methods over the years tend to expect that that must be the way to learn to read. Is rote memorization a common strategy for learning new words? Yes, but it is not nearly as efficient as reading for pleasure. Is programmed text with controlled vocabularies used in the teaching of reading? Certainly, but it will not help the reader become familiar with great literature and will not reveal the secrets of fine writing. Is it possible to learn to read from simple text? It is possible, but the approach takes a very long time and rarely leads to the pursuit of enriching literature. You may be faced with the dual tasks of debunking inappropriate notions about methods and redirecting the readers into the concepts of pleasurable practice. That is what this book helps to do.

> *So you're the little woman who wrote the book*
> *that made this great war!*
> —Abraham Lincoln, upon meeting
> Harriet Beecher Stowe.
> In *Abraham Lincoln: The War Years*,
> by Carl Sandburg (v. II, ch. 39)

Some Suggestions for Use

Readers may benefit from moving into increasingly more challenging material. To that end, you may want to show the individual reader how this progression can be realized.

Use will vary depending on the reader population. But the same titles can be employed for use

- with large classes,

- with small groups,

- with diverse student populations,

- in one-on-one settings,

- for self-study,

- at home,

- with family members,

- in the car,

- at the doctor's office, and

- in the community center or library.

Gathering as much data about the prospective reader as possible will make book selection easier. Here are some "always-ask" questions:

What is your favorite picture book?

What book have you most enjoyed reading?

What did you like about it?

Was it easy or difficult or so-so?

How often do you read for fun? (in any language)

Is this book for pleasure reading or for a class (on a deadline)?

Will you be reading this book to anyone else? (a child, another adult)

Have you ever tried listening to recorded books?

Although a teacher or a tutor or guide support is essential to getting a grip on the overwhelming world of books, over time readers can be taught to ask themselves questions about their literature choices and motives. Such questions can help them at once understand some of the cause and effect of the literature and make more informed requests for help in the library or bookstore.

In the following scenarios are guides for gathering information about the reader (what to keep in mind) and where in this book to look for appropriate titles (what to suggest).

> **An adult school or community college ESL teacher** has a very large class and wants to recommend a good book to a recent Russian immigrant, a former physician.

What to keep in mind

- The reader is literate in the first language. Because literacy transfers across languages, this person will probably understand the value of reading for pleasure.

- The reader probably already appreciates the classics.

- He or she may enjoy reading about Russia, or may want to focus on American culture.

- The reader may also need to hear spoken English to get pronunciation input.

- The student is probably not religious.

What to ask

The generic questions listed above will help the advisor get to know the reader.

- Did he or she read for pleasure in Russia? (If not, he or she will need time to acquire a love of reading.)

- What does he or she read in English now? (If it is the newspaper, it might be helpful to know what story he or she found most interesting recently.)

What to suggest

In chapter 4 there is a work by the Russian author Alexander Pushkin. It is an illustrated copy of *The Tale of the Golden Cockerel* and is only 20 pages long, indicating that it is a picture book. In the same section is a longer fiction book about a girl who owns a Pushkin book. Much more challenging is Leo Tolstoy's *War and Peace*, annotated in the same chapter. However, the Tolstoy has an accompanying audio book. If the reader has read the Tolstoy work in another language, or is familiar with and enjoys Tolstoy's work, the book and tape may be a good place to experiment. In case it is too difficult, the reader needs to have backup titles in hand to switch to. Many libraries have Tolstoy in print and audio forms, but it is essential to remind the reader to ask for unabridged audio.

Because you are probably unsure about the interests of the reader, you may want to recommend all of these, suggesting that the picture books would support comprehension, while the book on tape of the Tolstoy classic would give pronunciation input.

Encouraging this reader to work independently will allow you to spend more time on general class activities.

> **Diverse literacy levels.** A teacher is leading a large high school reading class, but has found that some students are reading well above grade level, while a surprising number are reading at the second and third grade levels. It is impossible to have them read aloud. It is also impossible for the teacher to keep track of every student. She wants books to have in the classroom during sustained silent reading time.

What to keep in mind

- The good students already know what they like. The challenge is to push them beyond that.

- The average-level students may feel pulled down by the low-level students and need many choices to be entertained.

- The bottom-level students are faced with more reading than they can handle in school already. They just wish there were some way to get away from all the testing of reading they get in English and social science classes.

- Review, if it is interesting, never hurt anyone, and can actually help readers at all levels.

So, re-reading a familiar tale, perhaps told in a new way, can offer new language to all levels.

What to suggest

The good students probably have a working familiarity with some classics. That background knowledge will support comprehension. Themes can expose these readers to more difficult reading material than they have previously encountered. The teacher may rotate themes (such as Greek myths, Don Quixote, Charles Dickens, illustrated Shakespeare, or James Baldwin) on an ongoing basis.

For the very new readers, the Whole Story edition of Jack London's *White Fang* from chapter 4 provides a beautifully illustrated story with a wealth of scientific information in the margins. It may be helpful to review periodically how much "real" information about science and history can be found in the short marginal passages of this series. From chapter 2, the illustrated books and ⅍ titles from the Canterbury Tales, Beowulf, and King Arthur collections will allow them to see that they can, indeed, access the classics and enjoy them. Even so, unlike readers brought up in picture book-rich environments, low level readers need to be coached in the art of seeking out information from the illustrations. Likewise, other titles that are supported by audio recordings will be both entertaining and useful in English and history classes.

Over time, one may be assured, the students will talk. If they have good books in hand, they will start to cross-pollinate. Occasionally, playing a few chapters from a well-recorded audio book will foster interest in the promoted book across reading levels. So will teacher reading of occasional chapters. Of course, if there is a class set of a title the teacher likes to read aloud, there is no substitute for hearing a real voice in real time, with time-outs for discussion and making connections between the events in the book and the individual students' lives. The voice of a good reader linking you to the lines read aloud makes the sound of the text immortal.

> **One-on-One Settings.** A tutor, reading specialist, or literacy volunteer may ask for help in selecting books for a particular adult or teen reader or English as a second language student.

What to keep in mind

- For the preliterate adult or teen, there is nothing more powerful than *language experience stories*. These are stories told by the learner to the teacher, who acts as secretary. These texts are unique to the learner. Unfortunately, some tutors are not confident about their ability to generate this kind of text, so more general materials must be substituted.

- Being read to is the way that good readers get the sound of reading in their heads. Tutors who spend a lot of their contact time reading to the learner will find that time paying off tenfold. Use of books on tape attempts to substitute for this, but it can never accomplish the "stop and talk" time a tutor provides. Yet when the tutor plays the tape for the learner and stops the tape as needed for clarification and to initiate dialogue, recorded books can provide a bridge between being read to—making meaning along the way—and reading for meaning independently.

- The tutor is a temporary support person, so the learner needs ways to gain independence quickly.

- The tutor needs several choices at hand so that during a lesson, if one thing doesn't work, another may be tried.

- Even a tutor working one-on-one with an adult learner may be misled by inaccurate test scores and student reports of prior achievement. That calls for a variety of levels of reading materials at hand.

- It may take a tutor several weeks to determine what the reader's interests are. Learners may initially report interest in topics that seem sophisticated, rather than topics of real interest. The tutor needs to be guided to ask questions that will lead to selecting desirable books to read.

- Adults and teens who have gone to American public schools have officially encountered a certain body of literature. The problem is, they may not have been there at the time or may not have been interested at the time. Helping to build the foundation assumed of a public school graduate can both enrich the learner and provide needed exposure for high school equivalency test takers and entry-level college literature courses.

- Often tutors only get one or two chances at very low-level learners before they disappear. Having irresistible bait is essential.

What to suggest

Try *The Race of the Golden Apples* by Claire Martin, annotated in chapter 1; *Chanticleer and the Fox* by Geoffrey Chaucer, retold and illustrated Barbara Cooney, or *The Legend of William Tell* by Terry Small, in chapter 2 (This book has a message about values that many adults enjoy. It can foster discussion that is essential to further literacy development.); John Milton's *Illustrations for "Paradise Lost,"* illustrated by Gustave Doré or *The Bard of Avon: The Story of William Shakespeare* by Diane Stanley and Peter Vennema, in chapter 3; Michael Bedard's true story of the Brontë children, *Glass Town*, in chapter 4; or Floyd Cooper's *Coming Home: From the Life of Langston Hughes*, in chapter 5.

> **For Self-Study.** An adult or teen who is able to read, but who is not able to read as fast as he or she wishes, has heard that reading for pleasure will increase reading speed. He or she wants help finding a good book.

What to keep in mind

- Learner interest is key.

- Learner need is key.

- Access is key.

What to suggest

If the reader is interested in returning to school and may want to build a literary foundation, he or she might begin with Margaret Hodges's retelling of *Saint George and the Dragon,* from chapter 3, or the three following illustrated easy reads from chapter 2: Sabuda's *Arthur and the Sword;* Chaucer's *Chanticleer and the Fox,* retold by Barbara Cooney; or Michele Lemieux's retelling of *The Pied Piper of Hamelin.* Any of these that grip the reader's imagination can easily be used to step him or her into more challenging reads. For more text-intensive selections that will give this reader hours of reading pleasure and will place the writer in a context, two famous names from chapter 5 may serve well. *F. Scott Fitzgerald: Letters to His Daughter*, edited by Andrew Turnbull, may be followed by *The Great Gatsby;* or try *The Misfits: Story of a Shoot,* by Arthur Miller and Serge Toubiana, followed by *The Misfits.* This progression can help the reader both connect to literature and to see that writers have mortal existence just as readers do. If the reader is a romantic, the works of John Steinbeck, starting with *Of Mice and Men*, may offer a literature hook. As a point of reference to that author's life, it might be noted that the funding for the public libraries in the California town of Salinas, Steinbeck's birthplace, was voted down in November 2004; even the Steinbeck library was consequently scheduled for closing.

> **At Home.** Although the guidelines for self-study may also apply here, when a person is addressing better reading from home, the circumstances may call for or allow a different kind of materials than for one who is not.

What to keep in mind

- Does the reader have a safe place to keep any materials away from children and other members of the household? This will temper what the person is able to do without undue stress over materials maintenance.

- Is there an audiotape player in the home?

- How much time does the person want to spend?

What to suggest

For the person who lacks a safe place for materials, it is best not to demand impossible maintenance. Secure Ⓧ editions, download copies, or make photocopies of appropriate passages and document the source on the copies. Many myths and legends from chapters 1 and 2 will serve this purpose. Having the source right on the copies will allow the reader to ask for more of the same easily. Store them in a jumbo-sized, clear plastic food storage bag with a pencil and pen. Encourage underlining.

After determining the interests of the learner, skim through the appropriate chapters for books that have audio books with them. Explain how listening to the book will, in fact, teach vocabulary and will foster faster reading. If a tape is abridged, explain that it does not include exactly the words that are in the book, but that listening first and then trying to read the book without listening will make the text easier to comprehend.

> **In the Car.** An ESL or new reader commutes several hours per day and wants to improve his or her skills.

What to keep in mind

- The adult may have some technical difficulties at first.

- When a person is driving, he or she will lose track of the story line from time to time.

- Good readers use audio books for pleasure.

- It is normal to be more attracted to one reader than another.

- Finding the difference between abridged and unabridged can be tricky.

What to suggest

Caution the reader that, while driving, it is easy to reverse a tape and suddenly be listening to the wrong side. It is also easy to pick up a new tape out of sequence. It takes a while to get a personal system going. The driving must be the priority. If things seem to have gone wrong on the tape, the reader should just turn it off. Mechanical difficulties are best handled in a parking lot.

The readers' advisor might advise the reader as follows: "Once you are very comfortable with listening to books on tape, don't plan to stop. It's a good idea to keep a record of what you have listened to and who that reader was. That way you don't borrow the same book twice by accident (on purpose is good). Also, you may identify certain tapes you want to buy for your own listening library."

Identify the words *abridged* and *unabridged* on several packages of audio books. When copies of both are available, compare the two with a copy of the text at hand. This will help the reader understand that a tremendous amount of text is missing from the abridged version. Usually that is not desirable. But, when the author is the reader, it can be informative.

A client may want to try listening to an unabridged copy first and then an abridged, just to get an idea of the kinds of things that have been cut. James Michener's *Mexico* (chapter 5) would be an excellent book to try with this experiment.

At the Doctor's Office or Awaiting Jury Duty. Readers who have to wait for long periods of time in doctors' offices or who must wait in holding areas during jury duty are well served by preselected reading materials.

What to keep in mind

- The reading may be interrupted without warning.

- The reader may need to hold the book up in the air while lying down.

What to suggest

Short stories and picture books can provide very short reads that can be closed in an instant. Begin with them. Later, very short books will also serve the waiting reader. From chapter 4, try *Oz: The Hundredth Anniversary Celebration*, edited by Peter Glassman, the Lewis Carroll tale *Alice's Adventures in Wonderland*, a pop-up adaptation, or Coleridge's *The Rime of the Ancient Mariner*. Illustrated by Gustave Doré; or the Renaissance author William Blake's *Songs of Experience* or Bruce Coville's retelling of *Hamlet*. From chapter 5, try the memories book *Pablo Neruda: Absence and Presence* or Neruda's *Love: Ten Poems from The Postman*, or James Thurber's collection of very short reads, *Fables for Our Time and Famous Poems Illustrated*. Select paperback whenever possible. It is just easier to hold up in the air. And it is less weight to carry around.

In the Community Center or Library. Libraries are great places to find collections of books on display to entice readers. In some the children's, young adult, and adult literature are combined; in others they are divided up. Though there are valid arguments for both arrangements, I opt for mixing them all together to allow readers to cross over from one genre to the next and to let the book, rather than the assigned category, drive the reader.

When setting up a reading area in a community center, the books do need to be arranged so that they can be picked up and put back without a lot of searching and shoving on the shelf.

What to keep in mind

- Not all adult ESL and new readers are at the same level of sophistication.

- Pictures always count.

What to suggest

Books that have dustcovers should always be displayed with them on. And new readers need to learn how to read the dustcovers to determine whether the book is enticing or not. A word about the historic importance of the early writings can set the stage for the START HERE! Ludmila Zeman sensuously illustrated *Gilgamesh the King* and its sequels, annotated in chapter 1. Once the reader understands how this man's epic poem fits into the grand scheme of literature, the story will sell itself. From there, more in-depth *Gilgamesh* editions or a fresh sampling of the essential illustrated Chaucer may help the reader overcome any negative impressions learned earlier in school. An informal discussion of freedom of speech issues can lead into the reading of books that went on to become classics, works by such authors as Nikolai Gogol, Louisa May Alcott, Oscar Wilde, D. H. Lawrence, and Arthur Miller.

> *In a hole in the ground there lived a hobbit. Not a nasty, dirty, wet home, filled with the ends of worms and an oozy smell, nor yet a dry, bare, sandy hole with nothing in it to sit down on or to eat: it was a hobbit-hole, and that means comfort.*
> —J. R. R. Tolkien, *The Hobbit; or There and Back Again* (ch. 1)

Reading Environment

All readers will benefit from reading in a place that is physically comfortable, a place where one may settle for a long, cozy time. So, if the children's section is best, that is the place to go. If it is too noisy, it is okay to take the big picture book to another area of the library or community center. Each reader needs to find the right nest so that that part of the reading is not a problem to be faced every time.

> *Great Literature is simply language charged with meaning to the utmost possible degree.*
> —Ezra Pound, *How to Read* (pt. 1, p. ii)

Conclusion

It probably didn't require a 20-year survey to convince us that literature reading is on the decline. It probably didn't take that survey to inform us that people who read for pleasure have better lives than those who don't. But it is very nice to have the National Endowment for the Arts survey on our side and at hand when we strive to help adults and teens convince themselves that reading good books is personally, socially, and financially beneficial.

Once readers begin to make connections between their reading of the classics and their own fuller, richer lives, they will easily move from one great book to the next. But for the new reader, the reluctant writer, the sensitized adult or teen, the first steps are difficult. Getting them to take a look at the classics wouldn't be so difficult if we could get at them before they were taught to dislike them. But that's not our option. We have the adults and teens we have. We can change the world for them . . . and for those whose lives they touch. That's what this book is about, and that's quite enough, isn't it?

References

"Agenda." In *Learning to Teach Reading: Setting the Research,* edited by C. Roller Newark, DE: International Reading Association, 2001.

Allington, R. L. "The Legacy of 'Slow It Down and Make It More Concrete." In *Learner Factors/Teacher Factors: Issues in Literacy Research and Instruction (40th Yearbook of the National Reading Conference,* edited by J. Zutell and S. McCormick, 19–30. Chicago: National Reading Conference, 1991.

Allington, Richard L., and Peter Johnston. "What Do We Know About Effective Fourth-Grade Teachers and Their Classrooms?" *The National Research Center on English Learning and Achievement, Report Series* 13010 (2000).

Bradshaw, Tom, and Bonnie Nichols. *Reading at Risk: A Survey of Literary Reading in America.* Washington, D.C.: National Endowment for the Arts, 2004.

Graves, Donald H. *Writing: Teachers and Children at Work.* 20th anniv. ed. Exeter, N.H.: Heinemann, 2003.

Krashen, Steve. *The Power of Reading.* 2d ed. Westport, Conn.: Libraries Unlimited, 2004.

Krashen, Stephen D., Lucy Tse, and Jeff McQuillan. *Heritage Language Development.* Language Education Associates, distrib., Burlingame, Calif.: ALTA Book Center, 1998.

McQuillan, Jeff. "Seven Myths about literacy in the United States." *Practical Assessment, Research & Evaluation* 6, no. 1 (1998). Available at http://PAREonline.net/getvn.asp?v=6&n=1 (accessed October 4, 2005).

Rosow, La Vergne. *In Forsaken Hands: How Theory Empowers Literacy Learners.* Portsmouth, N.H.: Heinemann, 1995.

Smith, Frank. *Insult to Intelligence: The Bureaucratic Invasion of our Classrooms.* New York: Arbor House, 1986.

———. *Understanding Reading.* 6th ed. Mahwah, N.J.: L. Erlbaum Associates, 2004.

Chapter 1

Myths and Legends of Ancient Civilizations: Egypt, Greece, Rome, and Beyond

The most clearly identifiable literature classics are perhaps those stories that date back to early civilizations. Now known and loved around the world, these stories have weathered the test of time. The appeal of myths is usually a strong story line with larger-than-life heroes, reflecting both history and cultural mores. The stories have substantial elements of adventure, or the hero may have a journey or quest that feeds the plot. There is always a problem to be solved, and usually time is running out, making for a fairly suspenseful, fast-paced read.

Having been translated into languages the world over for thousands of years, myths and legends provide literary allusions and idiomatic expressions that readers are expected to understand and apply instinctively when they are used. Students of history, geography, and anthropology will find useful references in the myths. Those same readers may want to read folktales or even fantasy, as many of the literary elements and devices are shared. Readers who are very interested in mythology might want to start keeping a record of the relationships of the gods and goddesses they come to know.

Titles in this chapter are grouped into individual geographical collections for Egypt, Greece, Maya, Mesopotamia (Sumeria) with embedded Gilgamesh collection, and Rome (alphabetical by geographical area). A final section is "Myths from Other Ancient Civilizations and Collections" (which are organized by location). The individual cultures in this category include Chinese, Irish, Maori (New Zealand), Native American, Norse, Russian, South Pacific, Viking, and more. **Within each section, titles are organized in reading order, and then alphabetically by author name.**

The Ancient Egypt Collection

Nolan, Dennis, reteller and illustrator. *Androcles and the Lion.* **Harcourt Brace, 1997. 32pp.**

Once a slave hid in a cave, where he found a lion howling with pain. Instead of running, he took time to remove a large thorn from the lion's paw. Much later, the lion had an opportunity to help the slave. This book tells how that happened. Big print on one page is countered by realistic, monochromatic drawings on the opposite. In his author's note Nolan says that this legend is based on a true story. Apion, an Egyptian living in Rome around t 40 C.E., was at Circus Maximus, where he witnessed a slave being spared by a lion, and then wrote about it in his book *Aegyptiaca*, which is now lost. But in the second century C.E., Aulus Gellius, a Roman, read it and copied parts of it, including the lion tale, into his own book, a collection of wise stories called *Noctes Atticae*. Over time, that collection was translated in to many languages.

Wildsmith, Brian. *Exodus.* **Eerdmans Books for Young Readers, 1998. 32pp.**

The Hebrew experience of Egypt was unlike other ancient tales. The Hebrews were slaves in Egypt when the pharaoh commanded that every Hebrew boy should be killed. One mother wrapped her child up and set him to float among the bullrushes, where he was found by the pharaoh's daughter. This is his story. Woven into the Old Testament story of Moses are the tales of the burning bush; plagues; the Nile turning to blood; plagues of frogs, insects, flies, boils, locusts, hailstorms, and three days of darkness; Mt. Sinai and the Ten Commandments; and the Jordan Valley. Each gilt-edged, two-page spread is so rich with color and detail it is frameable.

Fisher, Leonard Everett. *The Gods and Goddesses of Ancient Egypt.* **Holiday House, 1997. 40pp.**

Each two-page spread is dedicated to one of the ancient Egyptian gods. Large, stylized illustrations and one or two paragraphs of text in large print give the reader a chance to understand many of the mysterious images found on the walls of tombs. The language is not simple, but the pictures, map of Egypt, family tree, and pronunciation guide support the student of mythology. There is also a bibliography.

Related reads: Other ancient civilization titles by Fisher include *Theseus and the Minotaur, The Gods and Goddesses of Ancient China, Gods and Goddesses of the Ancient Norse,* and *Gods and Goddesses of the Ancient Maya.*

Farris, Geraldine. *Gods & Pharaohs from Egyptian Mythology.* **Color illustrations by David O'Connor; line drawings by John Sibbick. Peter Bedrick Books, 1981. 132pp.**

Stories of ancient Egypt are entwined with gods and pharaohs, who were considered gods. Topics include a seven-year-famine, King Khufy, Joppa, Phincas of Bakhtan, and the Book of Thoth.

Seton-Williams, M. V. *Egyptian Legends and Stories.* **Barnes & Noble Books, 1988. 137pp.**

Legends, fables, songs, and prayers of ancient Egypt are accompanied by many ink drawings. This is a fine carry-along and read-at-random book. Although some pages are solid text, most are not.

The Ancient Greece Collection

Amery, Heather, reteller. *Usborne Greek Myths for Young Children.* **Scholastic Inc., 1999. 128pp.**

Very short tales of Zeus and Prometheus and the gift of fire, the Chariot of the Sun, Pandora, Persephone and the seasons, Echo and Narcissus, Daedalus and Icarus, Bellerophon and the flying horse, King Midas, Theseus and the Minotaur, Pygmalion, and Eros and Psyche race across the pages, which are filled with richly colored illustrations and borders. There is an introduction to Greek myths and an extensive guide to pronunciation of Greek names. The clear telling and big print will be welcomed by readers of every age. This is a very fine reference book for personal, classroom, and homeschool libraries. Great read-aloud! Great discussion starter! Perfect for sustained silent reading time!

Barchers, Suzanne I. *From Atlanta to Zeus: Readers Theatre from Greek Mythology*. Teacher Ideas Press, 2001. 203pp.

This book is a treasure trove of three- or four-page skits about small parts of popular Greek myths. There are multiple speaking parts, making it possible for many members of a class (or a family) to perform without having too much to read during one performance. The play about King Midas, for example, has nine readers. With a small group of readers, this text is accessible to all levels of readers. The language is simple, but the key elements of the myth make it a good introduction to the ancient story. There is a pronunciation guide (much needed for some names), a names and places index, and a bibliography. ESL students who have heard a myth in their mother tongue will enjoy discovering familiar and interesting meaning in a new language.

Related reads: Other Barchers titles include *Fifty Fabulous Fables: Beginning Readers Theatre; Multicultural Folktales: Readers Theatre for Elementary Students;* and *Scary Readers Theatre.*

Fisher, Leonard Everett. *Jason and the Golden Fleece*. Holiday House, 1990. 32pp.

Jason's quest for the Golden Fleece is one of the most popular adventure stories in Greek mythology. Having been raised by a centaur after his father, the king, died, Jason had to fight for the crown. The large print text of this book is not simple, but the two-page drawings help tell the story every page of the way. After reading and talking about this book, homeschoolers may want to try the readers theatre skit of this same title found in Barchers's *From Atlanta to Zeus*, annotated above.

Aliki. *The Gods and Goddesses of Olympus*. HarperCollins, 1994. 48pp.

Whimsical illustrations intermingle in retellings of the Greek tales of Uranus, Chaos, Cyclopes, Hecatoncheires, and many others.

Blaisdell, Bob. *Favorite Greek Myths*. Illustrated by John Green, Dover Publications, 1995. 87pp.

The gods and titans, Hercules, heroes and monsters, the Argonauts, the Trojan War, and the *Odyssey* are presented in prose that tells these complicated tales clearly and provides an enjoyable listening experience to the read-aloud crowd. The six thematic chapters are broken into sub-stories that are neatly connected by words like "meanwhile" or redirected with "now let us hear." The stories of Hercules, Narcissus, Perseus, and Medusa are told in just two or three pages each. The whole book provides a fine introduction to Greek mythology. Of particular note is the last

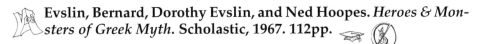

chapter, a deft retelling of the *Odyssey*. It does not read like simplified text. Rather, it can serve to entice the reader into more books on the individual myths.

Evslin, Bernard, Dorothy Evslin, and Ned Hoopes. *Heroes & Monsters of Greek Myth.* **Scholastic, 1967. 112pp.**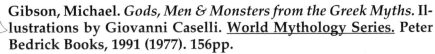

Evslin and Hoopes present stories about demigods (Perseus, Daedalus, Theseus, Atlanta) and fables (Midas, Pygmalion) in clear, everyday, conversational English. The chapters are short, but the stories are as exciting to today's readers as they were to the ancients. The one-page table of translations of Roman names for Greek gods gives a world of useful information. For example: *GREEK Zeus—King of Heaven, Ruler of the Gods/ROMAN Jupiter—Name derived from Zeus-pater, Father Zeus*, thereby demystifying the disparity between the names. A two-page glossary, "Mythology Becomes Language," explains how modern words such as *aphrodisiac, atlas, echo,* and *narcissistic* evolved. There are no pictures, and the print is small, but any reader with background or an interest in mythology will find this a rewarding little book.

Gibson, Michael. *Gods, Men & Monsters from the Greek Myths.* **Illustrations by Giovanni Caselli.** <u>World Mythology Series.</u> **Peter Bedrick Books, 1991 (1977). 156pp.**

A three-page essay "The World of the Gods," introduces readers to the history of Greek mythology, starting with the once-rich terrain that provided a variety of settings (before farmers overworked and destroyed the land); provides background on how the oral histories came to differ from one part of Greece to another; and explains how they were eventually written down, most notably in two epic collections by the poet Homer, 400 years after the fall of Troy.

Many of the well-known and popular tales of Greek mythology—of Zeus, Hera, Hades, Poseidon, Pandora, Aphrodite, Apollo, Pan, Midas, and others—follow, retold in exciting, though not simple, language. Sections of solid text are followed by brilliant pen-and-ink and full-color visual delights. There is a full page of short descriptions of symbols in Greek myths and an extensive index. This book fits beautifully into an ancient history or mythology unit. As a read-aloud, the first chapter also provides an informing introduction to the study of any Greek myths.

Related reads: Other titles in this series include *Gods and Pharaohs from Egyptian Mythology; Angels, Prophets, Rabbis & Kings from the Stories of the Jewish People; Gods & Heroes from Viking Mythology; Spirits, Heroes & Hunters from North American Indian Mythology; Warriors, Gods & Spirits from Central & South American Mythology; Heroes, Monsters & Other Worlds from Russian Mythology; Druids, Gods & Heroes from Celtic Mythology;* and *Kings, Gods & Spirits from African Mythology*

Hodges, Margaret. *The Arrow and the Lamp: The Story of Psyche.* **Illustrated by Donna Diamond. Little, Brown, 1989. 32pp.**

Psyche, a mortal, was so beautiful she inspired the wrath of Aphrodite, the goddess of love and beauty. Aphrodite sent her son Eros to ruin the young woman with bitterness, but the plan went awry when Eros fell in love at first sight of Psyche. Eros hatched a scheme to live as the husband of the forbidden lass. It worked well until she broke a rule that injured him, and he was forced to return to his mother. Psyche pursued him to the ends of the earth and beyond. This is the story of Psyche's journey in search of her god-husband. Realistic images in pastel tones make this enchanting story a joy to behold. A list of characters with name pronunciations and Roman myth counterparts will help ground the reader in Greek and Roman mythology. There are large blocks of solid print, but the language is easy to follow, and the conversations are in modern English. This book is appropriate for intermediate readers and ESL students who have an interest in Greek mythology.

 Martin, Claire. *The Race of the Golden Apples.* **Illustrated by Leo Dillon and Diane Dillon. Dial Books for Young Readers, 1991. 32pp.**

A babe is left in the woods. Her crime? She was a girl, so her father ordered that she be abandoned. The goddess Diana, goddess of the hunt, hears the crying just as a pack of wolves begins to circle. Beautiful illustrations grace every page. The long, sometimes complex, sentences may require more than one reading.

 Mayer, Marianna. *Pegasus.* **Illustrated by K. Y. Craft. Morrow Junior Books, 1998. 40pp.**

The magnificent flying horse, the Pegasus, takes his friend on death-defying adventures. The masterly oil on watercolor paintings of mysterious woods, dragons, and enchanted beings are worth a long, leisurely look before beginning to read.

 Yolen, Jane, and Robert J. Harris. *Odysseus in the Serpent Maze.* <u>**Young Heroes.**</u> **HarperCollins, 2002. 256pp.**

The young and foolish Odysseus, inclined to buffoon his way through thrilling encounters with supernatural adversaries, is counterbalanced by a female of poise and intellect in this first book of the series. Using archaeological research to provide information about the places and times in which their heroes would have lived, Yolen and Harris projected known mythological heroes and heroines back to their youths, thereby creating a new approach for this action-packed, history-informing series. Their first four main characters are Odysseus, Helen of Troy, Penelope, and Mentor. The language is very easy to follow. The episodes will provide a never before available foundation for reading Greek myths.

Related read: *Queen's Own Fool* by Jane Yolen and Robert J. Harris.

Maya Collection

Members of a complex and literate society, ancient Mayans believed in a flat earth with multiple layers above and below that represented the spiritual realms. Reflecting their love of many deities, the Mayans had festivals honoring gods of the winds, rain, birth, death, and war. The gods were related to different social classes and professions, particular lineages and families. Because they menstruated, women were considered impure and so were excluded from ceremonies, the exception being the virgins, who were essential to rituals. The beliefs of the gentle, peace-loving Maya stand in stark contrast to those of the nearby warlike Aztecs. In early times, human sacrifice was not a general practice, although own-blood sacrifices were. People in power would cut themselves and bleed onto a ritual paper, which was then offered to the gods. Because of a strong belief in astrology and numerology, the Mayans used three calendars that mandated events. Great stone temples were found throughout the Mayan empire, although the Mayans also made pilgrimages to the sacred city of Izamal and the island of Cozumel.

The Spanish conquest of the Yucatan led to "book-burning" and persecution of the indigenous people, forcing them to turn to an oral tradition to preserve their stories and belief system. Discovery of references to a Mayan sacred book called *Popol Vu* has led to controversy about the importance of the text and its origins. When a hieroglyphic record of the Mayan creation story, in which humans came from maize, was discovered in a 1,500-year-old temple in Chiapas, Mexico in 1997, there was debate over who might have carved it and when. Some suggest it is heavily influenced by Christian followers, while others consider it equal to the Christian Bible.

 Fisher, Leonard Everett. *Gods and Goddesses of the Ancient Maya.* Holiday House, 1999. 32pp.

The three-page introduction is all text, but after that each topic has a full-page caricature and one-paragraph story, with pages numbered in Mayan. This nonfiction book has a pronunciation guide, a bibliography, and a Mayan numbers code using fingers and toes.

Lattimore, Deborah Norse. *Why There Is No Arguing in Heaven: A Mayan Myth.* **Harper & Row, 1989. 28pp.**

The complicated, enchanting creation story of the Maya is made memorable by stonelike images. Lots of conversations among the gods. Humorous! A good one for readers theatre adaptation.

Mesopotamia (Sumeria)

The Gilgamesh Collection (ca. 2,700 B.C.)

Gilgamesh, a Sumerian warrior king, ruled over the territory known as Uruk around 2,700 B.C. (Sources vary on the exact dates.) The story of Gilgamesh, as written by this king, is the world's first epic. *Mesh* means *hero* in Sumerian. Gilgamesh was so proud of his remarkable accomplishments, achieved in concert with his friend, the wildman Enkidu (until Enkidu's death), that he had them written up in cuneiform on clay tablets and posted on the city wall. Actually, he had several copies made, which assured his posterity. Pieces of those tablets continue to surface and inform scholars about this ancient time, approximately the twenty-eighth century B.C.

It is now known that this work was a play script; perhaps, according to Robert Temple (see below), a sacred drama done with masks. In my own sixth-grade class, the students, inspired by the three Ludmila Zeman picture book interpretations, concocted their own drama, making huge masks, which the various characters carried rather than wore. The reader cannot help sensing a poetic rhythm in this tale.

The tales are aligned with some of the oldest biblical stories, though predating them by 1,500 years. There is, for example, reference to a great flood and an ark. Though the flood reported in the epic lasted only seven days, scholars now suggest that the story of the birds being sent to find land was first written in clay in the Gilgamesh epic, before the first prophet, and was later adapted as the flood of Noah. Translations continue to emerge, each making the epic tale easier to comprehend. There is one series of picture books referenced here, and detailed in the "Myths from Other Ancient Civilizations" section of this chapter, that I have used in my teaching. I enjoy re-reading them every time. Make no mistake: Gilgamesh is the original author. By retelling, reworking, or explaining the story, all these other writers are just providing us with ways to understand the autobiography of an extremely proud and powerful man.

Note: Most of the southern half of Mesopotamia (Iraq and parts of both Syria and Turkey on today's map) was known as Sumer, a 10,000-square-mile area of rich soil that was at once plagued by parching, hot drought and devastating spring and fall floods. Mesopotamia included both farmlands and the legendary cities of Ur and Kish.

If you have a scholarly interest in the topic of Gilgamesh, refer to Rivkah Scharf Klugar's *The Archetypal Significance of Gilgamesh, A Modern Ancient Hero* (Diamon, 1991). Throughout that book, comparisons are made between the Gilgamesh epic and the Judeo-Christian Bible. The author provides the background for a discussion on how a woman scorned can be a mortal enemy. Indeed, she denies Gilgamesh eternal life, a problem he takes so seriously that he ends up obsessed over it.

 Shepherd, Sandy. "Gilgamesh." In *Myths and Legends from Around the World*. Macmillan Books for Young Readers, 1994, 58-61 (annotated in the last section of this chapter). Contains a summary of the Gilgamesh tale.

 Zeman, Ludmila. *Gilgamesh the King*. Tundra Books, 1998 (1992). 24pp.

This is the first of three Zeman books about Gilgamesh, who was once king of the Sumerians in Mesopotamia. The epic tale of Gilgamesh was first written in clay over 5,000 years ago, making it one of the world's oldest stories. Some of the stories in it are aligned with Old Testament stories. Although the translations of the whole epic make for great reading, the retelling and brilliant, detailed illustrations in this book are the ideal introduction. This book has a summary of the tale with historical references and a map of Mesopotamia and Sumer.

 Zeman, Ludmila. *The Last Quest of Gilgamesh*. Tundra Books, 1998 (1995). 24pp.

Utnapishtim, not unlike Noah, tells Gilgamesh the story of angered gods who sent a great flood. First, however, they had told Utnapishtim to build an ark and to put his family and each kind of plant and animal aboard. After that, Gilgamesh sets out in search of immortality. This book features a summary of this part of the Gilgamesh epic, and makes critical connections between the epic and more recent ancient literature and art. For maximum enjoyment and comprehension, read *The Revenge of Ishtar* (below) before *The Last Quest of Gilgamesh*.

Zeman, Ludmila. *The Revenge of Ishtar.* **Tundra Books, 1998 (1993). 24pp.**

In this second Zeman episode of the Gilgamesh epic, the king of Uruk and his mighty friend Enkidu embark on a treacherous journey to conquer the monster Humbaba before it has a chance to strike their people again. No sooner have they dispensed with the unimaginable beast than Ishtar descends from the sky to propose to Gilgamesh. He shuns her. This scene does not end peacefully. This book has drawings of parts of the board game Pack of Dogs or Royal Game of Ur, and historical and archaeological notes.

 Temple, Robert. *He Who Saw Everything, a Verse Translation of the Epic of Gilgamesh.* **Rider, 1991. 144pp.**

The title of this book is a translation of the first line of the eleven-clay-tablet book, the oldest surviving work of sustained literature in the world. It is presented here tablet by tablet. Temple puts notes at the end of each tablet and notes along the way where pieces of clay are missing, giving the reader the right to fill in the blanks. The third-person story shows exactly how proud its author was. Conversely, Temple also is quick to appreciate his translator predecessors. Note that there are several translations that use the first line of the epic in the title, so searches need to be done with the translator's name.

The actual Temple-translated text of *Gilgamesh* can be found online, but it is the clearly written introduction that makes finding this very easy-to-hold little book worth locating. The endpapers are covered with cuneiform, and a very clear map details the location of the Gilgamesh kingdom. Temple acknowledges that he has translated only a handful of lines from the Akkadian, relying a great deal on earlier editions by other scholars. This edition also has notes on the translation and an extensive bibliography. Academic support is here for discussions on heroic characters, epic poetry, flood tales throughout various cultures, and Sumeria. Teachers may want to read the salient introduction before presenting the epic poem in any format. This little book can be held in one hand.

 Verniero, Joan C., and Robin Fitzsimmons. "The Journey of Gilgamesh." In *One-Hundred-and-One Read-Aloud Myths and Legends.* **Black Dog and Leventhal Publishers, 1999, 271–273** (annotated in the last section of this chapter).

Ferry, David. *Gilgamesh: A New Rendering in English Verse.* **Introduction by William Moran. Farrar, Straus & Giroux, 1992. 99pp.**

This book opens with the none-too-humble suggestion that Gilgamesh was the one who knew most of what there was to be known, including how the world was before the Great Flood, and who went to the end of the earth and returned to tell about it . . . in stone. Notes on all the tablets are at the end of the book. Although the print is small and there are no illustrations, the text is easy to read. It is the sentence breaks that make this story more difficult to understand than it would be if written in prose. Reading the three picture books in this collection will prepare the reader for this book.

Ancient Rome Collection

Founded by the twins Romulus and Remus, the Roman Empire was home to gods who looked after every aspect of life. Adopting many of the Greek gods, who lived on Mount Olympus, the Romans gave them new names and residences throughout the empire. Later, they imported gods from other cultures, too. There were gods in charge of events such as war and marriage, and gods in charge of the gratifying and concrete such as fame and food. The Romans believed that the gods had a great influence, and therefore they should be appeased. The average Roman called upon several gods per day, never being certain where the turf began or ended. The Romans also believed in predestination, assuring that a slave was a slave because the gods had willed it and a king, likewise, was supposed to be a king. Actions did not determine destiny. But Romans needed to take care not to annoy the gods.

References to Roman deities abound in modern literature. Those who would enjoy a macabre story with a heroine whose lineage traces back to Romulus and Remus, that addresses the goddess Isis in a new way, and that references many other names of that ilk, may want to read *Pandora*, a vampire story by Anne Rice.

 Lasky, Kathryn. *Hercules, the Man, the Myth, the Hero.* **Illustrated by Mark Hess. Hyperion Books for Children, 1997. 32pp.**

Beautiful, full-color illustrations and large print tell the ancient tale of the incredibly powerful man. Players in this Roman myth include Hera, Palaemon, and Zeus. After performing 12 labors, Hercules (son of the mortal Allemene and the king of the gods, Zeus), ascends to Mt. Olympus to live as a god. In addition to use in mythology units, this story is an excellent discussion starter about jealousy.

 McCaughrean, Geraldine. *Roman Myths.* **Illustrated by Emma Chichester Clark. Margaret McElderry Books, 1999. 96pp.**

Left to the mercy of the forest, the twins Romulus and Remus grew up to found the glorious city of Rome. Their story, from their beginnings with a surrogate mother-wolf, through growth and adolescence, to the murder of one by the other, is told with humor and clear language in just six pages and five brilliantly expressive illustrations. Here are 15 retold myths, an introduction to the Pantheon in Rome and related history, a short list of Roman gods and goddesses, and two pages of historical notes on the myths. This is a great read-aloud book and a very nice introduction to Roman mythology.

Related reads: Other McCaughrean titles include *Greek Myths* and *Greek Gods and Goddesses.*

 Usher, Kerry. *Heroes, Gods & Emperors from Roman Mythology.* **Illustrated by John Sibbick. Peter Bedrick Books, 1983. 132pp.**

In sometimes lengthy stretches using small print, with dramatic illustrations interspersed, here are some of the most popular Roman myths and some strange, unfamiliar ones. Included are tales about Aeneas, the Golden Bough, Rome, Romulus and Remus, the Sabine Women, Nuvia, and transformations.

Related reads: See also *Androcles and the Lion* by Dennis Nolan, annotated in the Egypt collection section.

Myths from Other Ancient Civilizations

This section covers books of ancient stories about women warriors, and Chinese, Maori, Norse, Native American, and Viking mystical beings, as well as several collections of tales from around the world. These tales provide an easy introduction to both the notion that unfamiliar cultures have their own ways of knowing the past and reconciling the unexplained and a chance to view the similarities among the spiritual concepts that humans have developed independently over time.

 Forest, Heather. *Wisdom Tales from Around the World.* **August House, 1996. 156pp.**

Fifty very short tales in big print open windows to people around the world, showing the traditions of Sufi, Zen, Taoist, Christian, Jewish, Buddhist, African, and Native American storytellers. Not every tale is a gripping adventure, but they each help the reader find another path to civilization. Perhaps as interesting as the tales themselves are the notes and bibliography pages at the end of the book, in which Forest gives detailed cultural insights. There are also two pages of one-line proverbs with their countries of origin. Readers may want to mark a map with the sources of each tale as it is read, thereby securing a geography lesson from the book as well as a reading excursion. Small groups could readily convert the tales into readers theatre scripts.

Mayer, Marianna. *Women Warriors: Myths and Legends of Heroic Women.* **Illustrated by Julek Heller. Morrow Junior Books, 1999. 80pp.**

Short tales form around the world, speak to the strength and achievements of women, mortal and immortal. Devi, meaning "diety" or "goddess" in Sanskrit, is the thousand-armed goddess who overcame the raging bull transformed into the evil Durga. Rangada, an Indian mortal found in the ancient Hindu text the *Mahabharata*, was stung by the sexism she faced when she discovered a handsome young Arjuna who was attempting to have a time of solitude in the forest. Semiramis, Queen Sammuramat of Assyria, is known to have lived, was abandoned in the forest, and was saved by doves. Hiera, of the lands from Asia Minor to the Black Sea known as Amazonia for 400 years, is documented in the writings of Herodotus, the "Father of History." Scathach, another Amazonian, was known for pole vaulting, underwater fighting, and her invention, the barbed harpoon. According to the oral history of the Zimbabwe Buhera Ba Rowzi tribe, Mella faced the python healer to save her dying father. Winyan Ohitika, a Sioux woman, rode into battle against the Crow to avenge her slain brothers. Stories of these and many more legendary women will fascinate readers.

There is a pronunciation chart for ancient names. A selected bibliography has categories: African, Amazonian, British, Celtic, General, Newark, Indian, Japanese, and Native American. The accessible index is annotated with phrases. Each story is three or four pages long, with one major illustration. Because there is lots of conversation, this book is a very good selection for ESL students, but others will also find the stories very entertaining. It will serve units on culture, history, mythology, and sociology.

Shepherd, Sandy. *Myths and Legends from Around the World.* **Illustrated by Tudor Humphries. Macmillan Books for Young Readers, 1994. 96pp.**

More than 50 tales, brilliantly illustrated, are presented in summary form. Although the tales lack the details that long stories provide, this collection gives readers a chance to get a taste of myths, legends, gods, and spirits that they might not ever hear about otherwise. If a reader finds a particularly interesting story, he or she can pursue more information in a more challenging and detailed text. Some of the stories are "The Birth of Japan," a story from a Chinese book called *Nihongi*, which tells how the Chinese taught the Japanese to write; "Romulus and Remus," the story of abandoned twins who started Rome; "Quetzalcoatl," about a king who became an Aztec god; "Gilgamesh, King of Uruk," who was part god because his mother was a goddess, and part human, making him mortal; "The Trojan War," a conflict that began when Paris of Troy went to Greece and kidnapped Helen, the wife of his host, King Menelaus; "Osiris and Isis," about Egyptian gods who were brother and sister as well as husband and wife; "Sedna," about the Inuit Goddess of the Sea, who was the child of giants; "Cagn," about the God of the San, once known as Bushmen of Southern Africa, who is a trickster and shows himself as a praying mantis. Tales from Tahiti, New Zealand, Scandinavia, Guatemala, India, Sierra Leone, Canada, Nigeria, Indonesia, the Maori, the Hindus, and others are introduced here. The print is very large, and some stories are just a paragraph long. Fascinating reading. There is an index to help readers find lost facts.

 Branston, Brian. *Gods and Heroes from Viking Mythology.* **Illustrations by Giovanni Caselli. <u>World Mythology.</u> Peter Bedrick Books, 1994 (1978). 156pp.**

Norse or Viking tales about the Creation, apples of eternal life, death, and doom are at once complicated and fascinating; they are told here with a mix of long passages of solid text and full pages of marvelous pictures.

Classified as nonfiction, this book has a mystical family tree at the front. A description of symbols in the Nordic myths greatly enriches the meaning of the text. For example, fire giants may have reflected the ever-present volcanoes of Iceland. Norse gods found here include Heimdall in Midgard, the Norns, Loki, Sigurd the Dragon-slayer, Thor, Fenrir the Wolf, and King Gylfi. This book supports academic units about Nordic myths, Vikings, creation myths, and concepts of eternal life.

 Osborne, Mary Pope. *Favorite Norse Myths.* **Illustrated by Troy Howell. Scholastic, Inc., 1996. 88pp.**

These Norse or Viking myths include "9 Worlds," "Odin," "Magic Stallion," "Thor," "Loki's Children," "Gait's Bride," "Golden Apples," and "Ice Maiden." Imaginative paintings of the earthly stories have spirits superimposed on them, visually delivering the double impressions these tales tell.

 Sanders, Tao Tao Liu. *Dragons, Gods & Spirits from Chinese Mythology.* **Illustrations by Johnny Pau. Peter Bedrick Books, 1990. 132pp.**

Chinese gods and symbols, creation, dragons, superstitions, heroes, Buddhist tales, Tao magic, and the Monkey Spirit are some of the offerings here. There is a lot of small text, but there are also two-page, full-color spreads of mind-boggling illustrations.

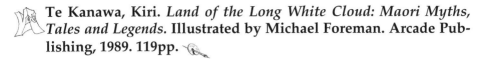 **Te Kanawa, Kiri.** *Land of the Long White Cloud: Maori Myths, Tales and Legends.* **Illustrated by Michael Foreman. Arcade Publishing, 1989. 119pp.**

Starting with a trickster tale, "The Birth of Maui," here are 21 tales from the land of the Maori and a brief glossary. Te Kanawa, whose father was Maori and whose mother was Irish—a Pakeha (a white person), was born in New Zealand and is an opera singer, educated at the London Opera Centre. These are tales from her childhood. They are written in clear prose with many stunning colored illustrations. This is a fine introduction to Maori culture and to New Zealand, the Land of the Long White Cloud.

Wood, Marion. *Spirits, Heroes and Hunters: From North American Indian Mythology.* **Illustrations by John Sibbick. Peter Bedrick Books, 1992 (1982). 132pp.**

Creation myths, mortality tales, and trickster tales, all magnificently illustrated, reveal much of the North American Indian mystique. Though the type is small and the language sometimes challenging (contains many Indian names, too), these are fascinating stories. Each tale is about three pages long. There is an index; this book supports units on North American Indians, North American legends, folktales, and creation stories.

Verniero, Joan C., and Robin Fitzsimmons. *One-Hundred-and-One Read-Aloud Myths and Legends.* **Black Dog and Leventhal Publishers, 1999. 336pp.**

Here is a collection of international short stories, each of which can be read aloud in about 10 minutes. The categories are Greek Myths; Roman Myths; Celtic Myths; Scandinavian Myths; and Other Stories from Egypt, Arabia, India, Nigeria, China, Japan, South Africa, Mexico, Hawaii, and North America. The language, although not simple, is clear. There are very few pictures. These are a great way to introduce history and cultural diversity to small groups at home, in homeschools, and in tutoring sessions. They also lend themselves to readers theatre at every level. Although this text is too challenging for beginner level readers—in part because of unfamiliar names such as Eurydice, Orpheus, Charon, Fragarach, and the like—listening to the familiar tales, such as "The Wooden Horse of Troy" or "Aladdin, or the Wonderful Lamp," will delight new readers and new speakers of English, who will soon after be able to open to the same tale and read through it. What this book doesn't have is an index.

Chapter 2

The Middle Ages

Although the Middle Ages are considered a time when little of cultural consequence happened, and much of the literature was communicated through the oral tradition, a number of literary masterpieces have survived. In some cases, the authors of these works remain a mystery—for example, Beowulf, the King Arthur legend. For others, the author is known. Therefore, this chapter is organized alphabetically according to author name, when it is known, and otherwise by character name. For example, the books about King Arthur are categorized under "King Arthur," and the William Tell books appear under "William Tell," whereas Chaucer's tales appear under the author name.

The chapter ends with "Other Literature about the Middle Ages," which contains a title that lends further understanding to the period. Titles within each section are grouped by reading levels:

 Start Here!

 Next Read

 Support Here

 Challenging Read

King Arthur (ca. 470–539 C.E.) Collection

Once there was a king named Arthur. He lived between the years 470 and 539 C.E. His life became a legend. The rest is speculation, myth, and research. He quite likely was born around 470 C.E., and he was killed at the Battle of Camlan in 539 C.E. as he slew Mordred, his son by his shape-shifting half-sister Morgan (or Morgaime) Le Fay.

The earliest textual reference to the mighty king is from the Welsh (ca. sixth century) poet known as Taliesim (who may be more than one person). Over the centuries, legends about King Arthur developed a cast of characters that included a soothsayer advisor named Merlin; a dazzling bride, Guinevere; a brave and honorable knight, Gawain; a sire, Uther Pendragon; and a rascally bastard son, Mordrid. King Arthur's desire for equity, a strange concept to hierarchical societies, gave rise to the famous Round Table, which in some stories leads to the meeting of Arthur and Guinevere.

The French added a knight of their own to the story, Sir Lancelot, and with him the notion of courtly love. Yet it was not until the thirteenth century that an English priest composed *The Brut*, the first of the Arthurian legends to be written in English. Fifteenth-century poet and storyteller Sir Thomas Malory delivered a compilation of Arthur stories in *Le Morte d'Arthur*, the most studied literary work on the topic of the legendary monarch. Tales of King Arthur have references throughout English literature today and are a delight to readers of all ages. Even today new stories are being added to the legend, particularly in the fantasy genre. Yet the volume of stories and variations on main events makes a sequential reading impossible. The two handsome glimpses of Sir Gawain below will allow the reader who is new to Arthurian legend to acquire a quick understanding that will likely whet the appetite for more text-intensive selections.

Because picture books are plentiful, frequently go out of print, and then come back into print quickly, there may be multiple books with the same title and multiple authors/illustrators. And there may be copies of the same book with more than one publisher name. Occasionally a well-told tale is re-illustrated; conversely, magnificent illustrations may acquire updated texts over time. This is particularly the case with the Arthurian legends. The best clue to identifying the books listed here is a match with title *and* author/illustrator. In the process, the very worst that can happen is that the reader will stumble onto a magnificent storybook that is not listed here.

Hodges, Margaret. *The Kitchen Knight: A Tale of King Arthur.* **Illustrated by Trina Schart-Hyman. Holiday House, 1990. 32pp.**

Here is the rarely told tale of Sir Gareth of Orkney, who faces the terrible Knight of the Red Plain. A damsel in distress—in a tower—gives this brave knight his just rewards. The Schart-Harman illustrations likewise give the reader rewards that may call for extensive pleasure looking.

Related reads: Other books illustrated by Trina Schart-Hyman include *The Fortune Tellers* by Lloyd Alexander; *A Child's Calendar* by John Updike; *The Serpent Slayer and Other Stories of Strong Women* by Katrin Tchana; and *Sense Pass King: A Story from Cameroon* by Katrin Tchana.

Latrobe, Kathy, and Mildred Laughlin. "A Connecticut Yankee in King Arthur's Court." In *Readers Theatre for Young Adults,* **65–69. Teacher Ideas Press, 1989. 130pp.**

This is a brief scene from the classic Twain spoof about a nineteenth-century mechanic who, after a blow to the head, lands in Camelot. His knowledge of science seems like sorcery to the medieval court. The five players in this scene can be portrayed by homeschoolers or students in cooperative learning groups. The pages are formatted for easy photocopying. Each reader can have a script for practice that will make the performance reading a public success. This readers theatre activity will at once introduce a contrast between King Arthur's time and provide an introduction to the many longer related texts in this collection. Other scripts in this book include passages from *Wuthering Heights, The Ingenious Gentleman Don Quixote de la Mancha, The Red Badge of Courage,* and other classics. Homeschoolers will want this and other Latrobe readers theatre titles handy as introductions to many classics.

Related read: Another Latrobe and Laughlin readers' theater title is *Social Studies Readers Theatre for Children: Scripts and Script Development.*

 Lehane, Brendan, and editors of Time-Life Books. *Legends of Valor.* <u>**The Enchanted World.**</u> **Time-Life Books, 1984. 144pp.**

Four chapters introduce various aspects of the lineage of the myths and legends surrounding the Arthurian tales. An illuminated, four-page "A Lineage of Enchantment" reveals one way in which an enchanted animal, in this case a doe, may in fact be an enchanted human, who charms the Irish Warrior Finn Mac Cumal, and bears him a feral son in the woods. The final story in this book of many short passages is "The Great King's Last Battle," in which King Arthur, Lancelot, Mordred, Agravain, Gawain, Gaheris, Gareth, Colgrevaunce, and Gueinevere are pitted one against the other and are sorted out by all manner of old alliances.

The dramatic paintings of the beautiful woman at the stake, Sir Lancelot sailing through on his white horse, and the once and future king sleeping "in the fairy isle of Avalon" support a thrilling read or read-aloud. Although the book is long, the stories are offered up in three-, four-, or five-page packages that are beautifully illustrated with realistic images that have clearly written, short captions. The print is large and easy to look at. Wide margins prevail.

Related reads: Other Lehane titles include *The Companion Guide to Ireland, The Complete Flea, The Quest of Three Abbots, The Power of Plants, Dublin, The Northwest Passage,* and *Wizards and Witches* (also in this series).

 Sabuda, Robert. *Arthur and the Sword.* **Atheneum Books for Young Readers, Simon & Schuster, 1995. 32pp.**

The Sword in the Stone was an early test of the future King Arthur's right to the throne. Stained glass-like images show this retelling of the first of Arthur's adventures, which is based on Sir Thomas Malory's fifteenth-century tale *Le Morte d'Arthur.* It is an art piece guaranteed to attract even the least willing reader. The teacher, tutor, or homeschooler will appreciate the single page of historical notes that provide context for whole lessons.

Related read: For a more detailed modern language retelling, see *The Acts of King Arthur and His Noble Knights: From the Winchester Manuscripts of Thomas Malory and Other Sources* by John Steinbeck.

 San Souci, Robert D. *Young Arthur.* **Illustrated by Jamichael Henterly. Doubleday Books for Young Readers, 1997. 32pp.**

Soon after Arthur Pendragon's birth to the beautiful Queen Igerna, she died, leaving a despondent King Uther unable to rule or father his son. Seeing enemies rising on all sides, the Magical Merlin spirited the babe out of harm's way and into the home of Sir Ector, whose wife had just lost a child. Knowing nothing of his identity, Sir Ector and his wife brought Arthur up as the brother to their older son, Kay. It was as a page to Kay that Arthur was embarrassed when he forgot to bring the older lad's sword to a tournament. As he raced for home, he noticed a sword sticking from a stone in the deserted village circle. He pulled it out, fully intending to return it at the end of the day, not knowing until much later that he had just proven himself the rightful heir to his long-dead father's kingdom. As he defended his coronation city, the sword from the stone was shattered and soon magically replaced by the legendary sword Excalibur. These were the beginnings of the time of King Arthur's court, which would herald the place known as Camelot. The language is easy to follow, the illuminations and illustrations splendid. This is a fine first read-aloud for an adult discussion group or for a parent to introduce the Arthurian legends to a child. The tutor may want to read this book with the learner and then read aloud the chapter "Merlin" in the Steinbeck book, annotated below.

Talbott, Hudson. *King Arthur and the Round Table.* <u>Tales of King Arthur.</u> **Books of Wonder, Morrow Junior Books, 1995. 32pp.**

Exciting battle scenes and sentimental close-ups of young Arthur and a young maid help deliver this interpretation of how the king met his queen and retrieved the legendary round table left by his father in safe-keeping with Guinevere's father, King Leodegrance. To get a taste of literary license, new writers may want to compare the Merlin character here with other depictions in this section.

Williams, Marcia. *King Arthur and the Knights of the Round Table.* **Candlewick Press, 1996. 28pp.**

Whimsical and detailed cartoons in comic book style present the key points of 12 Arthurian legends related to Excalibur, Morgan Le Fay, Guinevere, the Round Table, Sir Lancelot of the Lake, quests for the Grail, Princess Elaine, Sir Galahad, and Camelot.

Giblin, James Cross. *The Dwarf, the Giant, and the Unicorn: A Tale of King Arthur.* **Illustrated by Claire Ewart. Clarion Books, 1996. 48pp.**

After the young King Arthur's ship is cast up on an island during a storm, he comes upon a tower where an English dwarf tells him a strange story about his arrival there and the presence of the giant and a unicorn. The giant is an adolescent who, because he does not understand or know how to control his own strength, is a clear and present threat to the small humans. He is also key to their survival.

Originally written in French in the fifteenth or early sixteenth centuries for an adult audience, this was the final tale in *Le Chevalier du Papegau*. The 16-point Lucian font is at once beautiful to look at and difficult to stare at when it covers whole pages, which it does in many places. If a reader finds the text dizzying, he or she should simply set it aside, trying it just bit by bit. An author's note tells the full and interesting history of this episode.

Hastings, Selina, reteller. *Sir Gawain and the Loathly Lady.* **Illustrated by Juan Wijngaard. Mulberry Books, 1995. 32pp.**

Challenged by the Black Knight to answer a riddle, "What is it that women most desire?" King Arthur has only three days to answer, or he will lose his kingdom and his life. The noble knight of King Arthur's court, Sir Gawain, agrees to take as his bride the most loathly creature ever seen in order to save his king's word and his kingdom. But the tale, with many twists and turns, has more to offer, and all of it surrounded by illustrations as magnificent as the hag is horrible. To find out what happens on Sir Gawain's wedding night, you have to read the book.

This is one small part of the King Arthur saga. Sadly, the Hastings/Wijngaard team did not reveal every episode in this format, but what is here will delight a reader of any age and invite further exploration of the members of the Kingdom of Camelot. Because the text is not big and there are many lines on some pages, this is not a first book. Some may want to try it just to look at the pictures, though.

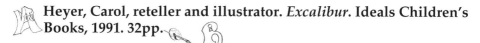

Heyer, Carol, reteller and illustrator. *Excalibur.* **Ideals Children's Books, 1991. 32pp.**

In this brief episode from the adventures of King Arthur, the young king breaks his famous sword from the stone as he battles the Black Knight in the forest. Minimally armed, he continues to fight, but he must be saved by Merlin's magic spells. Merlin then takes him to meet the Lady of the Lake, who loans him a new sword, Excalibur, which has a magic scabbard. With his new weapon, the king is restored to confidence. Large print and simply told events are accompanied by lovely detailed paintings on every page. This is a compelling story, one that will cause the reader to want to find out more about the enchanted king as told by Sir Thomas Malory in *Le Morte D'Arthur*.

Hodges, Margaret, and Margery Evernden. *Of Swords and Sorcerers: The Adventures of King Arthur and His Knights.* **Woodcuts by David Frampton. Charles Scribner's Sons, 1993. 96pp.**

From the birth of Merlin the Magician to the death of King Arthur and his noble knight Sir Lancelot, these nine fast-paced tales give a view into the kinds of people who may have lived in the splendor of Camelot.

Lang, Andrew. *King Arthur: Tales from the Round Table.* **Dover Evergreen Classics, 1967. 192pp.**

This is a republication of the Schocken Books collection of many of the most popular Arthurian legends, including the Sword in the Stone, Excalibur, the Round Table, Merlin, Morgan Le Fay, the Holy Grail, and Lancelot and Guinevere, told by the much admired Andrew Lang, known for his many colored fairy books. There are 28 black-and-white-illustrations.

Related reads: Other Dover books about King Arthur include *The Story of King Arthur* by Tom Crawford, *The Story of the Grail and the Passing of Arthur* by Howard Pyle, *The Story of King Arthur and His Knights* by Howard Pyle, *A Connecticut Yankee in King Arthur's Court* by Mark Twain, and *The Story of Sir Launcelot and His Companions* by Howard Pyle.

Osborne, Mary Pope, reteller. "The Sword in the Stone." and "Sir Gawain and the Green Knight." In *Favorite Medieval Tales,* **17–24 and 50–59. Illustrated by Troy Howell. Scholastic Press, 1998. 86.**

Two knightly tales are retold in this collection of medieval tales. The language is very accessible and the illustrations enchanting.

 San Souci, Robert D. *Young Guinevere.* **Illustrated by Jamichael Henterly. A DoubleDay Book for Young Readers, 1993. 32pp.**

Here is the story of the young Guinevere as she learns about the round table kept in her father's home for the future king. She also learns that the future king is to be her husband. San Souci's interpretation of the first Arthur/Guinevere encounter is quite different from the following one told by Hudson Talbott. These two books might be read in tandem, allowing the reader to speculate between fact and fantasy. Bold full-page illustrations are countered by miniature needlepoint scenes purportedly created by the young Guinevere. The author's note has one epilogue for the Arthur legend.

San Souci, Robert D. *Young Lancelot.* **Illustrated by Jamichael Henterly. Doubleday Books for Young Readers, 1997. 32pp.**

Lancelot, son of King Ban and Queen Helen of the Kingdom of Benwick in France, was orphaned while just a babe and taken by Ninane, the Lady of the Lake. But the lake was just a cover, an illusion that hid from passersby a paradise where Lancelot grew into a self-centered, willful young man. Though Ninane refused to tell Lancelot or anyone else who he really was, she ordered him called Son of King. Eventually, he insisted that Ninane give him the means to go to England to join King Arthur's Round Table. His intent was simply to become the most honored knight in the world. Unaccustomed to losing any challenge, his arrogance and boastfulness earned him many enemies in Arthur's court, not the least of whom was Sir Melyot. It was in a failed effort to save Sir Melyot from certain death that Lancelot's self-serving approach to greatness began to change, a change that eventually led to his earning and learning his name.

The language is straightforward and very easy to understand. Brilliant, realistic, illuminated text, full-color illustrations, and decorative borders enhance the pages.

 San Souci, Robert D. *Young Merlin.* **Illustrated by Daniel Horne. Doubleday, 1990. 32pp.**

Merlin the magician is traditionally cast in the role of the ancient mentor to the young King Arthur. But Merlin has a story too, and it begins with a miraculous birth. Here is the tale of young Merlin through the age of 17. Teachers may want to introduce this book and then read aloud "The Death of Merlin" from the Steinbeck book (annotated below). An International Reading Association Children's Book Council Children's Choice, this book is also fine for adults.

Related read: *The Wings of Merlin* by T. A. Barron is a good follow-up read to this book.

 Shannon, Mark. *Gawain and the Green Knight.* **Illustrated by David Shannon. G. P. Putnam's Sons, 1994. 32pp.**

When the party of the Round Table is visited by the immense Green Knight, young Sir Gawain eagerly accepts the challenge to chop off the monster's head. And off it comes. The problem is, it doesn't stay off. A year and a day later, the young knight, wearing the sash of his betrothed, Caryn, faces the Green Knight again, but he doesn't even know it . . . at first. He spends one night in the castle of Sir Bertilak and Lady Bertilak, a woman whose charms almost cause Sir Gawain to forget his knightly honor. When the lady of the house glowingly appears in his bedchamber, the young knight is tempted to accept her offer of a sash that will protect him from the Green Knight's powers. Magic and trickery, however, are overcome by Sir Gawain's honesty and faithfulness.

Illustrated with page after page of antique painting and needle-point-like images, this picture book holds an imaginative tale. Because it makes numerous departures from the early texts, it can be used effectively to illustrate how literature changes over time and retellings. For example, here Sir Gawain is a shy, hesitant lad who is the butt of other Round Tablers' jokes. Shannon supplies him with a girlfriend, to whom he remains faithful. No specific mention is made of sex or temptation in the way that the old classic does. A colorful introduction and well-told sampling, but surely the deficiencies are enough to drive adult students into more faithful retellings.

Yolen, Jane. *Merlin and the Dragons.* **Illustrated by Li Ming. Cobblehill Books, 1995. 40pp.**

In this story the fatherless lad Arthur has already pulled the sword from the stone and has been declared king, but he doesn't feel worthy of kingship. When he confronts Merlin (also known as Emrys) with a recurring dream of his, Merlin tells a tale of his own, a tale of two dragons, a tale that explains to Arthur that he wasn't fatherless after all and that he had been the son of King Uther Pendragon. Readers will also meet Vortigern, a self-appointed, evil king of Britain, and they will witness his cruelty to children. The dramatic scenes of battling dragons and fire-lit faces are the first picture book illustrations done by Ming. Hopefully there will be many more. The author's note gives full background on this episode and clarifies some of the complex relationships.

Crossley-Holland, Kevin. *The World of King Arthur and His Court: People, Places, Legend, and Lore.* **Illustrated by Peter Malone. Dutton Children's Books, 1998. 122pp.**

Biographies, stories, legends, hearsay, poems, practical information, and much more about the life and times of King Arthur are here to give the Arthur enthusiast background into the times when the man-turned-legend was king. Put into modern English are tidbits directly from the Middle Ages. For example, "Boys do not like work. They have big appetites and often get indigestion. Many little boys have bad habits. They shout and snatch greedily." So goes a quote from a medieval encyclopedia (page 22). There is a map of Arthur's Britain, including Colchester (sometimes referred to as Camelot), based on medieval sources, and there is an extensive index. Tutors and teachers may want to select passages that reflect the interests the individual reader has in King Arthur. Passages reflecting social attitudes, such as the quote above, will help the reader understand the value of both this book and other books about these times.

Steinbeck, John. *The Acts of King Arthur and His Noble Knights: From the Winchester Manuscripts of Thomas Malory and Other Sources.* **Edited by Chase Horton. Farrar, Straus & Giroux, 1993 (1976). 364pp.**

This book contains several Arthurian legends. Here is the story of the legendary King Arthur, beginning with his conception on a night when the lustful King Uther Pendragon tricked the beautiful and wise Igraine, wife of his vassal, the Duke of Cornwall, into thinking she was in bed with her husband. Here, too, is background on the capricious wizard Merlin—including a chapter on his death, the tale of the beautiful maid Guinevere, and stories of many others as recorded in the Winchester manuscript of Sir Thomas Malory's epic *Le Morte d'Arthur*.

"I wanted to set them down in plain present-day speech for my own young sons and for other sons not so young—to set the stories down in meaning as they were written, leaving out nothing and adding nothing," John Steinbeck wrote in the introduction. He took one episode at a time and told it clearly in clear language, weaving each into the circumstances of King Arthur's life. But he didn't finish. When he died, the incomplete retellings were left with letters that Steinbeck had written to Elizabeth Otis, aka ERO, his literary agent, and to Chase Horton, editor of this book. These letters comprise the appendix and reveal the thinking process of the author and his confidence, struggles, and determination.

Tutors and homeschoolers may want to match individual students' writing frustrations with selections from these letters. Steinbeck's storytelling is at its peak in these gripping tales. Although some of the chapters are quite long, the language is so clear and the details so obvious, it is tempting to list this as a . Support for this book can be found in the Arthurian picture books in this section. For example, the episode wherein Arthur volunteers to get a sword for his brother Kay and is obliged to grab the one stuck in the stone is a small part of the Steinbeck chapter called "Merlin." The same episode is enhanced by rich illustrations in the Robert Sabuda book *Arthur and the Sword* (see above). Readers not familiar with the tales of King Arthur can build background knowledge by going through this section and reading the single-topic books first.

 Yolen, Jane, ed. *Camelot*. Illustrated by Winslow Pels. Philomel Books, 1995. 198pp.

Here are 11 new tales to add to the Arthurian collection. Topics include Merlin, Excalibur, chivalry, gender issues, values, magic, sorcery, and enchanted places. Though they are told here for the first time, they well could have been parts of the original collection. Each by a different contemporary author with a different style, they stand separately as good reads in any order. Yet the reader is compelled to start another and another. Winslow Pels's dramatic full-color, full-page illustrations give a main picture of the topic at hand and a small perspective bar on the countryside along the bottom of the page, allowing the reader to see at once what is happening up close and where it is happening from a distance.

At the end of the book are one-paragraph biographies of each of the contributing authors. It is interesting to see how some of the author stories logically match them to the tales they have conjured for this collection. The language is easy to follow, though there are not enough illustrations to support the brand new reader or the entry level ESL student. They are excellent read-aloud discussion works for those who are already King Arthur fans.

Bulfinch, Thomas. *Bulfinch's Mythology: The Age of Chivalry and Legends of Charlemagne*. Doubleday Book & Music Clubs, 1967. 467pp.

This edition of part of the *Bulfinch Mythology* has a wealth of little Arthurian tales. Thomas Bulfinch (1796–1867), a Boston teacher, sought to preserve the classical tales commonly referenced in literature. He wrote *The Age of Fable, The Age of Chivalry,* and *Legends of Charlemagne*. These legends are found in various formats, and many are reprinted every year. Though simply sequenced and lively with detail, the sometimes long, scholarly sentences of the original Bulfinch stories can take more than one reading for meaning to become clear. Still, the Bulfinch works provide a historic basis for much of the Arthurian legends. Readers who are interested in a particular retold tale might find it worthwhile to track down whatever Bulfinch edition is in the local library or used bookstore.

Lacy, Norris J., ed. *The New Arthurian Encyclopedia.* **Garland Reference Library, 1996. 615pp.**

Here is a treasure trove of over 1,200 entries related to the growing body of Arthurian legends. At the very front are lists of entries by category and a bibliography. This is a collection of very short entries and some long ones. It is not magical prose. Neither is it encyclopedic. The content is thought-provoking. Did you know that A. W. Bernal reversed the Mark Twain *A Connecticut Yankee in King Arthur's Court* premise about time by using a time machine to bring Galahad forward in time to visit the 1940 World's Fair? Such tidbits make perusing a delight. Also an excellent resource for tracking down who is who.

Related reads: Other King Arthur titles include T. A. Barron's *The Wings of Merlin,* **which** tells of a new challenge to the old magician; William Faulkner's *Mayday,* a satirical update on courtly love; and Marianna Mayer's *Iron John,* about a wild man with magical powers and a penchant for kindness to animals. In the Iron John history, the author's note references a wild man who dates back to the twelfth-century wild man and prophet Merlin in Geoffrey of Monmouth's *Vita Merlini.*

Beowulf Collection

Beowulf, the epic poem about a heroic Scandinavian prince, is probably the most important piece of English literature in existence because it is the earliest English or even Teutonic text of its length—more than 3,000 lines. Key to its importance is that a single author conceived of it and wrote it down. Exact dates of origin vary from one reliable source to another. *The Norton Anthology of English Literature* suggests it may have been composed between "the first half of the eighth century" and "as late as the tenth century." Nobel Prize winner and Harvard professor Seamus Heaney places it between the "middle of the seventh and the end of the tenth century."

Beowulf's significance as a work of literature, according to Heaney, is explained in "Beowulf: The Monsters and the Critics," a scholarly essay by none other than Oxford scholar J. R. R. Tolkien, who asserted the work was the product of a literary effort—that is, the work of a poet. Tolkien said, "*Beowulf* is in fact so interesting as poetry, in places the poetry so powerful, that this quite overshadows the historical content." (**Note:** The Tolkien Society news indicates that this essay is scheduled for book-form publication.)

The debate about *Beowulf's* origins exists partly because the Old English epic poem is based in Norse legend and refers to known historical figures, and was delivered to the English by Danish invaders. But it was not just an old legend written down one day. It was an organized piece of literature, complete with literary features such as foreshadowing, background building, and character development, penned by a single poet who had a strong sense of the music of alliteration. Allusions to other stories and events (some historically documented) are woven into the poem so as to give a context for events in the current tale. This is one reason for reading a translation, rather than a summary or adaptation. After getting a taste of the fantastical events, a reader would be well served to sample the translated text. Translations are necessary for most of us because the Old English in which it was first written down is unrecognizable today. Sadly, the poet failed to give us his or her name.

The story is not linear. There are premonitions and stories within the story. But the main facts of the matter are as follows. Young, brave Beowulf, nephew of King Hygelac of the Geats, and some of his warrior cronies are the guests of Hrothgar, king of the Danes. During storytelling time, Beowulf hears that the murdering monster Grendel has made life impossible for his host in a nice palace on Zealand Island. Because Beowulf's father, now deceased, owes a big favor to Hrothgara, Beowulf decides to go do battle with the monster to settle things up. He doesn't have to wait long. Grendel appears on cue, whereupon Beowulf rips off the monster's arm. Grendel goes home to tell his mother, who becomes infuriated and comes back the next day for revenge and her son's arm. Then Beowulf charges into the pond, where he does battle with the hag. He returns to camp with both victims' heads. In due time, Beowulf becomes king of the Geats and does well . . . until a local dragon gets sorely vexed after being robbed by a human. Beowulf goes off to fight the dragon, but his troops, all except young Wiglaf, are reluctant to accompany him right up to the fiery face, so Beowulf is mortally wounded. So is the dragon. Wiglaf becomes heir to the crown and has a huge rock monument built in Beowulf's memory.

When approaching this legend, keep in mind that the original verse is about 3,200 lines long. The above retelling is, to say the least, truncated. The retellings in this collection are longer than mine and will help the reader discover the drama of this vibrant tale of heroism and terror. Just as the players in the story are drawn to the storyteller's forum, the adventures of the brave, strong, and ethical Beowulf will appeal to the modern reader's imagination.

 Crossley-Holland, reteller. *Beowulf*. Illustrated by Charles Keeping. Oxford University Press, 1982. 48pp.

Crossley-Holland tells the whole story of Beowulf in prose and pictures. This retelling uses modern conversational English and is supported by many graphic brown-tone illustrations. But the original character names will give the uninitiated a good way to get used to the unfamiliar sounds. For a quick overview of the story line, start with this edition and then move to the modern translations of the work that Tolkien praised as poetry.

Hinds, Gareth. *Beowulf: With Grimmest Gripe.* <u>**Beowulf Trilogy.**</u> **Book 1. thecomic.com, 1999. 40pp.**

Beowulf arrives at the great mead-hall, home of Danish King Hrothgar, whose lands and people have been under siege by the unthinkably horrible and vicious monster, Grendel. Beowulf is there to do battle. The gory images are dark and violent. There is no doubting the awesome nature of Grendel. And he is four times the size of Beowulf. The reader wants to cheer when the triumphant Beowulf stands like a wrestling ring champ, holding the monster's enormous arm over his head as Grendle runs toward the reader, cradling his shoulder. Of course, this is not the end of the story. This is Hinds's first in the <u>Beowulf Trilogy</u>, based on the Francis Gummere translation in the 1910 P. F. Collier & Son <u>Harvard Classics,</u> Volume 49, released into the public domain in 1992.

At the beginning, there are several blocks of explanatory storytelling. Unfortunately, the attempt at ancient-sounding language and a typeface that is way too fancy for visual comfort make reading difficult. Yet there is an interesting glossary at the front of the book that translates some archaic words. "Wyrd," for example, means fate or destiny. This list alone offers an opportunity for a discussion of language evolution. In this very thin graphic novel, Hinds has interpreted the tale in images that take readers right into the thick of these magical times and terrifying events. Many pages are just solid pictures, and that is very good.

Hinds, Gareth. *Beowulf: Gear of War.* <u>**Beowulf Trilogy.**</u> **Book 2. thecomic.com, 1999. 32pp.**

Grendel's supernatural and menacing mom is not amused at the injury of her beloved son. She is after revenge, but Beowulf is ready to face her on her own turf—underwater. This second book in the Hinds <u>Beowulf Trilogy</u> maintains the quality and suspense of the first book, with wonderful illustrations.

Hinds, Gareth. *Beowulf: Doom of Glory.* <u>**Beowulf Trilogy.**</u> **Book 3. thecomic.com, 2000. 40pp.**

This is the final work in the Hinds <u>Beowulf Trilogy</u>. The aging Beowulf of the Geats has been in power 50 years now. A fierce dragon has become enraged at a minor theft from the treasure it claims, so it has flown up to destroy Beowulf's village. More breathtaking illustrations, all grey tones, make the end of the saga as thrilling as the beginning. Hinds notes that he has taken some liberties with the story line in this final chapter. Even so, the pictures are the thing.

Gardner, John. *Grendel.* **Vintage Books, 1971. 174pp.**

Told from the perspective of Beowulf's adversary, this is a tongue-in-cheek retelling of how life was in Grendel's niche o' the woods. The fast-paced language makes this humorous story easy to keep on reading, though some passages bear re-reading. For example, at one point, Grendel is teasing a blind oracle who has fallen to his knees before the monster. Grendel observes the trembling man. "The old priest, kneeling, has one knee on his beard and is unable to lift his head" (page 131). One can imagine the terror of Grendel's victim, but Grendel isn't empathizing. If this is a fractured fairy tale, the evil stepfather is Grendel. The modern language in this story is very easy to follow. This book is a good one for showing how one literary work can inspire another.

Heaney, Seamus, trans. *Beowulf.* **Farrar, Straus & Giroux, 2000. 213pp.**

The epic poem of Beowulf is here in its entirety, but as a new translation. It is easy to grasp the meaning of every verse. In clear, modern English, this translation reveals the philosophy behind the tale. It is wise, for example, for a young prince to treat his father with respect, thereby building a reputation as an honorable fellow whom others will want to support when the prince becomes king.

This is a bilingual edition of the eighth-century classic with clear, modern poetic verse opposite Old English. There are also marginal notes to give more information to the reader. Regarding the passage above, for example, there is a note telling that the most famous warrior in Danish legend was Shield Sheafson, founder of the ruling house. Three family trees for *The Danes or the Shieldings, The Geats,* and *The Swedes* reveal the names contained in this epic.

The introduction to this book gives a fresh look at the background and historical content of this epic poem. It also explains the value of the work as a composition, providing clues to the reader, foreshadowing the important events, and presenting an integrated whole. Students who want to understand why this work is considered important to English literature teachers will benefit from reading Heaney's introduction. This translation is intended for general readers.

Hinds, Gareth. *The Collected Beowulf.* **thecomic.com, 2000. 120pp.**

Using perspective extremes—views through an open window to view the troops far below and from within the underbrush to look out from Grendel's lair—this graphic novel has such breathtaking illustrations, there is hardly a need for text. The back cover reads "One of the oldest and greatest classics of the English language, Beowulf was recorded around 1,000 C.E., during the late Viking Age. . . . The battles are lightning-paced contests of muscle and will, the speeches are filled with the courage of the ancient Norsemen, and the fjords are alight with burning funeral-boats." The text, though presented in elegant calligraphy, is hard to read because of the style and because of the poetic form. So the reader may want to read the story elsewhere. Yet here in these eerie and sensuous images is a support text for all Beowulf enthusiasts.

Katz, Welwyn Wilton, reteller. *Beowulf.* **Illustrated by Laszlo Gal. A Groundwood Book. Douglas & McIntyre, 1999. 64pp.**

An oral history for 200 years, the tale of Beowulf was finally written down in the West Saxon language as an epic poem in about 700 C.E. The year 751 C.E. has been historically established as the date when Hygelac was killed in battle, and it is from that that the other events of Beowulf are surmised. Some of the accounts in the poem may well be based on true events. In his author's notes, Katz explains, for example, how many details are verifiable. Even with the descriptive illustrations and clearly written prose, this is not a book for beginners. However, it reads like a Grimm's fairy tale, making it good read-aloud fare. Almost every other page is a full-page illustration. This book has the Great Royal House family tree, including the Waegmunding Clan; the Danish Royal House family tree; and an author's note discussing the known history of Beowulf.

 Osborne, Mary Pope, reteller. "Beowulf." In *Favorite Medieval Tales,* **8–16. Illustrated by Troy Howell. Scholastic Press, 1998. 86pp.**

When brave Beowulf twists the arm of the monster Grendel, the reader can feel the terror and torment from all sides. This retelling of the Beowulf legend, with its magical illustrations, gives yet another interpretation of this classic tale.

 Sutcliff, Rosemary, reteller. *Dragon Slayer.* **Illustrated by Charles Keeping. Viking Press, 1995 (1961). 108pp.**

In nine chapters of beautifully written prose, Rosemary Sutcliff describes the key events of the Old English epic poem. This book was first published as *Beowulf* in Great Britain by the Bodley Head Ltd. in 1961. Future English majors can use this as an introduction to Beowulf. Whimsical black-and-white drawings occur from time to time, adding sparkle to the narrative and helping the reader with comprehension. The print, although large, fills almost every page, making it a bit intimidating for new readers. In keeping with the tradition of this epic tale's first 200 years, this could be used as a read-aloud. It is up to the group whether they want to pass around the mead horns as was done in the great hall of Hygelac.

Related reads: Other Sutcliff titles include *Blood Feud, Bonnie Dundee, Dawn Wind, The Eagle of the Ninth, Flame-Coloured Taffeta, Frontier Wolf, The High Deeds of Finn Mac Cool, The Lantern Bearers, The Mark of the, Horse Lord, Outcast, The Silver Branch,* Three Legions (trilogy*), Tristan and Iseult,* and *Warrior Scarlet.* For another fantastical monster-slaying, see Mark Shannon's *Sir Gawain and the Green Knight* in the King Arthur collection above.

Rebsamen, Frederick, trans. *Beowulf.* **Icon Editions, 1991. 109pp.**

"Old English poetry cannot always be translated line by line. . . . I have therefore not hesitated to translate the words or half-lines from one line and place them two or three lines below or above in order to achieve the best effect" (page xx). In this translation, the poem is written with three- or four-word phrases, two phrases to a line, and line numbers appear in the margin by tens. The format of the lines allows the reader to hear the way in which the poem might have been recited—with a break in mid-line for a pause—as a harp accompanied the storyteller. The format reads:

> word word word   word word word
> word word word   word word word.

So the performance would go:
> word word word *music*   word word word
> word word word *music*   word word word.

Storytellers and others interested in chanting or singing the poem may want to read the author's introductory section about that. Genealogies of the Danes, the Swedes, the Geats, and the Waegmundings provide historical context. The modern tellings in this collection also provide support for study of this text. The work closes with an annotated list of suggested readings.

Gordon, R. K., trans. *Beowulf.* **Dover Thrift, 1992. 64pp.**

This is the translated poem that is summarized in the introduction to this section. It is challenging in this format, but other books in this collection will help make this essential literature accessible. Dover publishes out-of-copyright texts.

Miguel de Cervantes

The Don Quixote (1547–1616 C.E.) Collection

A peer of Shakespeare, Miguel de Cervantes (1547–1616) was born in Spain into a poor family of once good name. His own life experiences undoubtedly provided much of the grist for his literary mill. The child Miguel was educated by Jesuits, became a professional soldier, was imprisoned for five years by the Turks, was rescued by Trinitarian friars, went bankrupt, and was jailed for another 15 years. Though ever struggling desperately to provide for his mother, two sisters, an illegitimate daughter, and his wife Catalina de Palacios y Salazar Vozmediano, he never achieved financial stability. Yet amid the unpleasantness, he did become quite famous for his literary efforts. He wrote *Galatea*, a pastoral romance, in 1585; Part I of *Don Quixote* in 1605; *Exemplary Novels* in 1613; the satire against his fellow poets, *Journey to Parnassus*, in 1614; and Part II of *Don Quixote* and *Eight Plays and Eight Interludes* in 1615. Of all his works, however, it is the tale of the gallant Don Quixote, his faithful Sancho Panza, and the horse named Rocinante that makes the name Cervantes known around the world.

Cases showing how one artist's work influences another's are legion. To cite just one case here, one that spans across the centuries, when John Steinbeck began his now-famous trek across America with his dog Charlie, he named his noble steed—a modified truck actually—Rocinante.

Knowing about the life of the author will help ground the daunting name of Cervantes and the legendary name of his character Don Quixote in a place and time. Readers who view the writer as a human who, by an extraordinary series of misfortunes, was almost always down on his luck, will be able to appreciate the gift of stories Cervantes has left behind. Though his legacy is extensive, this collection provides an in-depth view of one of literature's most famous literary characters, Don Quixote.

Yet the texts are old and the original language remote. It is neither reasonable to ask contemporary readers to start reading about Don Quixote without adequate preparation, nor practical to expect appreciation to bloom unaided. However, the reader may enjoy just looking at the pictures in *Doré's Illustrations for Don Quixote* first to get an idea of the story line and to become familiar with the other important characters, such as his horse Rocinante, his partner in crime Sancho Panza, and the fallen and then reformed woman Dulcinea—and to revel in the glory of those majestic images. After that, the humorous picture book *How I Cured Don Quixote by Doctor Sancho Panza* will give license to reinterpretation of lofty literature.

The wake that a great work of literature leaves behind cannot be fully described in any introduction. Re-readings and rethinkings will generate far more than can ever be put to page. One contribution that Cervantes's imagery has made to languages around the world is the concept of chasing windmills. When the gallant Don does battle with the swirling windmill (and comes out much the worse for it), he gives a message that is at once idiomatic and philosophical. So, when the reader hears "Oh, he's just chasing windmills" or "Don't waste your time tilting at windmills," the phrase is laden with meaning that is over 400 years old and over a thousand pages long. The reader needn't get it all to gain a great deal from Don Quixote.

Barchers, Suzanne I., and Jennifer L. Kroll. "Episodes from Don Quixote." In *Classic Readers Theatre for Young Adults,* **25–38. Libraries Unlimited, 2002. 243pp.**

Scenes from *Don Quixote* are ready to use in a library, classroom, or homeschool dramatization, with a mix of long and short reading parts. There are 16 classic stories summarized, retold in a dramatic script format, and accompanied by other teaching ideas. This is very high-level comprehension support for the books addressed.

 Cervantes, Miguel de. *Doré's Illustrations for Don Quixote.* **Illustrated by Gustave Doré (1832–1883). Dover Publications, 1982. 153pp.**

This is a collection of 190 illustrations, reproductions of wood engravings made by H. Pisan after Doré's drawings. Each full page of illustration has a caption telling what part of the adventure is being depicted. This collection of drawings lends understanding to any modern translation of the epic tale of Don Quixote and his steadfast servant and accomplice in the pursuit of chivalry, Sancho Panza. New readers can begin by turning the pages, drinking in the illustrations, then later read the captions. This is a book for the personal library, homeschooler library, school library, and any other collection used by people who have an interest in history, fine art, illustrations, printmaking, classical literature, or drama.

 Evrard, Gaëttan. *How I Cured Don Quixote by Doctor Sancho Panza.* **Silver Burdett, 1986. 32pp.**

For the first time ever, readers discover that Sancho Panza was, in fact, a physician, who went along with Don Quixote to better observe and diagnose the strange malady that led him to assail monks and windmills. This humorous takeoff on the misguided hero gives the reader an overview of several episodes from the Cervantes novel—though not a word about the captivating prostitute Dulcinea, whose life he changed—and an impression that the Don's troubles were brought on by too much reading without glasses. That is how Don Quixote got his wild ideas about chivalry and damaged his vision. The large, colored pen-and-ink drawings reveal both what the Don saw and what he thought he saw. The language is quite simple.

 Latrobe, Kathy. "The Ingenious Gentleman Don Quixote de la Mancha." In *Readers Theatre for Young Adults,* **16–18. Teacher Ideas Press, 1989. 130pp.**

This is the famous windmill scene from chapter 8 of the original book. The three players have a chance to learn high-level vocabulary from short, meaningful passages that they must study in order to perform them. This is an excellent way of introducing the classic work to students at any level, English speakers and ESL students alike. Homeschoolers, tutors, classroom teachers, and community group organizers will all benefit from having these three pages (which are formatted for photocopying) in their resource files.

Cervantes, Miguel De. *Don Quixote.* **Translated by Samuel Putnam. Viking Press, 1949; Modern Library Edition, 1998. 1,239pp.**

In yet another translation of the story of the aging Don, this hardcover edition provides some interpretive notes not found in other editions, so the chance to compare translations is further extended.

Cervantes, Miguel de (Miguel de Cervantes Saavedra). *Don Quixote or Don Quixote of La Mancha.* **Translated and with an introduction by Walter Starkie. New American Library, A Signet Classic, 1964. 1,052pp.**

Don Quixote, a famous and well-to-do gentleman, becomes enamored of knighthood and begins a quest. Pressing his servant Sancho Panza into service as he goes about the world in search of daring and brave deeds to perform, Quixote accomplishes many noteworthy feats, among them his battle with windmills and his gallant treatment of the fallen woman Dulcinea. The most valuable feature of this particular edition is a nine-page table of contents that gives each chapter's opening sentences and with them key features of the Don's travels and the pages on which they occur.

This is not a book to be attempted at one fell swoop. Rather, the contents may lead the reader to one passage of interest and then another. The Don's adventures are bizarre enough that any one of them might stand alone for an evening's enjoyment. (In Kathy Latrobe's readers theatre skits, the windmill scene is played out, making that absurd part of the story abundantly clear.)

Cervantes, Miguel de (Miguel de Cervantes Saavedra). *Don Quixote or The Adventures of Don Quixote.* **Translated and with an introduction by J. M. Cohen. Penguin Books, 1950. 940pp.**

As in the previous entry, windmills, fantasies, romance, seventeenth-century chivalry, and Spain are cornerstones to a romantic drama. Readers are invited to take a close look at the difference in translator style in the first line of the prologue. Both of these skilled translators have tried to convey the spirit of the language, which is both foreign and several hundred years old. Obviously, it is not an exact science. Comparing translations will give the person who is newly acquiring English a way of seeing how the same thing may be said in more than one way, and grasping the fact that there is no single correct translation.

Geoffrey Chaucer (????–1400 C.E.)

The Chanticleer Collection

Geoffrey Chaucer's epic poem about the pilgrimage to the shrine of martyred St. Thomas Becket in Canterbury is revered both for its historic information about the times and for the often humorous morality lessons offered by the various people along the path. With a single purpose, these travelers from all walks of life, who are gathered together in a Southwark inn, are faced with many empty hours. The innkeeper comes up with an idea, a pre-radio drama game show, so to speak. Each of the pilgrims is to tell the others a tale. Upon their return from the shrine, the best storyteller will win a dinner. Thus, the tales from many folk are woven into the entertainment stream for one long voyage. Chaucer's language is now archaic, so scholars have done many translations, ever struggling to get at the hidden messages buried beneath the original words.

Like Shakespeare, Chaucer (who died in 1400, having finished only 21 of the more than 100 intended tales) is assumed to have drawn on current events (current for the year 1387) to spice up his turns of phrase. Unfortunately, we have no newspapers on file to give us definitive information about his life and times. So whenever an old letter from that time turns up or a diary is found, it is examined by scholars, who try to add new layers of meaning to the *Canterbury Tales*. Hence, there is no final text.

In this section, the focus is on one tale that has been retold for generations. Within "The Nun's Priest's Tale" is the story of a proud bird with a colorful comb and a sense of pride that almost leads to his demise. Because this popular fable has been re-created in picture books and many editions of modern English, it can be used to provide scaffolding for new readers and new speakers of English; as a scholarly, in-depth look at one of English literature's landmark tales; and as a rip-roaring good read at every level. The tale of Chanticleer the rooster and his close encounter with a fox is in the spotlight here.

Having a general idea of what the story is about will strengthen comprehension for any reader. Too often school assignments begin with the assumption that Chaucer (like Shakespeare) is to be revered first and understood almost immediately thereafter. Appreciation doesn't happen that way for anyone. Appreciation requires understanding, and understanding requires time and support. The titles in this section will give the student-who-would-become-a-scholar support for just one small part of the Chaucer literature, the story of Chanticleer.

Before touching a single book, you may want to give an overview of just how long ago that rooster lived—615 years or so. It may also be useful to know that his story purported to teach a lesson way back then, perhaps a moral lesson about the perils of vanity. With such an understanding, the picture book about Chanticleer and the fox that Barbara Cooney has illustrated can be appreciated as contemporary literature that gives readers a glimpse into Chaucer's time. After fully enjoying the Cooney edition, the value of McCaughrean's retelling of the Chanticleer dream episode may emerge. This is not to suggest that scholars plunge from one interpretation to the next in minutes or even weeks. Savoring the moment is one of the rewards that come from a little understanding.

Eventually, however, some readers will want to know more. It is helpful to understand that there is no definitive explanation regarding the tales Chaucer retold about the lusty and creative people on their pious pilgrimage to Canterbury. Discussions about the Canterbury Tales that can be appreciated by common researchers are also included in this section.

Who cares about these old stories, anyway? Well, for one example, Oscar Wilde did. In his humorous spoof about an American family vacationing in a haunted English manor, he conjures a scene that features the crow of a contrary rooster, a rooster named Chanticleer. This little literary joke will only be understood by the reader who knows who Chanticleer was. So it is that intellectual games may pass among eons of literary folk, waiting to enrich the informed.

Students who are assigned to write about the work of Geoffrey Chaucer may find it helpful to see how others have bitten off pieces of the topic, focusing on just one point or one idea. That, after all, is what Barbara Cooney did, isn't it?

Chaucer, Geoffrey. *Chanticleer and the Fox.* Illustrated by Barbara Cooney. HarperTrophy, 1989 (1958). 40pp.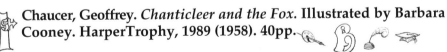

This is a picture book retelling adapted from Robert Mayer Luminasky's translation of the "Nun's Priest's Tale" from *The Canterbury Tales* by Geoffrey Chaucer. This morality tale uses the vanity of Chanticleer the rooster to show how such a sin will lead one into to the jaws of a fox. It includes a subplot of dreams and premonitions and the folly of ignoring them. Although the language is not simple and the plot has several twists, lively pictures and passages of just one or two paragraphs each make this ancient tale easy to comprehend.

Chaucer, Geoffrey. *Canterbury Tales.* **Translated and edited by A. Kent and Constance B. Hieatt. Bantam Classics, 1982. 448pp.**

This bilingual edition has the Middle English on one page and simple, modern English following phrase-by-phrase on the opposite. Here is a simple, straightforward version of a handful of the *Canterbury Tales.* The tales in this edition are "The Prologue," The Knight's Tale," "The Miller," "The Wife of Bath's Tale," "The Merchant," "The Franklin's Tale," "The Pardoner," "The Prioress," and "The Nun's Priest's Tale." There is also a glossary and a bibliography.

Cohen, Barbara, ed. *Canterbury Tales.* **Illustrated by Trina Schart-Hyman. Lothrop, Lee & Shepard, 1988. 104pp.**

Here is Chanticleer in all his glory, cozied up to by an adoring missy. The scrolling frame just finishing the page is as this proud bird would have ordered it. "The Nun's Priest's Tale," preceded by "Prologue to the Nun's Priest's Tale," is one of four featured here. The others are "The Pardoner's Tale," "The Wife of Bath's Tale," and "The Franklin's Tale," which likewise have their respective prologues and the prologue to all the Canterbury tales, which introduces the lot of travelers and sets them up for storytelling. Lively, clear modern prose (not simplified) tells the tales. Solid pages of text with lots of space between the lines are counterbalanced by stunning, full-page illustrations with realistic portraits of the featured four tellers and group shots of the rest throughout this gem of a book. By looking at the costuming and actions in the pictures, the reader will not only be entertained but will find a whole new level of meaning. This is an ideal next step for the reader who wants to hear more details from those pilgrims who went to Canterbury in 1387.

Hastings, Selina, reteller. *A Selection from Canterbury Tales.* **Illustrated by Reg Cartwright. Henry Holt, 1988. 75pp.**

The biography of the nun's priest and his full-page portrait (pages 44 and 45) are followed by five lively pages of text and four brilliant illustrations. A portrait of Geoffrey Chaucer; a brief introduction to Chaucer, his times, and the literary device he used to pull these varied tales together; and another brief introduction for the setup at the tabard introduce seven illustrated, two-page-spread biographies of the pilgrim storytellers and their respective tales. The clear, not simplified prose in large, clear print is just one reason for tracking down this now out-of-print edition. The contents pages show a small portrait of each teller (Knight, Miller, Reeve, Nun, Nun's Priest, Pardoner, Wife of Bath, and Franklin) below their respective page numbers. There is also an illustrated index, with an illustration of each of the seven locales above the seven descriptions and character lists. The organization of this book shows the reader how to set up a research paper. It is a classic worth having in the homeschool or personal collection.

Osborne, Mary Pope, reteller. "Chanticleer and the Fox." In *Favorite Medieval Tales,* **67–72. Illustrated by Troy Howell. Scholastic Press, 1998. 86pp.**

It is the duet of Chanticleer and his love Pertelote as they sing "My Love Steps Through the Land" that gets the attention of reader and, no doubt, of the fox in this retelling. By no means simplified, Osborne's retelling will introduce readers to new vocabulary. "Trying to salvage his pride, Chanticleer flew down from his perch and began strutting like a lion up and down the yard" (page 70). But that was before he spied the beast that had haunted his dreams. The fox invited him to sing as his father had sung, and he could not refuse. He stretched back his neck and in no time . . . .

Chaucer, Geoffrey. *Canterbury Tales.* **Translated by J. U. Nicolson. Dover Thrift, 1994. 135pp.**

A brief biography of Chaucer informs the reader about the man and his work in easy to follow language. Two pages give a Middle English sample of the "Prologue," allowing the reader to hear how this tale sounds when recited in many English classes. The "General Prologue" provides the same introduction in modern English and continues, introducing in rhythmical poetry each of the storytellers with a mini-biographical sketch that would lend itself nicely to small group or classroom interpretation. These character sketches make the pilgrims come alive in ways that few books do. "The Knight's Tale," "The Miller's Prologue," "The Miller's Tale," "The Wife of Bath's Prologue," and "The Wife of Bath's Tale" follow a poetic format using modern vocabulary. But the syntax still poses some stumbling blocks for the new speaker of English and the new reader. For the sake of making the lines rhyme, some sentences are turned about, still grammatically correct, but not in common use form.

These tales are reprinted from *Canterbury Tales: Rendered into Modern English by J. U. Nicolson* (Garden City Publishing, 1934). The print is small, but wide margins leave lots of room for notes. "The Nun's Priest's Tale" is not among these, but this little book does provide an affordable edition. "The Wife of Bath's Tale" gives entertaining detail about the Arthurian legend, wherein a rapist is saved only to be sent on a quest to find out "What thing it is that women most desire." For picture book support for this anecdote, look at Selina Hastings's *Sir Gawain and the Loathly Lady* in the King Arthur collection, above. The reader who has become excited about King Arthur or Chanticleer will assuredly enjoy these excerpts about war, compassion, loyalty, and many other human traits.

Mccaughrean, Geraldine, reteller. *The Canterbury Tales.* **Illustrated by Victor G. Ambrus. Rand McNally, 1984. 118pp.**

Each of the 15 tales in this book is illustrated by several colored ink drawings, sometimes humorous, sometimes chilling, always informing.

The print is easy on the eyes, but the prose is by no means simple. "From the tangle of reins, I sorted out my own, mounted, dismounted, told the Ship's Captain he was on my horse, and helped him on to his," reports the author in his prologue. This collection was first published by Oxford University Press. It is a delightful read-aloud collection, well-suited to introducing Chaucer to a small group, such as a homeschool session, or to an individual.

McCaughrean, Geraldine, reteller. "Nightmare Beast of the Firebrand Tail." In *The Canterbury Tales*, 28–37. Illustrated by Victor G. Ambrus. Oxford University Press, 1999 (1984). 117pp.

The Chanticleer tale is told in the chapter "Nightmare Beast of the Firebrand Tail" (pages 28–37), in which Chanticleer is introduced through language that is by no means simple, attempting an Old English flavor. ("Crowned at birth with the name Chanticleer, no cockerel in all the land could crow more graciously. His head was emblazoned with a comb-crest as scarlet as deep-sea coral, crenellated like the battlements of a castle wall," pages 28–29). But after getting the main idea of this tale from the Barbara Cooney picture book, the reader may want to first work through this rich retelling of the Chanticleer experience and then move on to other stories. Although there are a few pages of solid text, almost every one of the 117 pages of this book is illustrated.

Nardo, Don, ed. *Readings on the Canterbury Tales*. <u>Literary Companion Series</u>. Greenhaven Press, 1997. 192pp.

In this collection of 17 scholarly essays about various aspects of *The Canterbury Tales*, three entire chapters address language, themes, and the characters or the poem. Each essay is composed of sections that run for only one to two pages in length and can serve as independent readings. A heavy grey line runs below each section, a feature that helps readers find and keep their place.

Two sections will be of primary interest to the user of this guide. "The Moral of the Nun's Priest's Tale" by Saul N. Brody (pages 155–162) suggests that in all fiction there is an element of truth and compares this barnyard tale to George Orwell's talking animals in *Animal Farm*. Brody uses the J. U. Nicolson translation of the reporting by Chanticleer of his dream about the fox as the basis for his analysis of the poem. In "The Theme of Religious Pilgrimage in The Canterbury Tales" by Esther C. Quinn (pages 74–100) is "Becket's Murder and Martyrdom" (page 77), a clearly written background essay of less than a page long that explains why there is a shrine to visit (information that would have been common knowledge when Chaucer wrote about this gathering). There are also an English chronology for 1327–1400, an extensive index, and a bibliography for further reading. Because of the clear language and the reader-friendly, open-anywhere organization of this book, the small print and solid pages of text are much less off-putting than they typically would be. This is the kind of reference one might use for a Chaucer trivia game. It is also set up for easy bedtime reading. Teachers can use various sections to facilitate a student panel discussion. Homeschoolers may want to have it as a reference guide. It is appropriate for readers from an intermediate level on up. It is an ideal reader for units on medieval history, literature of the Middle Ages, morality tales, and Chaucer.

 Benson, Larry D. "The Nun's Priest's Tale." and "The Second Nun and Nun's Priest's Tale." In *The Riverside Chaucer*, 3d ed., 18–19 and 806. Houghton Mifflin, 1987. 1,327pp.

This is a scholarly analysis of *Canterbury Tales* and other Chaucer works that is not intended for leisure reading. But what are of interest are the discussions about the nun's priest who told the tale of Chanticleer and the fox. On page 806 a very short section refers to the Second Nun and Nun's Priest, spelling out the relationship of this storyteller to the Prioress. On this page we find the opinion that Chaucer expected to include biographies of several more characters like these and never got to it, and a projection regarding why the numbers of pilgrims and storytellers don't add up. On pages 18–19 there is an investigative analysis (or scholarly hypothesis), comparing this impoverished optimist to the well-endowed, but dour, monk. Also of interest to someone trying to forge a way through the old language, the copy of the Chanticleer episode (pages 253–261) in this book is glossed at the bottom of each page. That is, unfamiliar words in the poem can be found translated in the margins at the bottom of the pages. While no new reader would open this book alone, a walk through the sections and examination of the Chanticleer parts would help to demystify the research process.

 Chaucer, Geoffrey. *Canterbury Tales*. Introduction by Louis Untermeyer. Modern Library, 1994. 642pp.

The narrator tells of many colorful characters he meets, who share their strange and informing tales during a fourteenth-century pilgrimage. One of them is the Nun's Priest (here spelled "Nonne Preestes") , who relates the tale of Chanticleer the rooster, a proud bird fooled by a flattering fox and stolen from his barnyard. Chanticleer eventually manages to trick the fox into setting him free. This is an early trickster tale that demonstrates the roots of a character form enjoying a renaissance in children's literature today. This edition provides a familiar rendition of the poem with unfamiliar spellings, plus a lengthy glossary of obsolete words, rarely used words, and words that have changed meaning over time. This is not an easy read, but it is a fine tool for accessing some meaning buried in the text. The reader may want to use the glossary while reading another copy of the poem. Although this edition refers to the characters' names in old spellings and many current editions do not, there is enough similarity to make the connections, and the anecdotal notes are both informative and, at times, amusing. This book provides the reader with a chance to peruse other tales while in the neighborhood.

 McCaughrean, Geraldine, reteller. "Nightmare Beast of the Fire-brand Tail." In *The Canterbury Tales*, 26–32. Puffin, 1997 (1984). 113pp.

This newer edition contains the same text as the Oxford University Press edition listed above, but has no pictures. The lack of pictures makes this edition more challenging than the Oxford edition. Still, it will serve as a fine read-aloud book.

Omar Khayyám (ca. 1048–1122 C.E.)

The Rubáiyát Collection

Unknown as a poet during his lifetime, Omar Khayyám, a Persian mathematician, astronomer, and philosopher, also wrote poetry. According to some accounts, Khayyám was among the eight wise men selected by Malik Shah to revise the calendar into what is now known as the Jalali era. It was not until a collection of his quatrains (in a style popular during his lifetime) were discovered generations later by D. G. Rosetti and others and translated into English by Edward Fitzgerald (1809–1883) that Khayyám's poetry earned wide acclaim. (The heretical content may give a clue as to why the astronomer did not publish his poetry during his lifetime.) The 200 to 600 Rubiat or quatrains composed by Omar Khayyám are not one story or efforts at an epic work. They are independent philosophical observations about life, the meaning of life, and the relationship of man to the other, equally present, elements of the earth. Though many verses were traced directly to Khayyám, others appear to have been corrupted or entirely designed by later pens.

There are numerous editions of the Fitzgerald translations, only two of which are discussed here. Libraries, small independent bookstores, and used bookstores are great places to look for limited editions of large, illustrated copies. These tales lend themselves to colorful, romantic depictions.

Khayyám, Omar (ca. 1048–1122). *Rubáiyát of Omar Khayyám.* Illustrated by Edmund Dulac. Translated by Edward Fitzgerald. Introduction by A. S. Byatt. Quality Paper Back Book Club, Book of the Month Club, 1996. 189pp.

A poetic and farcical vision of life reveals how one Persian scientist perceived the meaning of life in the eleventh century. Suggesting that life is fleeting and one must enjoy the present, for once dead, there's no coming back, the poet ran against the traditions of control and restraint that were popular during his time. The pictures lend support to the reader of this edition.

Khayyám, Omar (ca. 1048–1122). *Rubáiyát of Omar Khayyám.* **1st and 5th eds. Translated by Edward Fitzgerald. Dover Publications, 1990. 52pp.**

The poet speaks of drinking wine (or the wine of life), enjoying the moment (or this one life we have), and yet respecting every living thing—birds and blades of grass—because they were dreams of lovers once. Having two editions in one book provides a walk into the process. From this little book readers can study the progression of the translator's craft into the poet's domain. A look at an illustrated edition will give needed support to the reader.

The Pied Piper of Hamelin Town (1284 C.E.) Collection

Here is the tale of the stranger who appeared in the rat-infested town of Hamelin, Germany, on June 26, 1284, the feast day of Saints John and Paul. It was on that day that 130 children simply vanished. Were they plague victims? Had they eaten rye bread contaminated by the fungus ergot? Were they lured into the Children's Crusade? Kidnapped and sold into slavery? Any of these explanations is possible. All that is known is that a man in colorful clothes was seen playing a colorful flute, and the children were last seen dancing around him. Based on real events, this haunting tale from the Middle Ages has been the stuff of literary inspiration ever since. In the selections below, readers can trace how an actual event inspired literature, and then how one literary work, Robert Browning's poem, inspired both the illustrator Kate Greenaway and the modern poet Shel Silverstein.

Note: Hamelin may also be spelled Hameln or Hamlin. The Web site for the town spells it Hameln.

 Biro, Val. *The Pied Piper of Hamelin.* **Silver Burdett, 1985. 32pp.**

Here is a retelling of the famous tale with the mystery solved and a happy ending. Full-page illustrations give the reader a delightful trip through the town and into the river. At first, only the rats go in. Then, after the Piper has taken the children into the mountain, the townspeople toss the self-serving, lying mayor and his administration in. Justice having been done, the Piper opens the mountain and restores the children to their now rat-free town. Purists may shudder at rewritten history, but those who require that everything turn out well will breathe a sigh of relief. Voters in search of subtle, literary ways of informing corrupt city officials may find this edition a perfect gift book.

 Lemieux, Michéle, reteller. *The Pied Piper of Hamelin*. Morrow Books, 1993. 32pp.

The once prosperous town of Hamelin, Germany has been overtaken by a scourge of rats. They are under doors, into beds, and eating everything in sight. Told in straightforward prose, the legend gets a new look from the oversized, dramatic, colorful drawings that fill almost every page. Very big print and just a few lines of text per page make this perfect for the adult new reader or English language learner.

 Browning, Robert [1812–1889]. *The Pied Piper of Hamelin*. Illustrated by Kate Greenaway. Dover Publications, 1997 (1888). 44pp.

Here are the words of the classic morality poem detailing how rats overran the little German town, how a bargain was struck between the mayor and a piper to get rid of the rats, how that bargain was broken after the services had been rendered, and how the piper then stole away the children in revenge. The illustrations were added subsequently. Pastel tones color the realistic drawings of the unhappy events. And at the end is Browning's warning, "If we've promised them aught, let us keep our promise!" Some of the pages have only a single line of text with a full illustration; others have two or more verses with no illustration; but every two-page spread has at least one image for support. Kate Greenaway was one of the best-loved illustrators of her day. This is a keepsake rendition of the poem that will also serve to introduce it to literature and English students. Though bits of archaic language surface throughout the text, the layout and illustrations make this a much-appreciated work for readers from middle school (and some elementary) through adult levels. Home and classroom libraries will be enhanced by this book.

 Silverstein, Shel. "The One Who Stayed." In *Where the Sidewalk Ends*. HarperCollins, 1974. 166pp.

This poem, inspired by Robert Browning's above-referenced "The Pied Piper of Hamelin," adds another literary coin to the coffers of a horrific event that cannot be forgotten. The Silverstein poem illustrates how one piece of literature inspires another. Art inspires art. This poem is long enough to be used as a readers theatre event and short enough for memorizing. Speech teachers will find a wide range of attitudes that can be demonstrated quickly through a single reading of this poem. In its twenty-fifth year of publication, this collection of 10 poems was released on CD, The poems are "recited, sung and shouted" by the author. Unfortunately, he did not choose to read "The One Who Stayed," a story about a child who was afraid to follow the Piper.

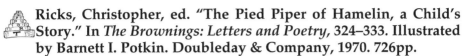 **Ricks, Christopher, ed. "The Pied Piper of Hamelin, a Child's Story." In *The Brownings: Letters and Poetry*, 324–333. Illustrated by Barnett I. Potkin. Doubleday & Company, 1970. 726pp.**

The tragic Hamelin tale is detailed in Robert Browning's (1812–1889) "The Pied Piper of Hamelin, a Child's Story" (pages 324–333). In this long poem, Browning suggests that a deal to get rid of the horrible rats went bad after the Piper had caused the rats to race into the river and drown. The mayor, it seems, having no further need for the piper's services, refused to pay him. Angered, the piper bedazzled the children with his music and led them away.

Support will be found both in the context of the letters in this book and in the 🎺 books in this section. Once the reader has the concept of the story, comprehension will come easily. Note that a 🏛 edition of this same text, having lots of illustrations to support comprehension, is listed above. Homeschoolers may want to use this book as a foundation for a Browning poetry unit and this excerpt in a social science unit on children's issues in Germany of the Middle Ages. The poem could also provide a context for a science unit on rodents and disease.

Skurzynski, Gloria. *What Happened in Hamelin*. Bullseye Books, Random House, 1979. 175pp.

When the cradle of the mayor's baby daughter was invaded by rats, the whole town was called together to pray for relief from the pestilence that had doubled and then tripled within the last week. Only the orphan Geist was around when the stranger entered the baker's door. As the boy reported the state of the town, the stranger ate a loaf of fresh bread. That is how Geist happened to know so much more than anyone else when the man with the silver pipe suddenly vanished, after the children had been driven into a killing frenzy. The events in this book are frighteningly possible. It demonstrates how the historical event (and probably the Browning poem) has inspired a modern novel.

Note: A suggested readers theatre skit about the meeting of Geist and Gast under the bridge is outlined on page 117 of *Readers' Theatre for Young Adults* by Kathy Howard Latrobe and Mildred Knight.

William Tell (ca. 1307 C.E.) Collection

The story of William Tell is a blend of historical fact and continuing bursts of the literary imagination. Though some sources maintain that William Tell was a real life superhero, most sources suggest he is a compilation of many brave men who were marked by physical prowess, unparalleled courage, and a willingness to do anything necessary for the right to gain freedom for their people.

The story tells us that Gessler (or Gryssler), bailiff of Uri and enforcer for Albert of Austria, was growing increasingly tyrannical in his demands of the forest dwellers, whose ancient (and not very desirable) lands Albert had decided were part of his property. Some time between 1260 and 1334 C.E., Gessler reportedly posted his feathered cap on a rail and demanded that all who passed it should bow. William Tell, who was already involved in intrigue and plans to overthrow the oppressors, passed the post as he walked with his little boy, Walter. Some say he didn't know about the bow rule, and others say he simply ignored it. In any event, Tell was challenged and refused to comply, whereupon he was told he must shoot an apple off his son's head in order to stay free. He took his crossbow from his shoulder and was successful, but he did not go free. The bailiff had lied, thereby setting into motion continued stories of revenge and trickery that fill many volumes.

The legend of the Swiss hero Wilhelm Tell may have begun in 1307 just prior to the struggle for independence from Austria. It was written into popular form in the *Chronicon Helveticum* (1732–1734) by Gilg Tschudi, who clearly introduced some historical fabrications. But that work inspired the 1804 dramatic interpretation by Freidrich von Schiller, which in turn inspired the 1829 opera *Guillaumi Tell* by Gioacchio Rossini. (It was in this opera that the English horn or alto oboe was given its first significant parts.)

As books on this topic quickly go in and out of print and are sometimes republished after remaining dormant for several years, it is impractical to settle on one or two favorite editions. The books presented here are just a few samples of those that readers may expect to find in libraries and can buy through the new and used book sources currently available. Because of translation differences and a lack of modern written documentation of dates and events, readers may discover a wide range of name spellings, locations, and dates attributed to this very popular tale of honor, courage, and risk-taking.

 Fisher, Leonard Everett. *William Tell.* **Farrar, Straus & Giroux, 1996. 32pp.**

Here is the tale of the legendary hero who refused to bow to the oppressive overlord's cap and, as punishment, was required to shoot an apple off his little boy's head. Placed "early in the fourteenth century," this edition has richly colored paintings with dramatic lights and shadows that provide comprehension support. But the text, superimposed on the illustrations, is less easy to read than black print on white paper normally is.

Small, Terry. *The Legend of William Tell.* **Bantam Little Rooster Book, 1991. 32pp.**

Gessler the Black, Viceroy of Austria, ruled the once happy people with an iron fist and tyranny. Furthermore, the people were expected to show deference to Gessler by bowing to his cap, an act of respect that William Tell refused to commit. So William was forced to shoot an arrow at an apple that was balanced atop his beloved son's head. That the lad stood still and trusted his father suggests both an extraordinary relationship between the father and son, and courage in both members of the family. Here the tale is told in verse, the strong rhymes causing the English-speaking reader to automatically pronounce words that might otherwise be difficult. This is a fine read-aloud or read-along book. The detailed pictures hold volumes of information and entertainment. Though out of print, this volume can be found in libraries and small independent bookstores.

Buff, Mary, and Conrad Buff. *The Apple and the Arrow.* **Houghton Mifflin, 2001 (1952). 80pp.**

The 1291 incident is told from the perspective of Walter, William Tell's son, rather than the typical storyteller's point of view. Swiss-born author Conrad and his wife Mary give many historical details about the real revolution as they retell this exciting legend. The language is clear, yet provides the reader with small details that make the story lift from the page. There are black-and-white and full-color illustrations every few pages in this Newbery Honor Book.

Other Literature About the Middle Ages

Hunt, Jonathan. *Illuminations.* **Bradbury Press, 1989, 44pp.**

Brilliantly illuminated medieval scenes fill the pages of what proves to be an alphabet book. Every illuminated letter introduces a concept, theme, or term that is illustrated with a big picture and detailed sidebars, borders, or insets. *A* is for the alchemist who, during the Middle Ages, might have been identified as a witch. *B* is for the Black Death or bubonic plague of 1347 to 1350, which wiped out one of every three people in Western Europe. *G* is for the Holy Grail, which revealed itself only to the purest Arthurian knight, Sir Galahad. *W* is for wattle and daub, medieval construction of a wooden frame filled in with woven mats—wattle—that was then covered with mud or clay. Topics include details about dragons, Excalibur, falconry, jousting, Merlin, the Normans, troubadours, and unicorns. There are 26 magnificent surprises in this book. The passages are only about eight lines long, and the reader will learn something on every page. There is also a bibliography for those who want to follow up on topics of special interest. The picture-text combination fosters comprehension of intricate details.

Chapter 3

Renaissance Literature

The term "Renaissance," which springs from the French word *rebirth*, refers to a return to a livelier secular society with a sudden surge of creativity, according to *Benét's Reader's Encyclopedia*, and denotes a period that begins in the "mid-14th to the end of the 16th centuries."

In this chapter Renaissance literature is represented by five literary icons: William Blake (1757–1827), John Milton (1608–1674), Alexander Pope (1688–1744), William Shakespeare (1564–1616), and Edmund Spenser (1552 or 1553–1599). Titles within each section are grouped by reading levels:

 Start Here!

 Next Read

 Support Here

 Challenging Read

William Blake (1757–1827) Collection

A self-taught poet, essayist, and artist, William Blake left a legacy of works that gives readers a glimpse into a man of genius who was at once a part of, and compelled to pull at the edges of, his times. Born to parents of modest means, Blake was engraving copies of Greek antiquities at the age of 10 and was apprenticed to an engraver when he was 14. At 21, his apprenticeship finished, he set up shop as an engraver. His first visions having occurred during his early childhood, Blake was recognized as unusual by his parents, who knew better than to force traditional schooling on him. Called a mystic by some, Blake considered himself a prophet. His art and poetry must be viewed together.

In 1782 he married Catherine Boucher, a woman five years his junior, who was preliterate (signing their wedding contract with an X), and he set about to teach her. She was eventually able to assist with his engravings, an enormous task considering that Blake wrote his poems, engraved the texts, created etchings to illustrate them, and hand-colored each. Over time, Blake came to believe himself spiritually connected to great persons such as Milton.

In this collection is a sampling of enduring work both by Blake and about him. Yet the unfamiliar reader may want to have a look first at Nancy Willard's picture book, *A Visit to William Blake's Inn: Poems for Innocent and Experienced Travelers*, with modern illustrations by Alice Provensen and Martin Provensen. It will help to set the stage for the power of Blake's language and his drawings. A look at the Dover edition of *Songs of Innocence* (or another edition that uses the Blake prints) will ease the modern reader into enjoying Blake literature as a visual as well as a linguistic experience. Even when leafing through, it is impossible to escape the emotional-spiritual messages of his images or the Christian moral undertones of his subjects. Yet reading directly from the reproductions of copper plates can be a difficult task, so having a modern typeset copy handy is essential for maximum enjoyment.

The Easson and Easson book is a scholarly work that will nonetheless support an appreciation of the whole Blake persona. It not only provides extensive discussions of the literary work, but also attempts to explain Blake's printing process in a way that will help the reader understand how extremely personal his work is, how Blake integrated visual and verbal experiences, and why each print must be considered a unique work of art. This is not a book to be read from start to finish. It is one that deserves to be referenced over and over as the reader develops both an understanding of and an appreciation for this man of genius.

Blake, William. *Songs of Experience.* **Color Facsimile of the First Edition with 26 Color Plates. Dover Publications, 1984. 42pp.**

The prologue to "A Little Girl Lost" reads

Children of the future Age, Reading this indignant page:
Know that in a former time,
Love! sweet Love! was thought a crime.

Like *Songs of Innocence*, this book has a mix of poems and illustrations. See *Innocence* for more detail on the presentation. It is difficult to imagine that school children were ever permitted to read Blake's empathetic poem *The School-Boy*, which is clearly addressed to parents, about the plight of children trapped in school during the best years of their lives. He considered school to be a form of child abuse. One passage reads:

How can the bird that is born for joy,
Sit in a cage and sing.
How can a child who fears annoy,
But droop his tender wing,
And forget his youthful spring.

 Blake, William. *Songs of Innocence.* **Color Facsimile of the First Edition with 31 Color Plates. Dover Publications, 1973. 55pp.**

Here is a mix of poems and illustrations, both on each page. They were originally designed to be mixed in random order. The hand-colored copperplate prints were different from copy to copy, per Blake's intention. Like the edition of *The Marriage of Heaven and Hell*, this palm-sized book has reproductions of the original prints with text and illustrations and a modern typeface copy of the text.

 Willard, Nancy. *A Visit to William Blake's Inn: Poems for Innocent and Experienced Travelers.* **Illustrated by Alice Provensen and Martin Provensen. Bt Bound Harcourt Children's Books, 1981. 40pp.**

Fifteen rhyming verses about an imaginary inn owned by William Blake demonstrate a love of that famous poet's work that Willard has had since her childhood. Of interest to the writer will be Willard's one-page introduction, in which she tells how she was first introduced to the work of William Blake as a child. Clearly this early introduction resulted in a lifetime of good experiences, including the inspiration for this book. Whimsical characters doing essential chores, such as dragons baking bread, have earned the book both Newbery and Caldecott Awards. Simplistic, full-page illustrations fill in all the blanks. Rhyme is a great tool for teaching pronunciation to ESL students and for teaching phonetic connections to all.

Related reads: Other titles by Nancy Willard include *Sailing to Cythera and Other Anatole Stories, Simple Pictures Are Best, The Well-Mannered Balloon,* and *Strangers' Bread.*

 Blake, William. *Blake*. Selected, with an introduction and notes by Ruthven Todd; General Editor, Richard Wilbur. The Laurel Poetry Series, Dell, 1960. 158pp.

This is a collection of poems from Blake's letters, epigrams, and individual poems and collections of prose and poetry about life, death, God, and Christianity. Although the print is small, there is very little text per page. In spite of the copyright date, the book is available through general public libraries and independent bookstores, and can be ordered through major chains.

 Blake, William. *The Marriage of Heaven and Hell*. Dover Publications, 1994. 43pp.

In this poem, Blake reverses many of the conventional norms, placing Heaven and Hell and devils and angels in unnerving juxtaposition. This, he claimed, was essential to creativity. This palm-sized book contains full-color reproductions of the original etched copperplate prints by the author, a modern typeset copy of the text, and a one-page introduction. Looked at carefully, this book gives its own support to the reader. There is also a scholarly discussion about the impact of Milton's Satan in *The Cambridge Companion to Milton*, annotated in the Milton collection section.

 Blake, William. *Milton*. Edited and with a commentary by Kay Parkhurst Easson and Roger R. Easson. Shambhala-Boulder in association with Random House, 1978 (1811). 178pp.

This is the story of a man, John Milton, who strove to find perfection through purification—"A spiritual pilgrim" the editors call him—who is back to overcome restrictive reason and Satan. Milton (returning from the heavens over a hundred years after his mortal demise and depicted as a Christ-like figure) and Blake are spiritually one in this epic work. Joined through imagination, they are at once the living prophet and the past master. (It is important to note that imagination *was* being to Blake.) Milton's preference of reason over inspiration and his allusion that sex is a base instinct were refuted by Blake, who otherwise revered the memory of Milton—or, to be more precise, revered the Milton in himself. Though published and distributed in limited editions, this was clearly also a work in progress, with various parts rearranged from issue to issue. There is also evidence to suggest that 12 Milton "Books" were intended.

Through the images, this book provides its own support for the reader. Even so, the tutor may want to select one small part of the book as an introduction to Blake's *Milton*. A desirable familiar quote, from the preface on Plate 2, is on page 62:

> Bring me my Bow of Burning gold;
> Bring me my Arrows of desire;
> Bring me my Spear; O Clouds unfold!
> Bring me my Chariot of fire!

Readers will want to peruse the images for some time before trying to get at the meaning of this spiritual journey to purification. They will also want to refer back to them as they read the modern type version.

John Milton (1608–1674) Collection

John Milton (1608–1674) benefited from the finest education his notary/composer father could devise. First tutored privately, eventually attending Cambridge, and then receiving five years of independent study, the young scholar commenced on a two-year European excursion, during which he began to prove his worth as a poet and writer of prose. He wrote in English and Latin, and in 1649 he became the Latin secretary to Oliver Cromwell. His own Puritan views stood in contrast to his humanist notions, which to some observers looked like heresy. Even so, his writing was much sought after. By 1652, he required the services of an assistant, having ruined his vision through strain. Yet he continued to work, producing his masterpiece *Paradise Lost* in 1667. On first publication, the book did not sell well; it took several other printings under more than one title and the eventual addition of illustrations to give the work the glamour appeal necessary for success.

In 1942, C. S. Lewis wrote a scholarly analysis called *Preface to Paradise Lost* (still available through Oxford University Press). In it, Lewis challenges the reader of *Paradise Lost* to first understand what it was that Milton had in mind to do. Too often, Lewis warns, the reader is disappointed for lack of knowing what the author's intent was in the first place. While Lewis's language is straightforward and clear, this treatise is also didactic and at times repetitious, but it could provide interesting background information for the educator or readers' advisor.

The literary periods to which Milton's works may be assigned are the Caroline Age (1625–1642) and the Commonwealth Interregnum (1649–1660). Milton's literary efforts included political literature, sonnets, elegies, lyric poetry, masques, epics, essays, and poetic drama.

Milton, John. *Doré's Illustrations for "Paradise Lost."* **Illustrated by Gustave Doré (1832–1883). Dover Publications, 1993 (1866). 50pp.**

Man's fall from the grace of God and loss of the right to live in Paradise was detailed in John Milton's epic poem *Paradise Lost* in the seventeenth century. Two-hundred years later, Milton's poem was detailed by Gustave Doré's enchanting wood engravings, all 50 of which have been reproduced in this volume. The book opens with a historical accounting of the poem, followed by Milton's own plot summaries of the 12 books of the poem. Then there are the 50 full-page plates, with brief quotes from the original poem and reference to the exact book and line quoted. This awesome picture book, illustrating Paradise, Satan, Adam, and Eve, is a must-see for anyone who wants to learn more about the poem, the poet, the artist, or the biblical story. The print is small, the pictures monumental. Used as a picture book, this suits every reader.

Related read: William Blake's *Milton* is annotated in the William Blake collection, above.

 Danielson, Dennis, ed. *The Cambridge Companion to Milton.* **Cambridge University Press, 1995 (1989). 297pp.**

Here are 18 scholarly articles by contemporary authors on Milton and his works. Some are much easier to comprehend than others. The first, and perhaps of most interest to readers using this guide, is "The Life of Milton" (pages 1–19) by John T. Shawcross, in which the author gives a detailed accounting of the author from his high birth and royal contacts to his death as a blind man, estranged from his three daughters. There is also considerable discussion of Milton's influence on other writers, notably on Percy Bysshe Shelley and William Blake, as the two responded to Milton's Satan (pages 252–253). In the twentieth century alone nearly 10,000 items have been published about Milton. This book is a very readable sampler. The half-dozen historic illustrations are not enough to carry the very new reader along. There is a list of significant dates and works and an extensive index. The biographical chapter aside, this book is best used as a reference guide or for read-aloud passages, such as Milton's rhetoric of prophesy and Milton and the sexes.

Alexander Pope (1688–1744) Collection

Born in London on May 21, 1688, to a papist couple, the prosperous linen merchant Alexander Pope and his second wife Edith Turner, Alexander Pope grew up a Catholic and died one during an extremely anti-Catholic time. The family had to relocate to Binfield in order to comply with a statute forbidding Catholics to live within 10 miles of London or Westminster. These laws no doubt restricted the professional prospects and quelled any political aspirations of young Alexander, who was educated sporadically by tutors of Latin, Greek, French, Italian, and other liberal arts, who encouraged him to become an avid reader. Left physically disfigured by a childhood illness, possibly tuberculosis of the bone, he grew only to about four feet six and had a severely hunched back. Intuitively skilled in poetic technique, at the age of 11 he was writing poetry and, in 1711 at only 23, he published the scholarly *An Essay on Criticism*. This work instantly gave him literary recognition. In 1704, upon reading some of his poems, William Wycherley introduced the young Pope to members of the London literary establishment. His understanding of metrics emerged in *Pastorals* (1709), which he had written when he was only 16. His style, perhaps reflecting the personalities of some tutors, was didactic and at times cuttingly sarcastic. These characteristics showed themselves in his essays and poems. Yet he had gained a great understanding of classical themes and history. His neoclassical style served him well as he translated the *Iliad* (in six volumes) and the *Odyssey*. He found unending support in his friendship with Jonathan Swift, who secured for him many patrons to purchase the *Illiad* work. The money from this enterprise and the subsequent *Odyssey* gave him enough, when combined with his inheritance from his father, to live independently for the rest of his life. Those efforts were much praised, but when he produced an annotated Shakespeare, he lacked the scholarly foundation and was roundly criticized by some of his contemporaries, among them Theobald. Pope, ever the sardonic wit, returned the criticism by naming names in *Duncaid*, a spoof on literary critics and criticism, sporting Theobald as the first edition hero. Appearing in various forms from 1728 to 1743, the cutting couplets assailed the empires of Emptiness and Dullness. Even as he labored over this voluminous enterprise, Pope added insults via The *Grub Street Journal,* a weekly bulletin. Yet those he damned in verse and handbill did not lose all; some would be unremembered were it not for their unenviable places in *Duncaid*, often considered the pinnacle of Pope's literary work.

Pope, Swift, John Arbuthnot, and other Tories established the Scriblerus, a literary group that produced satirical portrayals of their political enemies. The *Miscellanies* and other products of their collaboration put them in the direct line of fire from the literary establishment. Pope lived with his widowed mother in a villa named Twickenham. Because of his caustic criticisms of his contemporaries and didactic diatribes on many common themes, he became known as the Wicked Wasp of Twickenham. Meanwhile, he also began to dabble in the metaphysical, writing philosophical essays that were of lesser importance but that earned him more wrath than he had expected. Though he was far from reticent over his offensive behavior, his health began to deteriorate after *Duncaid*, and Pope took the advice of a Catholic friend to see a priest; he died the next day, May 30, 1744, much at peace, and was buried near his parents' memorial at Twickenham. He was 57.

Among his best-known titles are *Messiah* (1912), *The Rape of the Lock* (1712 and revised in 1714), *The Spectator* (1712), *Windsor Forest* (1713), *An Elegy to the Memory of an Unfortunate Lady* and *Epistle from Eloisa to Abelard* (1717), and *Epistle to Dr. Arbuthnot*, a scathing reference to Joseph Addison.

Note: There are over 4,500 volumes of Alexander Pope books available today. Some are extremely costly volumes. Most public libraries hold several hardbound copies. Following are just two affordable examples.

 Pope, Alexander. *Essay on Man and Other Poems*. **Dover Thrift Edition, 1994. 128pp.**

    Small print on newsprint makes this book less attractive than many books of poetry and critical thought, but the contents provide a treasure-trove of wit, sarcasm, and literary genius. Included are *The Rape of the Lock, 'Ode on Solitude, The Dying Christian to His Soul, Elegy to the Memory of an Unfortunate Lady, An Essay on Criticism, Epigram Engraved on the Collar of a Dog*, and *Epistle to Dr. Arbuthnot*.

 Pope, Alexander. *The Rape of the Lock*. **Illustrated by Aubrey Beardsley. Dover Publications, 1968 (1714). 47pp.**

    Missy's elegant curls enchant one lighthearted lad, who dares to cut one off for himself. This much is true, though the parties to the offense were no ordinary English folks. Both close to the royal family, their families commenced to feud over the incident. In 1712, in an effort to stop the bickering, Pope wrote this mock-heroic poem—a spoof on the incident blown out of proportion. He presented it to Mrs. Fermor, the de-locked, who was so pleased she gave out copies of it. Subsequently, Pope worked on the poem, extending it to the level of a classical epic and adding his own notes, included here. The language is a bit forced to make the rhymes, and some of the words are archaic. Furthermore, there are references unknown to modern readers. So, it is for the gist of the tale that a reader would take on this text. But, having been illustrated by Aubrey Beardsley, it is the collection of his highly stylized, black-and-white ink drawings that make this book a treat.

William Shakespeare (1564–1616) Collection

Born into very comfortable circumstances in Stratford, England, on a large parcel of land overlooking the Avon River, William Shakespeare had the leisure time to pursue his interest in stories told in pubs by travelers from far and wide. So the young man—who would one day be acclaimed as the greatest English writer of all time—accumulated a wealth of information about current and historical events, facts and folklore, which provided him with details about people from all walks of life for the tales he wrote down as poetry and plays. Most of his plays were based on real events or conventional wisdom that his audiences were somewhat familiar with. A career thespian, Shakespeare played in most of his own dramas, making changes to the texts in mid-rehearsal to ensure that his audiences would understand and therefore enjoy what was going on. He also used the vehicle of a prologue: an actor would face the audience before the play began and explain what was about to happen. The prologues of Shakespeare's productions might be thought of as audio program notes. Shakespeare never meant for his plays to be delivered without a great deal of support. His plays, comedies, tragedies, and histories were written to be performed by actors dressed in colorful costumes and surrounded by fanfare and music, not as silent reading material. Only after his death—in fact seven years after his death—did two members of his acting company publish and in 1623 facilitate the wide distribution of a volume of his plays, the "First Folio." So, it is in the spirit of Shakespeare's day that this collection is intended for those who are first meeting his work and for those who are revisiting the once-familiar works. This section provides the literary version of the Bard of Avon's color, spectacle, and a thespian delivering a prologue.

 Coville, Bruce, reteller. *Hamlet*. Illustrated by Leonid Gore. Dial Books, 2004. 40pp.

Hamlet was away at school when his father was murdered through "murder most foul" and his mother became the all-too-quick-bride of her brother-in-law, Claudius. The ghost of Hamlet's father appears to advise him. Hamlet takes on the guise of madness to facilitate his investigations into the crime. The beautiful daughter of Polonius, Ophelia, whom Hamlet had pursued, is frightened by the face of the Hamlet she saw after his first encounter with the ghost. The new king calls in Hamlet's school buddies, Rosencrantz and Guildenstern, to study the bereaved prince. Polonius is also sent to spy on Hamlet; when he asks the mad prince what book he is carrying, Hamlet says, "Words, words, words," a line that some may recognize from more recent literature.

The demise of almost everyone close to Hamlet is presented in very clear prose. Many of the famous idiomatic expressions, now commonly used in English, are planted in the dialogue so that the reader will quickly understand where these lines have come from. Haunting acrylic paintings allow the characters of Hamlet, Ophelia, and other ill-fated members of the cast to drift through the pages. Readers will not only experience an introduction to one of Shakespeare's most famous stories, but also will see how expressions find their way from popular literature into everyday language.

Coville, Bruce, reteller. *Macbeth.* **Illustrated by Gary Kelley. Dial Books, 1997. 48pp.**

Coville retells Shakespeare's story of a sixteenth-century Scot, Macbeth, Thane of Glamis, and his friend, Banquo, who encounter witches. Using riddles, the witches suggest to Macbeth that he is destined to greatness, to become king. So informed, Macbeth, egged on by his wife, Lady Macbeth, begins a quest for power that leaves a trail of death in his wake and makes him a king who is at once rewarded and haunted. In his introductory remarks Coville spells out the features of the original play that he has chosen to leave out. He also shares some of the lore about the play, including the fact that thespians prefer to call it "The Scottish Play" rather than bring on bad luck by speaking the word *Macbeth* aloud. The very big print and dark, ominous, shadowy pictures deliver an effective set of "program notes" for the drama. (This book is not in script format.) A perfect introduction to this play for readers of any age or level, this book would enhance the school or public library, the classroom reading center, and the homeschooler's library.

Audio version: *Shakespeare's Greatest Hits Volume I.* Full Cast Audio, 2003. 2 cassettes, 2 hours. Read by Bruce Coville, Cynthia Bishop, and the Full Cast Family. Here are four beautifully delivered summaries of *A Midsummer Night's Dream*, *Macbeth*, *Romeo and Juliet*, and *Twelfth Night*. The actors play critical plot points, reading directly from Shakespeare's lines, with narrators filling in the rest. Each play is a 30-minute presentation that invites a weeklong introduction to Shakespeare, with one play per day and a summary discussion on Friday. The voices are so clear that even the nearly beginning English learner will understand the words. The telling is so direct that even those with no background will be caught up in these tales.

 Coville, Bruce, reteller. *William Shakespeare's A Midsummer Night's Dream.* **Illustrated by Dennis Nolan. Dial Books, 1996. 40pp.**

The beautiful Athenian Hermia and the poet Lysander are deeply in love and plan to marry. But this is not the plan of Hermia's father, who prefers the level-headed and noble Demetrius, who had just recently been betrothed to Hermia's best friend, Helena. It was either marry Demetrius or die, her father said. Not so, claimed Duke Thesus, the legal authority over such matters; Hermia had the option of going to live in a religious order for the rest of her days. Meanwhile, the Duke's own wedding was being prepared. A carpenter, Peter Quince, and his friends were arranging a play for the festivities; a weaver, Nick Bottom, was to play the hero. But Shakespeare then introduces a volley of fairies, a hobgoblin, and all manner of magic and mischief-making. Bottom becomes an ass, and the entire play takes a turn toward the absurd. And they live happily after.

Nolan's realistic graphite and watercolor drawings deliver the characters enchantingly. Coville's note to readers begins with a story about E. Nesbit's daughters requesting that she write this and other Shakespearian plays in language they might appreciate. This is a book a new reader or speaker of English might readily read.

Video version: *A Midsummer Night's Dream.* Miramax, 1996. 1 cassette, 120 minutes. Starring Alex Jennings, Lindsay Duncan, Desmond Barrit, and Barry Lynch. Director Adrian Noble. Seen through the eyes of a young boy who has just been reading the play, the intrigue and fairy pranks quickly bring the tale to life as believably as it must have been to those watching it for the first time at the Globe Theatre. This is one of several well-done interpretations.

Front, Sheila. *Never Say Macbeth.* Illustrated by Charles Front, Esq. Doubleday, 1990. 32pp.

Young Jeremy Lamb has a chance encounter with the famous actor-stage-manager Sir Montague Worthington-Browne. He is offered a job that has but one unbreakable rule, "Never say 'M____h'." That name is considered extremely bad luck. The reader travels onto the stage of this Shakespearian presentation and is able to learn a great deal about the behind-the-scenes activities of the London stage and theatrical superstition. Then Jeremy makes that fatal mistake. Everything changes—chaos is king.

Koscielniak, Bruce. *Hear, Hear, Mr. Shakespeare: Story, Illustrations, and Selections from Shakespeare's Plays.* Houghton Mifflin, 1998. 32pp.

Presented in comic strip format, this book takes readers on a walk down a country lane, actually past Stratford-upon-Avon where Shakespeare lived, showing how a play came together. It may at first seem to be all whimsical illustrations, but the progression gives insights into such mundane details as rain and such important issues as the queen's interest i in the play. Many of the characters' lines are Shakespearean quotes, complete with citations. This book also has a timeline of Shakespeare's life and a list of his plays grouped into four periods.

Stanley, Diane, and Peter Vennema. *The Bard of Avon: The Story of William Shakespeare.* Illustrated by Diane Stanley. A Mulberry Paperback Book, 1992, first Mulberry printing, 1998. 48pp.

This richly illustrated biography walks the reader through the life of the most important English-language writer of all time, revealing the ways of the English in the late 1500s and the majesty of the original Globe Theatre. Stanley and Vennema report that they have only used information that is verified by historical documents.

An interesting activity is for readers to compare the school scenes illustrated by this same team in *Charles Dickens: The Man Who Had Great Expectations* with those shown here. There are full-page illustrations on the right-hand side of each two-page spread. The 14-point Bernhard Modern font is very easy on the eyes, and there are only one, two, or three para-graphs on each page. For those wanting even more, there is an author's note describing her research, a spellings and idioms discussion, and a bibliography.

Burdett, Lois. *The Tempest for Kids.* **Firefly Books, 1999. 64pp.**

During a spellbound storm, Alfonso, King of Naples, is shipwrecked on an enchanted island, where the great sorcerer Prospero plays mind games with those washed up on his shores. Hidden identity and magic make this tale fantastic entertainment. Here is an illustrated retelling of *The Tempest* in verse, with sidebar statements by the players about the situ-ation. Though the rhyme is pushed a little too hard in places, the story co-mes through. It is purportedly designed to be acted out, but the parts are not marked, so it works better as a read-aloud (teacher reading to stu-dents) introduction to the play. The exception is with a small group, such as homeschoolers or tutor groups using it for readers theatre practice. The foreword is by Richard Monett (artistic director, Stratford Festival); teaching activities are provided.

Coville, Bruce, reteller. *Romeo and Juliet.* **Illustrated by Dennis Nolan. Dial Books, 1999. 38pp.**

The feud between the Montagues and the Capulets has gone on for as long as anyone can recall. What no one can remember is why. This is the state of affairs in which the lad Romeo Montague and the lass Juliet Capulet are entangled as their forbidden love attempts to bloom and ends in a double suicide. The tale has come a long way. Coville's retelling is based on Shakespeare's play, which was based on an English translation of a French poem, which was a retelling of an Italian folktale. The gentle drawings on every page move the tragedy along, but the famous balcony scene is delivered in a dramatic vertical foldout. This presentation will help prepare the newcomer for the young lovers' dilemma, and will en-chant those who have known it in other forms. New readers will be sur-prised at how simple this famous love story is. Homeschoolers may want to trace the progression of the famous story through literary ages. Educa-tors may find this a powerful discussion starter about how unresolved conflict can prevent friendships from developing.

Video version: *Romeo & Juliet.* Fox Video Premier Series, 1996. 1 cassette, 120 min-utes. Starring Leonardo DiCaprio and Claire Danes. Director Baz Luhrmann. Relo-cated to the futuristic Verona Beach, the story is retold for modern audiences.

Related read: *The Coffin Quilt: The Feud between the Hatfields and the McCoys* by Ann Rinaldi.

Coville, Bruce, reteller. *The Tempest*. Illustrated by Ruth Sander-son. A Picture Yearling Book, 1994. 40pp.

Retold in fairytale style with magnificent classical-style paintings on almost every page, this book provides a delightful way to introduce the story line of a great play. It does not present the play in the one-day format, but presents most events sequentially to eliminate lengthy explanations. It also eliminates the subplot regarding an assassination attempt on King Alfonso. The book can be used with many different ages of students at many levels. Because the pictures and text work so well together, even new readers and new speakers of English enjoy it. Those with prior expo-sure to Shakespeare also enjoy reading this book.

Note: Those who have seen Bruce Coville will quickly observe that he posed for the pictures of the leading man, Prospero. There is a summary discussion in the author's note that will support the tutor or teacher who needs a quick refresher on this play.

 Coville, Bruce, reteller. *William Shakespeare's Twelfth Night*. Il-lustrated by Tim Raglin. Dial Books, 2003. 40pp.

This convoluted mix of disguise, misguided romance, trickery, and "he loves her, but she loves another, who loves another yet," is retold well by Coville and Raglin. The realistic, full-color, ink illustrations do help keep the reader in touch with all the comical characters. On the first page the handsome Duke Orsino pines for the lovely Olivia, who is committed to mourning her dead brother for seven years. "If music be the food of love, play on!" Orsino commands his musicians, hoping music will fill the void in his heart. Meanwhile, a shipwrecked lass, Viola, mourns her ship-wrecked twin brother, Sebastian, who may have drowned or also may have survived the storm that cast Viola onto the coast of Illyria with the ship's captain, a native of the place. Viola knows it is not good to be a stranger in a strange land, and she alights on the idea of dressing as a man—named Cesario—so that she can get work in the duke's service. Soon after, she/Cesario is hired as the duke's confidant and messenger be-tween Orsino, who thinks Viola/Cesario is a young man, and the noble-woman Olivia, who is instantly attracted to Cesario and attempts to get his attention. Viola/Cesario is twice troubled because she has begun to fall in love with the duke.

This is only part of the story. There are other characters, with their subplots, and other shunned lovers afoot. Sebastian does turn up, as does the captain who had plucked him from the angry sea. Still there is more. The language in quotes gives hints of Shakespearian turns of phrase and notable quotes. For example, the servant to Olivia says, "Some are born great. Some achieve greatness. And some have greatness thrust upon them," as he foolishly imagines she is wooing him.

Although the print is very easy on the eyes, the story and language combine to make this prose retelling of the play just a tad more difficult to follow than others in this collection rated 🎭 It is a fine introduction to *Twelfth Night*, but should not be used as the introduction to Shakespeare's plays. The presence of so much dialogue makes this a good candidate for readers theatre. For more advanced students, or as a group writing project, participants might write a prologue that would set up the audience, much the way the prologue did in Shakespeare's time.

Davis, J. Madison, and A. Daniel Frankforter, eds. *The Shakespeare Name Dictionary.* **Garland Publishing, 1995. 533pp.**

When Shakespeare wrote his popular plays, he drew upon events of the day to convey hidden meanings that his audiences would quickly understand. Such understanding eludes modern readers because the news of the 1500s and 1600s is not on our minds. So the editors of this huge dictionary researched every name and word they could find and explained how a name selection for a character would capitalize on audience prejudice or how reference to a particular location would bring to mind a litany of events. A simple name may deliver a pun to informed audiences. This is a book that can be perused randomly. Though few readers of Shakespeare would attempt to dig out every name in any play, just knowing that there is so much more meaning behind the words will give the reader a greater respect for the bard and his efforts. Look at this book as a collection of *very* short passages.

Early, Margaret. *The Most Excellent and Lamentable Tragedy of Romeo and Juliet.* **Harry N. Abrams, 1998. 32pp.**

Here is the story line of the fabled feud between the Montagues and the Capulets, retold with rich vocabulary and complex sentences, filling every left-hand page. Opposite each text section is a full-page, full-color, realistic representation that is loaded with fine details. Oddly, speakers' words are set off in single quotations marks, a point that tutors or teachers may want to mention to students who have been advised to learn punctuation from their reading. That said, this is a fine introduction to the famous tale. The author's note at the end provides some information not commonly told.

Garfield, Leon, abridger. *The Tempest.* **Illustrated by Elena Livanova.** <u>Shakespeare the Animated Tales</u>. **Heinemann Young Books, 1992. 48pp.**

After all that has been said about abridged presentations of classical works, I must include this one. It is a retelling in play form, complete with stage directions and colorful illustrations that clarify the actions, making it a natural for an introduction to drama and for classroom production. There are parts for 16 players. It is one of six Shakespeare plays that Garfield adapted for a series of animated films presented by the BBC and S4C (Channel 4 Wales).

Special features include a lengthy introduction to the theater in Shakespeare's day and a detailed biography of Shakespeare. Here is a quick pitch for the Bard that can be delivered as a readers theatre or read-aloud.

 Hopkins, Andrea, reteller. *Romeo & Juliet.* **Illustrated by Marine D'Antibes. Barnes & Noble Books, 1998; originally by Grimm Press, 1995. 56pp.**

The love of Romeo Montague and 13-year-old Juliet Capulet was forbidden by both families and complicated by the fact that a suitor of means and sufficient station had expressed an interest in marrying the girl. The tragic tale of feuding families and secret love that ends in a double suicide is presented here as prose, rather than in the dramatic form of Shakepeare's original. The language is clear, as is the type. The ethereal paintings contribute a great deal of meaning to the star-crossed lovers' tale. This book works in combination with *The Bard of Avon* and *The Tempest* (retold by Coville) with sixth graders, community college students, and university graduate students. As an introduction to Shakespeare, it works very well. This book also has a brief biography of Shakespeare.

 McQuain, Jeffrey, and Stanley Malless. *Coined by Shakespeare: Words and Meanings First Penned by the Bard.* **Merriam Webster, 1998. 273pp.**

Did you know that before William Shakespeare's time not one person was ever accused of elbowing another? It all began with *King Lear*. Neither did people do things *instinctively*. That got started with the rats of *The Tempest*. Two to four paragraphs, each paragraph being two or three sentences, are devoted to each of the Shakespearian words and phrases in this fascinating reference book. Though there are no pictures and the print is small, this is a fun, open-anywhere book. Readers will enjoy simply reading it. ESL students may want to study it as a source of many idiomatic expressions. Teachers may want to pass out different words to different student groups for presentations. And others will enjoy coming up with Shakespearian trivia.

 Miles, Bernard. *Favorite Tales from Shakespeare.* **Illustrated by Victor G. Ambrus. Checkerboard Press, 1988 (1976). 125pp.**

Here are retellings of *Macbeth*, *A Midsummer Night's Dream*, *Romeo and Juliet*, *Twelfth Night or What You Will*, and *Hamlet, Prince of Denmark* in very colorful, not at all simplified prose. In his two-page introduction, Miles reveals the sources from which Shakespeare got his original ideas and explains that he, Miles, has tried to return to those original stories that inspired the Bard of Avon. The lively, colorful illustrations add to the meaning and support comprehension of these stories. Unfortunately, the book is out of print, but it can still be found in libraries and online. It is a great read-aloud.

Related reads: Other Miles titles include *Well Loved Tales from Shakespeare, Robin Hood: His Life and Legend*, and *Curtain Calls* by Bernard Miles and J. C. Trewin.

 Nesbit, E. *The Best of Shakespeare: Retellings of 10 Classic Plays.* Introduction by Iona Opie. Afterword by Peter Hunt. Oxford University Press, 1997. 110pp.

Story lines and photographs of their dramatizations are given for *Romeo and Juliet, The Merchant of Venice, Twelfth Night, Hamlet, The Tempest, King Lear, Macbeth, As You Like It, The Winter's Tale*, and *Othello*. These are useful program notes for anyone planning to read or watch one of the Bard's works. The language is clear.

 Shakespeare, William. *A Midsummer Night's Dream.* The Folger Shakespeare Library, 1993. 204pp.

The wedding festivities of the Duke of Athens and the enchanting Hippolyta set the mood for a tale of love and potions, fairies and fantasies. This lighthearted play is delivered in a solid little book that is guaranteed to help the newcomer to Shakespeare's world. The actual text of the play is shown on the right-hand page, with story summary notes and vocabulary translations on the left. This book also has several mini-essays on the background of the play, Shakespeare's language, his theater, folio publications, and an introduction to the play. A further reading list, annotated with practical details, will be useful to the student of Shakespeare, and the key to famous lines is just interesting to read through. The good news is that this is a very small book, to be held in one hand, perhaps while the reader enjoys a glass of tea in the other. The bad news is that the print is also small. That said, this is a book worth looking through. Teachers and tutors will find it provides everything needed to set up an introductory lesson for this play.

 Williams, Marcia. *Tales from Shakespeare.* Candlewick Press, 1998. 32pp.

Formatted like a small newspaper, this is a fascinating collection of retellings. There is not a simple, thought-free inch on any of these wildly imaginative presentations. Williams has authentically interpreted each play (*Romeo and Juliet; Hamlet, Prince of Denmark; A Midsummer Night's Dream; Macbeth; The Winter's Tale; Julius Caesar;* and *The Tempest*) and has enhanced them in ways I'm sure would please the Bard. The three strangest witches I have ever seen appear before the bewildered Macbeth, who rightfully has a very white face. Unlike the traditional cartoon strip, the margins of these pages are fleshed out by members of the court and peanut gallery, who put in their two cents' worth at every scene. Of Lady Macbeth, one fellow remarks, "She's more wicked than the witches." It is all in modern English, but it works.

Chute, Marchette. *Stories from Shakespeare.* **New American Trade, 1991 (1956). 319pp.**

Describing her reason for retelling the complete plays of Shakespeare, Chute said, "I wrote it to share as far as possible the joy I have had in Shakespeare's plays. I hope I have made a small but clear path of entrance to the most varied and glorious world ever created by one man." This book is a delightfully written collection with "program notes" that will help the reader understand the many intricacies of the plays. After the three sections (Comedies, Tragedies, and Histories), you'll find a nine-page index that will prove useful to the student who is writing about Shakespeare. Though written half a century ago, this collection is still clear and useful to today's readers. Look for it in public and university libraries, used bookstores, and small independent stores. New readers will benefit from hearing passages from this book read aloud.

Related reads: Other Chute titles for young people include *An Introduction to Shakespeare*, and for adults. *The Search for God, Geoffrey Chaucer of England, The End of the Search, Shakespeare of London,* and *Ben Jonson of Westminster.*

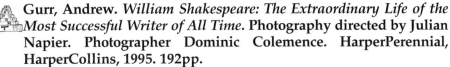 **Gurr, Andrew.** *William Shakespeare: The Extraordinary Life of the Most Successful Writer of All Time.* **Photography directed by Julian Napier. Photographer Dominic Colemence. HarperPerennial, HarperCollins, 1995. 192pp.**

This fascinating reference book is chock-full of background on the Bard, his times, his players, his successes, and his disasters. A detailed description of the rural region on the Avon River where farming was the primary activity, the scene of Shakespeare's childhood, is illustrated with authentic, historical photographs. Also included are play summaries, a Henry VII family tree (with Tudor and Stuart intermarriages), a diagram of the Shakespearean Company, and chronologies of Shakespeare's plays and influential world events (1564–1587).

This is such a rich document, opening it at random inevitably uncovers fascinating facts. Good for short reads and for serious research on the writer, his work, and his times. Any teacher intending to prepare a lesson about Shakespeare will find helpful information, and it makes a fine school library or classroom reference book. Of particular interest to thespians may be the photo-reenactment of the ghost in *Hamlet*, emerging magically from a trap door in the stage floor. Readers will find support in a chronology of Shakespeare's plays, including the play, date, playhouse, and related historical events (pages 182–183); a chronology of the world, 1564–1587 (pages 184–187); and an extensive index. For the very new Shakespearian fan, Diane Stanley and Peter Vennema's *The Bard of Avon*, annotated above, will also lend support.

Norwich, John Julius. *Shakespeare's Kings: The Great Plays and the History of England in the Middle Ages: 1337–1485.* **Scribner, 1999. 401pp.**

In this scholarly nonfiction work, William Shakespeare is examined as a historian, with comparisons of the actual events and the ways he wrote about them. This brilliantly organized and researched companion to the Bard's works is a reference tool for any scholar. It details 19 historical periods, from Edward III and the Black Prince (1337–1377) to King Richard III (1471–1485). The 13 period illuminations and paintings give worlds of details. Three lineage tables help keep the many characters straight and show the interactions between the Royal Houses of England and France. This book will help any student of Shakespeare's work grasp the historical connections between the events and characters. The reader need not use the whole book at once. Just opening to a table that explains who the Lancasters, Tudors, and Yorks were will give insights into the royal lines. Readers will discover the mass of information behind the Bard's plays that distinguishes his information-intensive presentations that are anchored in posterity from literary fluff that has blown away with the winds of time.

Teachers may want students to compare the research behind one of Shakespeare's works with the modern research project *Midnight in the Garden of Good and Evil*, a book by John Berendt that has also yielded a great drama production, albeit in movie form. As support for the reader this book has color plates; lineage; maps of the 1300s and 1400s in Scotland, England, Flanders, Normandy, Brittany, France, and Gascony under the English; drawings of royal figures; a chronology of the book's contents; a bibliography; and an extensive index. It is a fine reference work for units on the Middle Ages, Shakespeare, or drama.

Pollinger, Gina, ed. *Something Rich and Strange: A Treasury of Shakespeare's Verse.* **Illustrated by Emma Chichester Clark. Kingfisher, 1995. 96pp.**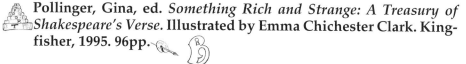

Original passages, both long and short, familiar and unknown, from Shakespeare's plays and poems are grouped by category. For example, in the section "Youth, I do adore thee" we find:

> My salad days,
> When I was green in judgment.
> (*Anthony and Cleopatra*, act I)

Such quotes are fine discussion starters, and students see that there are layers of meaning in Shakespeare's words. The discussion may also address the notion that famous quotes come from authentic sources, such as Shakespeare. For example, the section entitled "The King Is But a Man" has:

Some are born great, some achieve greatness, and some have greatness thrust upon 'em. (*Twelfth Night*, act II, scene v)

Humorous and appropriate illustrations appear with almost every quote, giving support. This is a great source of passages on emotional topics such as death, envy, and romance that one might want to copy down to keep or to commit to memory. The book is introduced by an easy to understand, critical analysis of Shakespeare's work. There is also a one-page biography of William Shakespeare, a list of plays and poetry cited, an index of first lines (three pages), and a glossary that could serve as a discussion starter for several meetings.

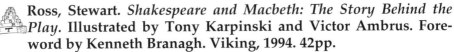 **Ross, Stewart.** *Shakespeare and Macbeth: The Story Behind the Play.* **Illustrated by Tony Karpinski and Victor Ambrus. Foreword by Kenneth Branagh. Viking, 1994. 42pp.**

Supported by dramatic paintings and whimsical pencil drawings, this is the story of how one Shakespearean play was conceived and evolved from a people's play into a court presentation. Though there are brief citations from the play *Macbeth*, most of this book is *about* the play. Politics, economic considerations, social issues (e.g., only men could be players); technical matters (e.g., no electricity), and other problems of the day give the reader a deeper understanding of the times. A great history lesson. Users of this book are supported by a time line of Shakespeare's life; a history of the play *Macbeth* ; a list of Shakespeare's plays and the approximate dates when they were written; an index; a bibliography and suggestions for further reading; and a detailed, two-page illustration of the Globe Theatre, with a brief history of its construction, shape, size, and capacity. The Bruce Coville retelling of *Macbeth* and the books by E. Nesbit, Sheila Front, and Bruce Koscielniak in this section will support reading of this book.

Edmund Spenser (1552 or 1553–1599) Collection

When London-born, Cambridge-educated Edmund Spenser (1552 or 1553–1599) began writing *The Faerie Queene*, his tribute to Her Majesty Queen Elizabeth I, he bestowed on her a great honor. Already he was considered by many the finest English-language poet of his time. *The Faerie Queene*, about Queen Glorianna's magical world, was six books (and an unfinished seventh) on six different virtues—Holiness, Temperance, Chastity, Friendship, Justice, and Courtesy—which were published during the 1590s. Spenser's work was appreciated immediately, though no more than it was half a century later, when eminent children's book illustrator Walter Crane decided to illustrate it. Even today, however, the myths that entertained Spenser continue to attract creative folk such as Margaret Hodges. Her treatment of one small part of the story is in children's book form, annotated below.

The sampling of books here was specifically selected for new readers and learners of English. Because of the popularity of Edmund Spenser's themes and poetry, new books are published each year, forcing earlier ones out of print or keeping them from being replaced in libraries when they are lost. Readers are encouraged to peruse all the books in a Spenser section in the library when one of the titles below is unavailable.

The Spenserian scholar will find more of his works both in sixteenth- and seventeenth-century form and in modern works of literary criticism; a few are *Complaints*, a collection of short poems, printed for William Ponsby in 1590; "A Vewe of the Present State of Ireland," in *The Historie of Ireland*, printed by the Society of Stationers in 1633; *Spenser: Poetical Works*, edited by C. Smith and Ernest de Selincourt (Oxford: Clarendon Press, 1912); *The Mutabilitie Cantos*, edited by S. P. Zitner (London: Nelson, 1968); and *Edmund Spenser's Poetry*, 3rd ed., edited by Hugh Maclean and Anne Lake Prescott <u>Norton Critical Edition Series</u> (Norton, 1993).

More difficult, however, is to find Spenser in forms that make access easy for the newcomer to Spenser's world. This section, therefore, is quite short. The offerings will allow the reader to dip into the works of an author often known only to academics, but whose influence extends to contemporary literature. After a period of digestion, some readers may want to revisit the annotated books and then plunge deeper into Spenser's works. The few challenging offerings listed here may be a good starting place for them.

Crane, Walter, illus., and Carol Belanger Grafton, arranger. *Illustrations and Ornamentation from The Faerie Queene.* **Dover Publications, 1999. 137pp.**

Walter Crane (1845–1915), the most notable illustrator of children's literature of his time, began to illustrate Spenser's poem featuring *The Faerie Queene* in 1891. Here are 352 of the images of Queen Glorianna and company that Crane used to help the reader enjoy the virtuous allegory. With the combination of captions and pictures, the reader will be able to grasp the general meaning of a given story. While the old spellings may be confusing at first, all readers tend to enjoy the phonetic quality. Furthermore, the illustrations are so powerful that the meaning of the old text is immediately clear. For example, there is a close-up of the soon-to-be Saint George about to run his long sword through the soon-to-be dead dragon. The caption for this full-page illustration is *The Knight with that old Dragon fights Two days incessantly: The third him overthrows, and gayns Most glorious victory*. Modern spell checkers disallow the spelling *gayns*, but new readers quickly comprehend the sound/symbol connection and may wonder why it ever changed.

This is a fine way to introduce this piece of great literature. It also clearly illustrates how one art form may inspire another, 250 years later. Designed to be sold to a highly literate book-buying elite, these images make the story enchanting even to very young children. The economical, oversized paperback format makes this an attractive addition to personal, homeschool, and public school libraries.

Tip: To understand more about how English language spellings got the way they are today, read about the work of Professor James Murray in *The Professor and the Madman* by Simon Winchester. It is available both as text and audio recording at public libraries.

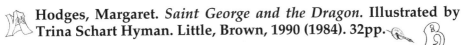

Hodges, Margaret. *Saint George and the Dragon.* **Illustrated by Trina Schart Hyman. Little, Brown, 1990 (1984). 32pp.**

A small part of the Edmund Spenser tale *The Faerie Queene* (ca. 1575) comes to life as the brave Red Cross Knight follows the instructions of the Queen of the Fairies to challenge a terrible dragon to a dual. Stained glass-like images of the knight, his princess, the dragon, and others grace every page. Published as a children's book, this is a book adult readers of all levels find irresistible. It is a fine introduction to Spenser for adult new readers and high school students.

Hadfield, Andrew, ed. *Cambridge Companion to Spenser.* **Cambridge University Press, 2001. 298pp.**

A chronology accompanies 14 essays about Spenser, his reading habits, and the influences they had on his work; religious and historical issues of his time; sexual politics; and many other details that help the newcomer to his work understand who he was as a poet and as a person. This dense text is too difficult for a new reader, but a tutor might find a single element within one of the essays and use it as a model for modern essay writing. Homeschoolers may want to reference this book for background information on classical literature.

Spenser, Edmund. *Shorter Poems.* **Edited by Richard A. McCabe. Penguin Classics, 2000. 816pp.**

This collection reveals why Spenser was a popular poet in his time and is so to this day. His revelations about human nature offer a glimpse of ourselves, no matter what century we are from. The publisher says, "The *Amoretti* and *Fowre Hymnes* reveal an acute sense of how erotic and even religious love are shot through with vanity and narcissism. Mother Hubbards Tale—an Elizabethan Animal Farm—savagely satirizes the sexual jealousy and political disarray at the heart of the Queen's court. And even the Epithalamion, a rare celebration of consummated desire, is offset by far darker echoes." This book, although challenging, provides discussion that the tutor and new reader may want to consider in bits and pieces.

Chapter 4

The Romantic Movement and the Victorian Age

The Romantic movement is designated as occurring ca. 1780–1832. Queen Victoria reigned from 1837 to 1901. This explains, in part, the frequent confusion over how to categorize literary works based on a movement or major influence. This chapter covers literature from the late eighteenth century through the end of the nineteenth century, encompassing both eras. Emphasis is on British and American authors, but some French and Russian authors, for whom good English translations exist, are also included.

Authors in this section are arranged alphabetically by author name. Author titles are grouped by reading levels:

 Start Here!

 Next Read

 Support Here

 Challenging Read.

Louisa May Alcott (1832–1888) Collection

Born to poor and politically radical parents (her father was philosopher, author, and teacher Amos Bronson Alcott), nineteenth-century American author Louisa May Alcott always had radical political inclinations and always intended to be a writer. Because her father did not believe in taking meaningless work and lacked the necessary resources to support his wife and four daughters through work he found meaningful, finances required Louisa to take odd jobs to provide day-to-day sustenance. She began to write "rubbishy novels" under the pen name A. N. Barnard, and also wrote gothic tales, among them "Pauline's Passion and Punishment," "The Abbot's Ghost: or Maurice Trahern's Temptations," which she was reluctant to claim at all until years afterward. In support of the abolition philosophy, during the Civil War Alcott worked as a nurse in a Union hospital in Washington. It may be noted that, just as her father lacked the skills to be the many noble things to which he aspired, so, too, Louisa was untrained as a nurse. But it was there that she wrote letters for wounded soldiers. Her *Hospital Sketches*, published in 1863, were based on that experience and were her first popular work. The book that gave her (and her family) the first financial security they had ever known was *Little Women*. As an advocate of women's suffrage, abolition, education for blacks, integration, and gender equity, both her personal activities and literary efforts reflect characters and events that supported forward thinking as a matter of course. At the family gathering in *Little Women*, for example, there is a quadroon baby, an obvious product of the amalgamation espoused by Louisa and her father, who had for a time run an unsuccessful school for children of all races.

Annotated in this collection are *Little Women* and the much less familiar *Louisa May Alcott on Race, Sex, and Slavery* (which has a fascinating introduction about Alcott's family, friends, associates, life, and times); a three-in-one containing *The Quiet Little Woman*, *Tilly's Christmas*, and *Rosa's Tale* (a collection of stories she wrote as a gift to a newsletter written by five enterprising young sisters); *Transcendental Wild Oats and Excerpts from the Fruitlands Diary* (a wry report on her father's experimental commune in the woods); and *Invincible Louisa* (a lively biography of this very lively author).

 Alcott, Louisa May. *The Quiet Little Woman: A Christmas Story*. Edited and with an introduction by Stephen W. Hines. Illustrated by C. Michael Dudash. Honor Books, 1999. 122pp.

    In a letter to Carrie, Maggie, Nellie, Emma, and Helen Lukens on their venture into publication inspired by the characters in *Little Women*, Louisa May Alcott assured them she was in favor of helping women help themselves. To that end, she submitted the stories in this book for publication in their family paper, called *Little Things*. Two of the stories remained otherwise unread, until the newsletters were discovered by Stephen W. Hines, who has reproduced them here. Included here are "The Quiet Little Woman" (pages 15–53; first published in 1872 and then in a magazine in 1920), "Tilly's Christmas" (pages 59–76), and *Rosa's Tale* (pages 77–106).

Hines's introduction suggests that Alcott obligingly wrote them for the girls when she was at the peak of her career. These sentimental stories were obviously written to teach positive values to young people. That said, they are also a snapshot of social issues of the time, issues that were no doubt of concern to the, at a minimum, radical thinker Alcott. This charming little book can be held in one hand and read. The print is comfortable, with lots of white space; the language is vintage Alcott—very accessible—made even more so by the attention to her audience. This book is perfect for units or lessons dealing with nineteenth-century orphans, class distinctions, or morality tales.

 Barchers, Suzanne I., and Jennifer L. Kroll. "Little Women." In *Classic Readers Theatre for Young Adults*, **1–25. Libraries Unlimited, 2002. 243pp.**

This modern language readers theatre script will help new readers and ESL students develop an understanding of this classic story. In this two-part selection, two narrators and eleven other distinctive voices offer a variety of difficulty levels. It is Christmas in the March home, and the little women are speaking from their characteristic roles.

Related read: There is a brief but detailed biography of Louisa May Alcott in Kathleen Krull *Lives of the Writers: Comedies, Tragedies (and What the Neighbors Thought)*, an illustrated collection of literary biographies.

 Meigs, Correlia. *Invincible Louisa*. **Scholastic, 1991. 247pp.**

Louisa May Alcott, author of the autobiographical *Little Women*, one of the world's best-loved family novels, began writing plays when she was 13. Her creative energies were hardly the fruits of a stable lifestyle. By the time she was 28, her family had moved 29 times. This book gives the history behind Louisa May Alcott's writing and illuminates her writing career, which provided much-needed money to her struggling family.

Full of rich detail, the language in this book is not simple. Colorful turns of phrase make this text too difficult for the beginner ESL student. It is, however, a gripping story for the intermediate level ESL student, and passages that discuss the difficulties of getting an education and how Louisa's father first learned to write by tracing letters in the white sand on his mother's kitchen floor serve as fine read-alouds for small groups of adults at all levels. And of course this book is a wonderful companion to Alcott's *Little Women*. This Newbery Medal winner has a four-and-a-half page chronology of Louisa May Alcott's life. It will serve well as a discussion starter on family values, parent–child relationships, siblings, or writing.

Related read: A similar biography is *Louisa May Alcott: Young Novelist,* by Beatrice Gormley.

See also: *The Louisa May Alcott Encyclopedia,* edited by George Eiselein and Anne K. Phillips, for research support about the author's life or her work.

 Alcott, Louisa May. *Transcendental Wild Oats and Excerpts from the Fruitlands Diary.* **With an introduction by William Henry Harrison. Illustrations by J. Streeter Fowke. The Harvard Common Press, 1995 (1873). 92pp.**

When Louisa May Alcott was 10 years old, her father led the family into a utopian forest setting to establish a Transcendental commune. The chief bill of fare was apples. Sex was forbidden. The project attracted a very colorful lot, so colorful that thirty years later, Alcott was able to put the tale of the doomed experiment on paper, changing only the names of the main characters for their protection. Episodes in the story may have received some exaggeration from the woman who had never related to the experiment or the spiritual quests of her father, but surviving diary entries and corroborating historic documents attest to much of what is told.

This little book has historic photographs, including the tombstone portrait of Joseph Palmer, who chose to go to jail rather than pay the fine for having a full beard. Beards were not socially acceptable at the time. This palm-sized book is a small treasure, with clear print and very easy to follow prose.

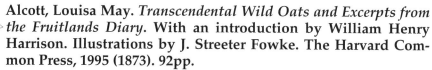 **Alcott, Louisa May (1832–1888).** *Little Women.* **Illustrated by Jame's Prunier, <u>The Whole Story.</u> Viking, 1996 (1868). 285 pp.**

Louisa May Alcott wrote this book on consignment. Her editor wanted a "girl's" book. Alcott was unsure how to do that, never having known or liked many girls, but she managed *Little Women* in 1868 based on her own home life with her sisters. The story is told through traditional prose with lots of conversation and letter exchanges. The main character, Jo March, who writes in the book, is based on the author.

Though the book was an instant hit, the editor demanded a revised edition for reprints, a revision reflecting popular values. Alcott complied, making the stout Marmee tall and Laurie less foreign looking, and having those characters given to slang clean up their language. Here is a delightful picture of how life really was during the Civil War and during the Industrial Revolution. Planners of <u>The Whole Story</u> series chose not to protect their readers from the stout Marmee or Jo's inclination toward rough language, so this book has the original unadulterated 1868 text. It also has rich full-color illustrations on nearly every page and historic sidebars to help bring the period even more to life. For example, when the family is doing a shared storytelling, Jo jumps into Meg's passage with the word "snuff-box," whereupon the story takes a new turn. In the sidebar are illustrations of two snuffbox labels of the day and a brief explanation of how tobacco was marketed during the time of the *Little Women.*

An all-time favorite girls' book, this edition will give the new reader and ESL student even more than those early readers got. Though the print is not big, there is lots of space between the lines, and the margins are generous. The slick paper not only shows the colors well, it feels nice to the reader's touch. This book supports discussions about poverty, sibling relationships, problem solving, and the American Civil War.

Video version: *Little Women*. Columbia TriStar Home Video, 1994. 1 videocassette, 119 minutes. Closed-captioned for hearing impaired. Director: Gillian Armstrong. Producer: Denise DiNovi. Co-producer: Robin Swicord. Starring Winona Ryder, Susan Sarandon, Gabriel Byrne, and Trini Alvarado.

Related read: *Short Stories* by Louisa May Alcott is available in an AFFORDABLE edition through Dover Publications.

Alcott, Louisa May. *Louisa May Alcott on Race, Sex, and Slavery.* **Edited and with an introduction by Sarah Elbert. Northeastern University Press, 1997. 101pp.**

In her introduction, Sarah Elbert gives background not only on the political attitudes held by Louisa May Alcott and those around her, but also on the mores of the country during the time when Alcott was teaching black men to read and write and black women both literacy skills and management skills needed to conduct business not traditionally thought possible by women or blacks. Alcott, whose radical activism included support for John Brown's raid on Harper's Ferry, and whose fiction clearly reflected a belief in amalgamation, was an aggressive mover for women's rights and abolition of slavery. She came by such attitudes naturally; her own father's school had been forced to close when all the children had been withdrawn because he held the notion that the relationship between human sexuality and the birth of babies should be common knowledge. During the Civil War, Louisa joined the military, serving in a hospital in Washington.

Readers will also learn of the relationships between the Alcotts and author-revolutionary Margaret Fuller, Ralph Waldo Emerson, Henry David Thoreau, Dorothea Dix, Clara Barton, and other notables of the day. The collection of essays in this book give readers of *Little Women* background knowledge that may make that simple girl's book appear subversive. They provide a wealth of read-aloud material for units on slavery, civil rights, women's suffrage, gender issues, disease, military health care, the Civil War, and U.S. history.

Jane Austen (1775–1817) Collection

As her family went about its daily business in their eighteenth-century Georgian home, Jane Austen, the seventh of eight children, quietly wrote, documenting the morals and mores of her time, poking fun at them, and forging a path into literature where no woman was invited to trudge. She was at once protected by her circumstances as the daughter of an impoverished clergyman and trapped as a member of a social class that placed strict conditions on what a young woman was and was not allowed to do. Women lived with their parents until they were paired with a respectable mate and then moved in with him.

Ultimately, Austen decided it was more important to write than to wed. Austen's writing carved a new chapter in literary history, creating a mold for novels that would be imitated into the next century and books that would be read forever after. Her fully developed characters bounce off the pages as though they were bouncing down a contemporary avenue. It is remarkable that a young woman who was living in what appeared to be near-seclusion had such extraordinary understanding of human nature and the various social classes of her time.

Jane Austen kept no diaries or other journals of her inner thoughts. Much of what is known of her today is based on the letters between her and her older sister, Cassandra, with whom she had a stormy, but enduring, relationship, and in whose arms she died. Fortunately family members and friends recorded anecdotes about the way life was for Jane as she struggled to make her way in literature. Earlier reports suggest that she had a rather dull life and began writing as an escape. More recent biographers have begun to learn that her life was filled with as much intrigue as her books, perhaps more. It is clear that she read books from her father's library and, as a consequence, started writing very early on.

It should be noted that not all her works were published in the order they were written and that some appeared only after her death at the age of 41. Her works are *The Three Sisters* (1792); *Sense and Sensibility* (1811); *Pride and Prejudice* (1813); *Mansfield Park* (1814); *Emma, Northanger Abbey,* and *Persuasion* (published jointly, 1818); *Juvenilia* (written 1790–1793; published as vol. I in 1933, vol. II in 1963, and vol. III in 1951); *Lady Susan* (1817); *The Watsons* (begun in 1804 and abandoned, 1817); and *Sandition* (a fragment abandoned because of her illness, 1817).

Though her heroines became progressively older and more mature as Austen's writing matured, there is some disagreement over whether the novels are actually autobiographical. What can be seen from her novels is the development of a writer, from a struggling observer with things to say about those observations to a polished and sophisticated designer of characters in complex webs made of everyday situations.

The works of Jane Austen, read aloud to the new reader via audio recording or by a teacher, will provide background for the eighteenth-century genre that paved the way for what is written today. These books also show how simple, everyday events can be made into stories that others want to read. Jane and Cassandra attended the Abbey School in Reading, England, from 1785 to 1787. Literature reading was an integral part of the Austens' lifestyle, and the girls' education also encouraged it. By the age of 14, Jane Austen had written her first novel, *Love and Freindship* (sic). Reading begets writing . . . and often spelling.

 Austen, Jane. *Emma*. **Dover Publications, 1999 (1816). 328pp.**

"Handsome, clever, and rich" Emma Woodhouse of Highbury is a busybody, who believes that she knows exactly where every person should stand in her rigid social stratosphere. The marriage of her best friend, Anne Taylor, has left Emma in search of a new close companion. She settles on the simple Harriet Smith, whom she elevates to a position of such unwarranted importance that Emma's hair-brained matchmaking schemes for her fail. Through false assumptions about people, their values and worth, and their stations in life, Emma manipulates romance, foils marriage proposals, and humiliates many of those around her. She eventually is forced to grow up, albeit minimally, and discovers that her greatest oversight in matters of the heart has been her own.

The exaggerated tone of everything that Emma believes about her life and times reveals Austen's strong satirical sense, almost to the point of slapstick. This story will amuse anyone who has been manipulated by secret insights or a meddling matchmaker. This Dover edition is printed on newsprint-like paper, is lightweight, and is very easy to carry around. For support, readers may want to begin with the less-complicated works of Louisa May Alcott. There are also audio recordings of Austen's books, and new recordings have begun to show up as a result of recent moviemaking activity.

 Austen, Jane, and Stephen M. Parrish. *Emma: Norton Critical Edition*. **3d ed. W. W. Norton, 2000 (1816). 449pp.**

In addition to the original text annotated above in the Dover edition, this hardbound book contains letters to the author's sister, Cassandra (providing internal support); critical reviews by Virginia Woolf, Sir Walter Scott, George Henry Lewes, Henry James, and E. M. Forster; film reviews; and a chronology.

Audio version: *Emma*. Books on Tape, 2002. 11 cassettes, 11 hours. Read by Donada Peters (British).

 Austen, Jane. *Mansfield Park*. **Dover Publications, 2001 (1814). 322pp.**

Austen, Jane. *Mansfield Park: A Norton Critical Edition.* **1st ed. Edited by Claudia L. Johnson. W. W. Norton, 1999 (1814). 538pp.**

Saved from her poverty-stricken Portsmouth home by her well-to-do aunt and uncle, the two-faced Mrs. Norris, and Sir Thomas Bertram, sweet, 10-year-old Fanny Price views the Mansfield Park lifestyle through the eyes of a commentator. Although she is caught up in the romantic intrigues of her cousins, Fanny's unassuming demeanor eventually opens the doors to the hearts of these relatives and romance. Readers will find a witty outsider's perspective on the times in which Jane Austen lived. This is considered one of Austen's most sophisticated works. Listening to the recording and then reading the book may be most beneficial to one new to Austen's work.

Audio version: *Mansfield Park.* Books on Tape, 1983. 13 tapes, 19 hours, 30 minutes. Read by Jill Masters (British).

 Austen, Jane. *Northanger Abbey.* **Signet Classics, 1996 (1818). 240pp.**

Catherine Morland falls in love while at Bath. She is caught up in the social mores of the upper crust and begins a series of misadventures that stem from her being targeted as a young woman of means. The tale is a near parody of the Gothic novel of Austen's day. It was originally written under the title *Susan* in 1803, and although it was purchased by a publisher, it was not published during Jane's lifetime.

Note: This title is also available in an AFFORDABLE Dover edition.

Audio version: *Northanger Abbey.* Books on Tape, 1982. 7 cassettes, 7 hours. Read by Donada Peters (British).

Related read: There is a detailed summary of the life and work of Jane Austen in Kathleen Krull, *Lives of the Writers: Comedies, Tragedies (and What the Neighbors Thought)*, an illustrated collection of literary biographies.

 Austen, Jane. *Persuasion.* **Dover, 1997 (1818). 188pp.**

On the advice of the very elegant Lady Russell, the teenaged Anne Elliot broke off her engagement with naval officer Frederick Wentworth . . . and regretted it ever after. About eight years later, a prosperous Captain Wentworth returns to find his sister living at the Elliot estate with the impoverished Elliots. Will the love rekindle? This book was written just before Austen's death and was published in 1818 with *Northanger Abbey* (first accepted by a publisher in 1803). The audio recording will support new readers as they experience Austen's powerful satirical wit.

Audio version: *Persuasion.* Books on Tape, 2001. 6 cassettes, 9 hours. Read by Donada Peters (British).

Austen, Jane. *Sense and Sensibility.* **Modern Library, 2001 (1811). 282pp.**

Two sisters are born to the simple lives of middle-class English women in the early nineteenth century. These sisters, however, are emotional opposites: Elinor is the epitome of *sense*, advising her frivolous mother on things proper; Marianne is the picture of *sensibility*, illustrated by her yielding to every impulse, particularly romantic impulses, and that is the key to life in this satire of the times, in which husband-finding is the most pursued sport. This is old-fashioned romance, albeit replete with deceit, suitable for general audiences. The audio reading by Saral Badel will support the reader who starts this long book, puts it down, and then tries it again. Her use of many voices helps keep the web of characters untangled. This dramatic reading will also support the drama student and readers theatre participant.

Audio version: *Sense and Sensibility.* The Audio Partners Publishing Corp., 1986. 8 cassettes, 10 hours, 30 minutes. Read by Saral Badel.

Video version: *Sense and Sensibility.* Columbia/Tristar Studios, 1995 (2003 video release). Starring Kate Winslet, Emma Thompson, James Fleet, Harriet Walter, and Hugh Grant. Director: Ang Lee.

Related read: Austen's *Pride and Prejudice* (1813).

L. Frank Baum (1856–1919) Collection

Although he used many pseudonyms for his books, plays, poems, and songs (among them Floyd Akers, Edith Van Dyne, and Captain Hugh Fitzgerald), Lyman Frank Baum is best remembered as Frank Baum, author of *The Wonderful Wizard of Oz* and the creator of the most magical road in children's literature, the yellow brick road. Illustrated by his good friend W. W. Denslow, this was the book that captured the imagination of his own generation and of Walt Disney, who adapted the themes and imagery in the 1939 classic film *The Wizard of Oz,* starring legendary film star Judy Garland when she was young.

Although *The Wonderful Wizard of Oz* was filled with fantastic elements, such as a magical rainbow and terror from a very wicked witch, readers, among them Baum's own children, got the message that "There's no place like home." The book enjoyed so much success, Baum wrote 13 sequels (illustrated by John R. Neill). In 1902, Baum created a theatrical version of the book for adults.

 Baum, L. Frank. *The Wonderful Wizard of Oz.* **Illustrated by W. W. Denslow. Oz. HarperCollins Juvenile Books, 2000 (1900). 272pp.**

When a cyclone blows through Kansas, the young orphan Dorothy, unable to reach the cyclone cellar (actually just a hole in the ground under the house), is caught in Auntie Em and Uncle Henry's one-room farmhouse as it is swirled into the air—Dorothy managing to grab onto her beloved dog, Toto, by an ear just in the nick of time. After the house and its occupants are dropped into the mysterious Land of Oz, the young girl is greeted by Munchkins, and she joins forces with Scarecrow, Tin Woodman, and Cowardly Lion, all of whom follow the yellow brick road to find the Wizard of Oz. However, the road to the Wizard, with his powerful message, "There's no place like home," is fraught with trials that prove to the members of the party that they are more than they had imagined.

This facsimile copy, the first of 14 Oz tales, contains the 24 original color plates and 130 two-color illustrations that support the reader in enjoyment of this classic book. The occasional unfamiliar word will hardly pose a problem for the new reader. This is straightforward, old-fashioned, fanciful storytelling with emotionally charged classical drawings and clear print. There are lots of other editions available, but readers are encouraged to look for this one. This would be a starter reading, if there were fewer pages. As it stands, it is a fine introduction to one of the all-time great stories of the twentieth century. Many wonderful dramatizations—which do not match the book word for word—have been recorded, two of which are listed below. Furthermore, the movie—which does not exactly match the book—is a classic well worth watching for its own sake.

Note: Only the first in the Oz series is annotated here. Multiple editions are listed in copyright date order. At the end there is also a reference to a commemorative edition of tributes to Baum.

Baum, L. Frank. *The Wonderful Wizard of Oz.* **Illustrated by W. W. Denslow. Oz. Dover, 1976 (1900). 267pp.**

This book also has full-color facsimiles of the original illustrations.

Baum, L. Frank. *The Wonderful Wizard of Oz.* **Illustrated by W. W. Denslow. Dover Large Print Classics, 2002 (1900). 256pp.**

This large print edition has the whole story as Baum wrote it, flying monkeys, wicked witch and all, and it has many, but not all, of the original illustrations.

Audio versions: There are many audio versions of Baum's tale, including

> *The Wonderful Wizard of Oz.* Blackstone Audio, 2002. Unabridged reading by Cindy Hardin and Walter Zimmerman.

> *The Wonderful Wizard of Oz.* The Colonial Radio Players, 2001. 10 cassettes, 11.5 hours. Dramatization of the first five books of the Oz series, including *The Wonderful Wizard of Oz, The Marvelous Land of Oz, Ozma of Oz, Dorothy and the Wizard in Oz,* and *The Road to Oz.*

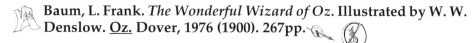

The Wonderful Wizard of Oz. Otherworld Media Productions, 2001. 3 cas-
settes, 4 hours. Fully dramatized benefit performance for the Los An-
geles Children's Museum; adapted by Firesign Theatre's David
Ossman, produced and directed by David and Otherworld Media's
Judith Walcutt, and originally heard over Public Radio International.
Featuring Phyllis Diller as the Wicked Witch.

Glassman, Peter, ed. *Oz: The Hundredth Anniversary Celebration.*
Books of Wonder, 2000. 55pp.

Thirty award-winning artists and illustrators give their earliest impressions of L. Frank Baum's *The Wizard of Oz* in words and pictures. Dip
into the minds and souls of Maurice Sendak, Tomie de Paola, Uri
Shulevitz, Madeleine L'Engle, Jules Feiffer; Kinuko Craft, Peter Sis, Lloyd
Alexander, and many others who pay tribute to this enduring story. The
print is not large and in some places it is quite dense, but never for more
than a page. The ideas and illustrations are enchanting, promising to strike
a chord with anyone who ever saw the movie or read the book. At the end
of the book there are paragraph-long biographies of the contributors and a
two-page spread showing the covers of many Oz titles.

Charlotte Brontë (1816–1855) and Emily Brontë (1818–1848) Collection

There were six Brontë children, five girls and a boy, when their
mother died, leaving them to the care of their seemingly uninterested,
Puritanical parish vicar father and an aunt. The four older girls were
shipped off to school (immortalized by Charlotte in her 1847 *Jane Eyre* as
Lowood School), where the two oldest girls contracted tuberculosis and
died. Subsequently, Charlotte (pseudonym Currer Bell) and Emily
(pseudonym Ellis Bell) were brought home, where the sisters, young
Anne (Acton Bell) included, were left to the pastoral countryside and
stories they invented among themselves for entertainment. (Not as
much is said about their brother Branwell, who eventually found his so-
lace in alcohol and opium.)

In addition to playing with toy figures (some accounts say lead, others wooden), the children devoured the tales of the Arabian Nights, the
works of Shakespeare, popular poets, and other literature, thereby making up for the reportedly barren environment of their small, unheated,
austere quarters. They invented countries and kingdoms with histories
and current events. Charlotte and Branwell invented "Angria" and began to write stories about it in tiny books scaled to Branwell's little soldiers. Emily and Anne developed the North Pacific Island kingdom of
Gondal in 1832 when the older girls had gone off to school. Critics who
learned about the Brontë sisters' imaginary town (featured in

Michael'Bedard's picture book *Glass Town*) and discovered that the sisters continued this self-teaching activity as adults were sometimes most unkind.

Before attempting to sell their works, young Anne became a governess and Charlotte and Emily moved away and became teachers. Charlotte became enamored of a married man. The three sisters finally ventured into a singularly unsuccessful self-publishing operation. Tenacity worked for them, though. Anne did sell her manuscript for *Agnes Grey* (1847); Emily sold *Wuthering Heights* (1847); and in 1847 Charlotte, after much rewriting, sold *Jane Eyre*, which became an overnight success, with reviews at both ends of the spectrum. The character Jane Eyre was considered by some to be much too liberated for a lady. Charlotte, meanwhile, fairly boasted about her own simpleness and lack of education. Even so, when set against the backdrop of their times and circumstances, the characters of Emily and Charlotte's creation are now considered to be brave pioneers in feminist thinking.

This section offers the biographical picture book *Glass Town*, then a readers theatre support title for *Wuthering Heights*, followed by various editions of *Jane Eyre* and *Wuthering Heights*.

Bedard, Michael. *Glass Town*. Illustrated by Laura Fernandez and Rick Jacobson. Atheneum Books for Young Readers, 1997. 40pp.

When the Brontë children were emotionally abandoned by their widowed father and compelled to amuse themselves in the cold upstairs rooms of their isolated country home, they began to invent stories, creating an imaginary town to their liking. The children wrote their stories down in miniature books, which were much later found among Charlotte Brontë's papers. The notion that the gifted sisters sprang into adulthood as unschooled novelists is belied by this proof that, indeed, they had had many years of intensive novel-writing practice and that their imaginary childhood glass town was the foundation for later writings. While the picture book details how the Brontës lived as children, the foreword gives a brief history of the strange collection of miniature books. This book has eerie images and chilling insights into the lives of Charlotte, Emily, and Anne Brontë.

Related read: There is a colorful overview of Charlotte and Emily Brontë in Kathleen Krull, *Lives of the Writers: Comedies, Tragedies (and What the Neighbors Thought)*, an illustrated collection of literary biographies.

Latrobe, Kathy Howard, and Mildred Knight Laughlin. "Wuthering Heights." In *Readers Theatre for Young Adults*, 11–15. Teacher Ideas Press, 1989. 130pp.

This is support for *Wuthering Heights*. In this skit, the willful Catherine discusses with her nurse her plans to marry. This is a five-page dramatization drawn from chapter 9 of *Wuthering Heights*, with narrator passages at the beginning and end extending the story. This particular skit offers many opportunities for parent–daughter discussions, for small group analysis of marriage, and for three readers to work together, reading lengthy passages.

 Brontë, Charlotte. *Jane Eyre*. Introduction by Diane Johnson. Notes by James Danley. The Modern Library, 2000 (1847). 717pp.

Told from the perspective of the plucky orphan, Jane Eyre (whose literary references because of her voracious reading will inspire all readers to think of daily life in allusions to literature) this novel and case study in self-perception became an overnight success, giving readers and publishers alike great cause to speculate on who the elusive author, using the androgynous pseudonym Currer Bell, really was. Key features in this paperback edition are two prefaces, one for the second edition (December 21, 1847) and the other for the third edition (April 13, 1848), signed by Currer Bell (Charlotte Brontë's pseudonym), notes that clarify biblical references and terms not used today; commentary by eight notable writers (including a response letter from Charlotte herself); and a reading group guide with points for discussion that might well inform a homeschooling, library, or classroom discussion. In her prefaces, the author responds to criticism by her contemporaries, not unmindful, we might guess, that the masses were clearly willing to buy this book in numbers. In the 1847 preface Bell tells her readers "Conventionality is not morality. Self-righteousness is not religion." In a letter to the *Jane Eyre* publisher, William Makepeace Thackeray, to whom the book is dedicated and who became a close friend of Charlotte's, claimed he was unable to put the book down, losing a whole day's work on his own novel. "It is a woman's writing, but whose?" Thackeray asked. George Eliot said she wished the characters would "talk a little less like the heroes and heroines of police reports." Virginia Woolf said the work has exhilaration that "rushes us through the entire volume, without giving us time to think, without letting us lift our eyes from the page." These messages are much easier to read and understand than the actual text of the book. Readers may want to begin with the informing introduction, the prefaces, the readers' guides, and the commentaries.

Related reads: Other works by Charlotte Brontë include *Shirley; Villette; The Professor; The Twelve Adventures and Other Stories; The Spell; Legends of Angria; Poems by Currer, Ellis and Acton Bell; and Complete Poems.*

Brontë, Emily. *Wuthering Heights.* **Wood Engravings by Fritz Eichenberg. Introduction by Royal A. Gettmann 1991 (1847). 400pp.**

In addition to the thrilling wood engravings that occur at chapter breaks, this edition has a September 19, 1850 "Biographical Notice of Ellis and Acton Bell" in which Currer Bell [Charlotte Brontë] discusses the gossip and confusion over the names Currer, Ellis, and Acton Bell. There is also an editor's preface to the new edition of *Wuthering Heights,* also written by Currer Bell. These little teasing essays are very easy to understand and provide a look at the personality behind the pen.

 Brontë, Charlotte. *Jane Eyre.* **Introduction by Diane Johnson. The Modern Library, 1993 (1847). 682pp.**

The romance of Jane and Rochester has become a mainstay of the romance genre. Charlotte Brontë, pseudonym Currer Bell, first wrote *The Professor* (not sold), based on her involvement with a married headmaster, then transformed it into *Jane Eyre,* about a governess with an open mind. Mores of the day caused some critics to declare that if the author was a woman, she was a *fallen* one. (That was before it was commonly known that reading begets writing, and the three sisters had been immersed in all sorts of literature out there on the moors.)

This easy-to-hold hardbound book has clear typography, with ample space between the lines. The font is small, but it is much easier to read than many current volumes of this text. There is also a brief biography of the author. Readers needing more support may want to begin with the 🕯 and 🖼 titles in this collection.

Related reads: Other titles by Charlotte Brontë include *The Professor* (published posthumously in 1857) and *Villette.*

 Brontë, Charlotte. *Jane Eyre.* <u>**Great Illustrated Classics.**</u> **Dodd, Mead, 1941 (1847). 474pp.**

This edition of Charlotte Brontë's romance masterpiece may well be unavailable except on library shelves. It bears mentioning, however, because of the remarkable prints and photographs that show where the author lived and some of the sources of her inspiration. The anecdotal captions by Basil Davenport have informing historical references. If this edition is available, I suggest going through and looking at the plates. Then get a version of the book with a font that's easier to read.

 Brontë, Emily. *Wuthering Heights.* **Introduction by Katherine Frank. Everyman's Library, Alfred A. Knopf, 1991 (1847). 385pp.**

Catherine and Heathcliff have a relationship based on secrets that hail back to the imaginary place of the Brontë siblings' making. The dark, brooding, unhappy orphan, Heathcliff, who was taken in by Catherine's father and who eventually won the father's favor over his natural son, loves Catherine more than life itself. But his failure to win her hand in marriage begins a downward spiral into lust for power and merciless cruelty to those near to him, and it leads the lives of many into shadows.

Some of the phrases in *Wuthering Heights* are borderline archaic, such as "Her features were so sad, they did not seem hers: she evidently regarded what she had heard as every syllable true" (page 268). Emily's usual plain talk and clearly stated ideas, however, make the meaning emerge from the context.

This is still an intriguing read for romance buffs and those interested in gender issues. As a discussion prompt, the path has been well-prepared. There has been much controversy over the motives and values of the characters, particularly Heathcliff (hero or villain?). (See the Kathy Latrobe readers theatre skit referenced in this collection. It will make one passage of the book very easy for all participants to follow.) This book has a 15-page introduction, a bibliography, and a chronology starting with the Battle of Waterloo in June 1815 and ending with Louis Napoleon's coup d'état in December 1851.

Related read: See also Deborah G. Felder's "44/45 Charlotte Brontë/Emily Brontë," in *The 100 Most Influential Women of All Time: A Ranking Past and Present*, 155–158. Though it focuses on only Charlotte and Emily, this entry has summary life stories of all the Brontë siblings. Felder finds the Brontë authors' strength of character and will to survive emotionally quite remarkable, all things considered. Among the hostile environmental issues the Brontë children had to deal with was the fact that when their father was displeased, instead of speaking about it, he would open the back door and fire off pistols in rapid succession.

Lewis Carroll (1832–1898) Collection

Known to the world as Lewis Carroll, Charles Lutwidge Dodgson, a logic and mathematics professor, used satire and puns to deliver multi-level messages enjoyed by audiences of all ages. Through entertaining images that targeted the social and political absurdities of his time, the stories of Lewis Carroll reflected a need to challenge the logic of how things worked. His writings have contributed metaphors and idioms to the English language used by all generations since. Even those who have not read his books will readily recognize, for example, a "house of cards" that may soon come tumbling down. It is the language as much as the imagery or the message that makes Carroll's works classics.

His most famous books are *Alice's Adventures in Wonderland, Through the Looking Glass,* and *The Hunting of Snark.* Since it was first published in 1865 (illustrated by John Tenniel), there have been over a hundred editions of *Alice* alone. Some editions, unfortunately, have attempted to improve upon the Oxford man's text. Some have attempted

to spare the reader the trials of going through such a long story, and have cut, bent, mutilated, simplified, or abridged the text. (Such folks should be dipped in a barrel of glue and covered with shredded dictionary pages—simplified dictionary pages.) Others have made attempts at illustration that under-present or insult the tale.

Alice's Adventures in Wonderland is the story of a bored child who, as she falls asleep, glimpses a rabbit going down a hole. It is the story of a child who observes a rabbit who is in a hurry going nowhere. It is the story of a society of people doing absurd and meaningless things. And it is an example of character development that is so subtle the reader hardly notices the evolution from a foggy-headed child to an awake, aware evaluator who responds decisively to her environment. This story can be enjoyed by the child, the adolescent, and the adult. Indeed, there is something for everyone, and the story invites revisiting.

Two editions of *Alice* that appear here state: "This book contains the complete text of the first edition published by Macmillan in 1865 and incorporates additions made by Lewis Carroll during his lifetime." This gives the reader the benefit of Carroll's rethinking and self-editing, something rarely possible to find in contemporary works. In both books the print is large and easy on the eyes. But the words are not simple, and the sentence structures are not simple. The references to political issues of the past require contemplation. Some social matters, however, span the generations. Take, for example, Carroll's observation of the Duchess singing to her baby, the one she was repeatedly tossing in the air:

> "Speak roughly to your little boy,
> And beat him when he sneezes;
> He only does it to annoy,
> Because he knows it teases."
> CHORUS
> (In which the baby joined):
> "Wow! wow! wow!"
>
> "I speak severely to my boy,
> I beat him when he sneezes;
> For he can thoroughly enjoy
> The pepper when he pleases!"
> CHORUS
> (In which the baby joined):
> "Wow! wow! wow!"

Child abuse is not a new phenomenon. Nor has it ever been limited to a single socioeconomic group. But the "blame the victim" attitude seen in the second verse is one that applies to broader interpretation, as governments crack down on the homeless and teen mothers are punished for not working enough. The depth of Carroll's offerings calls for reading and re-reading, discussion and contemplation.

The conversations in Alice may well have influenced the thinking of Antoine Saint-Exupery as he wrote *The Little Prince* in 1943. Nonsense questions of the Alice caterpillar, for example, sound much like the unnecessary questions of the adult in the Saint-Exupery parable. Readers may want to compare the two works.

Many of the pages in some of these books are solid text. Still, the illustrations matter, giving visual relief, pleasure, and notions to contemplate that extend the story. The books below offer very different, though realistic, styles of illustration. Readers are invited to seek out these and others to compare approaches. In none of these books does Alice smile. The artists acknowledge that these are absurd situations with profound implications, both when Alice is just a child falling asleep in her sister's lap and as she suddenly finds herself much bigger at the end of the book.

It cannot be overlooked that there have been numerous attempts at movie interpretations of *Alice in Wonderland*. Before or after reading the whole text , the reader may want to view one or two such videos or DVDs to identify what has been left out, what has been left in, and what has been modified to suit popular contemporary political notions. A group of readers may want to analyze those sections Sabuda chose to highlight through his pop-up treatment; are they the ones the readers would have selected? This kind of critical questioning is part of what makes reading so rewarding. The answers are never simple.

 Carroll, Lewis. *Alice's Adventures in Wonderland.* **A pop-up adaptation by Robert Sabuda. Little, Simon, 2003 (1865). 7pp.**

> Here is a summary that delivers the goods in just a few pages and will take hours to read. This is the epitome of capturing the main idea. This stunning work of paper engineering retells the highlights of Carroll's classic through fold-out forests, an incredible tea party, little sidebar books, and more. This book may not last long on library shelves, but is well worth tracking down as an introduction to Carroll and to paper sculpture for all ages. Of interest is the Sabuda Web site, which gives a fundamental lesson in this craft that can be used with small groups or whole classes.

 Fisher, Aileen. "Hearts, Tarts, and Valentines." In *Plays from Favorite Folk Tales,* **31–41. Edited by Sylvia Kamerman. Plays, Inc., 1987. 293pp.**

> This skit is a reenactment of the absurdity of the Queen of Hearts and the tarts fiasco from the Lewis Carroll story *Alice's Adventures in Wonderland*. There are nine speaking parts and any number of townspeople. Given a teacher, tutor, or higher level native speaker of English, this skit is

an excellent way for new readers and new speakers of English to become familiar with the pronunciation and the Carroll story line.

Carroll, Lewis. *Alice's Adventures in Wonderland.* **Illustrated by Michael Hague. Holt, Rinehart & Winston, 1985 (1865). 121pp.**

A graduate of the Art Center College of Design in Los Angeles, Michael Hague has taken a very personal approach to the persona of Alice, modeling her on his own youngest daughter, Brittany. He tells us she is a "daydreamer with an analytical mind." Almost half the pages of this book have large, stunningly detailed, carefully wrought, full-color images. The art connoisseur will notice the influence of Maxfield Parish in brilliant background skies and the breath of Arthur Rackham in the twisted bark of a tree that almost appears human. Hague conveys messages about the story that are not explicitly told. For example, the illustration introducing the Queen of Hearts, clearly the star of the scene, shows the glib face of the king with a very rosy nose. Hague gives the reader much to study beyond the text.

Related reads: Other titles illustrated by Hague include *The Wizard of Oz, The Velveteen Rabbit, Mother Goose,* and *Aesop's Fables.* Also, check *The Little Prince* by Antoine De Saint-Exupery.

Carroll, Lewis. *Alice's Adventures in Wonderland.* **Illustrated by Lisbeth Zwerger. A Michael Neugebauer Book, 1999 (1865). 103pp.**

Vienna born and educated Lisbeth Zwerger has won numerous awards, including the lifetime achievement award, the Hans Christian Andersen Medal. In this book, her flat, simple, images show faint pencil lines with color washes. Three cards brush red onto white roses, revealing through their dialogue that their heads are at risk for having planted the wrong color. The Zwerger delivery shows the cards in unanimated poses with deadpan faces, clearly following nonsense directions without emotional connection. It is what Zwerger does not portray in these images that tells the story.

Related reads: Other books illustrated by Zwerger include *The Wizard of Oz* and *Noah's Ark*, both recipients of *the New York Times* Best Illustrated Children's Book of the Year award.

Carroll, Lewis. *Alice in Wonderland.* **Illustrated by John Tenniel. Dover Publications, 2001 (1906—a slightly corrected Macmillan Company edition). 105pp.**

Here again is the story of the little girl who chased the rabbit. This charming little edition has an introductory note giving a full and detailed story of how the mathematics professor made up the tale for the three little girls of a colleague, then wrote it down and illustrated it as a gift for young Alice as *Alice's Adventures Under Ground*, whereupon it was so praised, he submitted it to Macmillan under the new title *Alice's Adventure's in Wonderland* (with no mention about the name change used in this edition, *Alice in Wonderland*.) and with the illustrations of *Punch* magazine artist John

Tenniel. This edition is an exact copy of the modified, improved text published in 1906, and has all of Tenniel's original drawings. The dark ink on newsprint is clear, with plenty of space between the lines. Because of the inexpensive presentation ($2 at this printing), this edition lends itself to large group distribution for read-aloud sessions.

Anton Chekhov (1860–1904) Collection

If anywhere, the power of experience on literature shows in the work of Anton Pavlovich Chekhov, born in the southern Russian town of Taganrog, the third of six children, to the son of a former surf. The suffering underclasses were to become a recurrent theme in his literary works. Chekhov attended the School of Medicine at the University of Moscow. During that period he developed tuberculosis, a disease that would eventually shorten his life.Under a number of pen names (Antosha Chekhonte Ch. and The Doctor Without Patients), he began earning money from short stories, jokes, and essays he wrote in part to help support his family.

These literary efforts caught the attention of noted writer Dimitry Grigorvich, who introduced him to leading publisher Aleksey Suvorin, who in turn began to publish Chekhov's stories. A visit to a prison island resulted in *Sakhalin Island*, published in 1893. Chekhov also worked in the relief effort during the 1892 famine, an enterprise that gave him a storehouse of impressions about human suffering that would resurface in his writing. Then he moved to a small village near Moscow, where he wrote short stories and wrote and produced two plays.

His was not a smooth literary journey, however. Chekhov gave up playwriting after the critical failure of *The Seagull.* (Later the same play was so celebrated by the Moscow Art Theatre, the seagull became its logo.) Because of his health, he was obliged to move again, this time to Yalta, where he formed literary relationships with the writers Maksim Gorky and Leo Tolstoy. He married the actress Olga Knipper, who remained in Moscow much of the time because of her work. Readers may find themes reflecting failure to communicate in many of Chekhov's works. But he did communicate through his plays, writing *The Cherry Orchard* and *The Three Sisters* for his wife's theatrical company shortly before being moved to a German health resort, where he died.

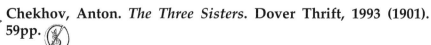

Chekhov, Anton. *The Three Sisters.* **Dover Thrift, 1993 (1901). 59pp.**

Three sisters, Olga, Masha, and Irina, have come down in the world. Once cultivated young ladies in Moscow, they are now stuck in a rural berg where nothing is going on, save their longing to escape. There is a surprise ending. This four-act play has many short sentences and is very easy to follow, making it a readers theatre natural.

 Ford, Richard, ed. *The Essential Tales of Chekhov.* **Translated by Constance Garnett, with an introduction by Richard Ford. The Ecco Press, 1998. 337pp.**

Here are 20 of Chekhov's best-loved tales, including "A Misfortune," "Difficult People," "The Kiss," "Peasants," "About Love," and "The Lady with the Dog," averaging 17 pages each. These subtle wanderings into the psyches of adults allow the reader to empathize with the characters while observing another time and place. "The Lady with the Dog" reveals a love affair between two very ordinary people, who are married to two other very ordinary people; all of the excitement is in their illicit liaisons, which both find increasingly addictive. The language is very simple; though Chekhov does not give graphic details, the reader is drawn into the relationship by innuendo. The print in this volume is not large, but it is clean and easy on the eyes.

 Pitcher, Harvey, ed. *Chekhov: The Comic Stories.* **Translated from the Russian, with an introduction by Harvey Pitcher. Ivan R. Dee, 1999. 217pp.**

These 40 very short stories, most less than five pages long and some less than three, are perfect for read-aloud and discussion activities. The jacket states: "By 1888, when he was just twenty-eight, Chekhov had published a staggering 528 stories, about half of them comic." Now the new reader and speaker of English may enjoy these interludes by one of the most prolific storytellers. The print in this book is small.

Related reads: Chekhov's *Five Great Short Stories*, an affordable volume produced by Dover Publications. Also, *Chekhov's Doctors: A Collection of Chekhov's Medical Tales.* Edited by John L. Coulehan. Kent State University Press, 2003. 232pp. Shows doctors in their day-to-day and professional lives.

 Chekhov, Anton. *The Cherry Orchard.* **Dover Publications, 1991 (1904). 49pp.**

This four-act play is a portrait of changes in the Russian class system in the late 1800s. First produced by the Moscow Art Theatre on January 17, 1904, the last birthday of Anton Chekhov, this play, which centers on the sale of Madame Ranevsky's cherry orchard (and the memories associated with the act of moving), presents most of the main action offstage (a dramatic form called "indirect action," which Chekhov introduced). The Ranevskys represent the aristocracy that found itself ill-prepared to deal with a rising middle class. In the end, the businessman Lopakhin buys the orchard and takes his own advice—chopping down the orchard in the name of redevelopment.

This is a fine readers theatre presentation text for a class. Using it for readers theatre or a general production will give all participants the support needed to become a very smooth at reading these lines. Russian history units will be greatly enhanced by a reading of this play. It is also a high-interest selection for Russian immigrants.

Samuel Taylor Coleridge (1772–1834) Collection

Samuel Taylor Coleridge was born the last of 10 children to an uninterested Ann Bowden Coleridge and the vicar of Ottery St. Mary, John Coleridge, on October 21, 1772. The victim of bullying by his older brother Frank, Col, as he was called, was subject to horrid nightmares that over the years found their way into his work. His father died when Col was nine, whereupon Col was sent to a charity school for clergy children.

A voracious reader, particularly impressed by the tales of the Arabian Nights, the young boy early on had expectations of becoming a famous and rich poet. The former began to happen, though his production never reached its full potential. He was physically ill, and the treatment at that time for suffering from the damp of the Lake District, laudanum, may have led to his addiction to opium. When Coleridge was a young man, the high cost of women, alcohol, and opium forced him to leave Cambridge. Desperately poor, he joined the army under the pseudonym Silas Tomkyn Comberbache, much to the consternation of his family. Thanks to his poor horsemanship skills, he narrowly missed an opportunity to fight in France.

Col was recalled to Cambridge by his family on grounds of insanity. He had a habit of falling in love with whatever socially acceptable woman was at hand. Sara was a favorite of his—two of them at least. He married at least twice, and began making literary contributions by way of critical reviews and lectures. Yet fortune eluded him. All of his adult life he fought the twin devils poverty and opium dependency. He went for long periods without contact with his children, but his friends thoroughly enjoyed his company and conversation. With William Wordsworth he wrote "Lyrical Ballads." Charles Lamb praised him. But he was not, according to his peers, meeting his potential. Shelley proclaimed that he was a "hooded eagle among blinking owls." His epitaph, written by himself, reads in part:

> Beneath this sod
> A Poet lies; or that which once seem'd he.
> O, lift one thought in prayer for S. T. C.
> That he, who many a year with toil of breath,
> Found death in life, may here find life in death.

Remembered most of all for his handful of poems, Coleridge also contributed to our language. For example, he coined the word "selfless."

 Coleridge, Samuel Taylor. *Kubla Khan*. Illustrated by Nick Bantock. Viking, 1994 (1798). 10pp.

Reported by Coleridge to be a dream—or nightmare—half-remembered, perhaps the product of an opium-induced trance, this very short poem introduces the famous Xanadu. Kubla Khan (Kublai Khan, 1216–1294, Yuan dynasty founder), a well-known figure from the Far East, begins a decree that references many experiences that would have been in the news in 1797 and 1798, thanks to Marco Polo and company. Standing alone, this poem, with its many elusive references and images, is inaccessible to the casual reader. This Nick Bantock interpretation in dark and sensuous paper sculptures, however, will cause any adult to pause and struggle. Readers will want to compare the Bantock take on this poem with their own, line by line. A teacher or tutor may want to attempt making a visual model of one line or one passage as a way of introducing this visual conversation with Coleridge.

 Coleridge, Samuel Taylor. *The Rime of the Ancient Mariner*. Illustrated by Gustave Doré in 1878. New introduction by Millicent Rose. Dover Publications, 1970 (1907). 77.

A wedding guest is about to enter the church, when a shockingly intense old man detains him. The hoary old man is the sole survivor of a ship that was doomed by his arrogance and self-importance. Now he must do penance by telling the dreadful details of his fateful journey. By divine instinct, he knows to whom he must speak; neither speaker nor listener has a choice in this. As the wedding music beckons, the guest is compelled to stay outside to listen, to learn, and to evolve into a better sort of man by the time the rice is thrown. This morality poem has myriad lines that have become idioms and axioms of the English language. Yet it is poetry . . . 1796 poetry, and there are many allusions the first-time reader may miss.

Doré's illustrations make this classic poem accessible to the modern reader and may encourage those who are seeking passages to memorize to consider this poem as a source. The awe-inspiring engravings give life to the text and would have likely enchanted even the author. The verses of this classic poem are largely on the left-hand page (pages are 9¼ by 12 inches), often with modern English notes in tiny print, leaving lots of room for the reader to apply sticky notes or write comments. This edition is "[s]lightly rearranged (from the 1878 Harper & Brothers, Publishers edition) to conform to the authoritative 1834 edition." The seven interesting pages of double-spaced introduction by Millicent Rose deal primarily with the life and times of the artist and critique the 42 illustrations themselves.

Homeschoolers and cooperative learning groups can use the stanzas of this poem as readers theatre choral readings. The poem also lends itself to units on enchantment, ghosts, morality, penance, and values.

Related reads: *The Raven* by Edgar Allan Poe is also illustrated by Doré in a 9¼-by-12-inch format. *Doré's Illustrations for the Fables of La Fontaine* has just a one-line story and a one-line message. Both *Doré's Illustrations for "Paradise Lost"* and *The Doré Illustrations for Dante's* Divine Comedy offer one or two lines of text beneath dramatic, full-page, black-and-white drawings.

 Coleridge, Samuel Taylor. *The Rime of the Ancient Mariner*. Illustrated by Charles Mozley. Franklin Watts, 1969 (1907). 50pp.

A very old seaman is obliged by the forces of life and death to make penance for having killed a bird of good omen—an albatross—that senseless killing having heralded terrible storms and windless skies and caused the deaths of all his mates. The penance for this deed is to repeat his tale to those who need to hear it. He stops a wedding guest, who, although hearing the music start, is still compelled to listen to the old man's story. Describing a time when there was no drinking water left and the boat stood still, the story continues with these often-memorized lines:

> As idle as a painted ship
> Upon a painted ocean.

And these famous lines:

> Water, water, everywhere,
> Nor any drop to drink.

And these frequently reinterpreted lines:

> He prayeth well, who loveth well
> Both man and bird and beast.

The final stanza is about the wedding guest:

> A sadder and a wiser man,
> He rose the morrow morn.

Marginal notes and dramatic black-and-white drawings provide information about this classic poem. It is not a book to be read alone by any novice, but it is a fine introduction to the poem from which several modern allusions come. Readers may want to go through this poem several times to find familiar phrases that have come into modern language from Coleridge.

Coleridge, Samuel Taylor. *The Rime of the Ancient Mariner and Other Poems.* **Dover Thrift, 1992 (Edited by Ernest Hartley Coleridge and published by Humphrey Milford/Oxford University Press, 1917). 76pp.**

Here are more than 20 poems, including "The Rime of the Ancient Mariner," "Kubla Khan," and "To William Wordsworth," offering a variety of reading levels and lengths, some being just a handful of lines. "The Knight's Tomb" laments the loss of a landmark, reflects on mortality, and kicks up a surprising punch of humor in the last line. This little volume is very easy to carry about and allows even the reader with a modest budget a chance to add a classic collection to his or her personal library.

Guy De Maupassant (1850–1893) Collection

Best known for his ironic portrayals of everyday life with strange twists of fate, the French-born Guy de Maupassant was a protégé of Gustave Flaubert, who taught de Maupassant to structure his tales carefully. Focused on the peasants of his time, war, and Parisian fashion trends, he did not poke direct fun at his subjects, but in de Maupassant's writing, seemingly mundane details are paramount to the plot. Almost like clues to a mystery, he provides the reader with much-needed points of information and then hides them in plain sight. He is best known for "The Necklace," "The Umbrella," and "Le Rendezvous," simple stories that fail to warm the heart but do twist the mind of the reader. His storytelling is clear, making the translations of his short stories and novels a perfect choice for new readers.

 Barchers, Suzanne I., and Jennifer L. Kroll. "The Necklace." In *Classic Readers Theatre for Young Adults,* **39–45. Libraries Unlimited, 2002. 243pp.**

These modern language readers theatre scripts will help new readers and ESL students develop an understanding of this classic story. Two narrators and three other characters have a scripted introduction to the story as Matilde borrows the diamond necklace for a party and then loses it, and a scripted closing as (10 years later) she learns the necklace she has labored to replace was costume jewelry. These are combined with one-paragraph plot summaries for the rest of the story. This provides both dramatic reading and scriptwriting opportunities for small groups.

de Maupassant, Guy (1850–1893). *The Necklace and Other Short Stories.* **Dover Publications, 1992 (1884). 119pp.**

The surprise ending is a trademark of Guy de Maupassant. Best known is "The Necklace," the story of a woman whose life was wasted because she spent it slaving to replace a borrowed diamond necklace that she had lost, only in the end to discover that the necklace had been fake. These short stories are fine read-alouds and discussion starters. The stories in this book are "Ball of Fat," "The Necklace," "A Piece of String," "Mme. Tellier's Establishment," "Mademoiselle Fifi," "Miss Harriet," "A Way to Wealth," "My Uncle Jules," and "The Horla."

Discussions supported by these tales include the human condition, pride, innocence, and human frailty. Reading from those short story collections identified as NEXT READ or START HERE in this chapter will help the new reader gain the needed vocabulary and speed to read these easily.

Charles Dickens (1812–1870) Collection

One day when nine-year-old Charles and his father were out walking, they came upon a mansion that positively captured the imagination. On that stroll, John Dickens told his son that, with hard work, he might well live there one day. Little did either know that first the family would fall into the depths of English poorhouse poverty, that eventually Charles would indeed possess and live in that great house, or that he would die there. The Diane Stanley/Peter Vennema picture book *Charles Dickens: The Man Who Had Great Expectations* includes these anecdotes and many more. The book provides a basic understanding of the writer and his times. Reading the picture book aloud first and discussing it by drawing comparisons between the nineteenth and twenty-first centuries would be enough to connect the new reader with the author, but there are other texts that will promote a deeper understanding of the times and of the poor whom Dickens championed through his work.

To get started, try reading the picture book and then reading some of Dickens's classic work, referring back to the picture book as connections come up. The literary source of the famous exclamation "Bah! Humbug!" is one readers of all persuasions enjoy discovering. "A Christmas Carol" (first published in 1843) is a good choice during the holiday season, when readers are going to be exposed to many references to the story and the characters, from Disney cartoons to advertisements to dramatizations of the classic tale. The severity of the times in which Dickens lived is difficult to discover from one book. To better understand the conditions of those times, the student may be encouraged to peruse the works and illustrations in other books referenced here. For comprehension support of "A Christmas Carol," readers may want to view the latest movie version, or they may well enjoy listening to an unabridged recording, one of which is listed in this collection.

The readers theatre activities titles annotated in this unit will also help readers become familiar with Dickens's world. But the actual reading of the original texts will deliver details that show (rather than tell) so much about the author's times and demonstrate how this author could cast a mood, and within the mood, a spell. We learn to write by what we read, and from reading these stories readers will gain insights into literary devices so subtle they will be absorbed unconsciously.

Barchers, Suzanne I., and Jennifer L. Kroll. "A Christmas Carol." In *Classic Readers Theatre for Young Adults,* **47–64. Libraries Unlimited, 2002. 243pp.**

Support for "A Christmas Carol." These scenes are ready to use in a classroom or homeschool dramatization. There is a mix of long and short reading parts, accompanied by other teaching ideas. This is very high-level comprehension support for the books addressed.

Barchers, Suzanne I., and Jennifer L. Kroll. "Hard Times." In *Classic Readers Theatre for Young Adults,* **65–92. Libraries Unlimited, 2002. 243pp.**

This readers theatre unit specifically addresses the Dickens novel *Hard Times.* The summary reveals: "Mr. Gradgrind, a school superintendent, believes that children should be exposed only to facts, nothing fanciful, artistic, or sentimental." It goes on to explain that this philosophy has profound negative implications for the lives of his children. Eighteen scenes from this book, written in simple, direct, modern English, provide a great deal of reading practice that will familiarize the readers with this book, the author, and the social attitudes of industrial England in the 1800s. It is excellent support for academic units in English history, the Industrial Revolution, and philosophies of education.

Latrobe, Kathy. "The Personal History of *David Copperfield.*" **In** *Readers Theatre for Young Adults,* **23–25. Teacher Ideas Press, 1989. 130pp.**

This skit, based on chapter 8 of *David Copperfield,* "My Holidays: Especially One Happy Afternoon," provides five reader roles that allow the lead character to have remarkably few words to read, none of which are difficult. The scene gives a very clear look at poor Little David's predicament as he is belittled by his stepfather and step-aunt in his own home. The benchmark Dickens themes of orphanhood and despair are quickly identified by readers. Here is an excellent introduction for both players and audience members to Dickens's work.

Stanley, Diane, and Peter Vennema. *Charles Dickens: The Man Who Had Great Expectations.* **Illustrated by Diane Stanley. Morrow Junior Books, 1993. 48pp.**

This extensively researched biography captures the spirit of Dickens's life and times: the gossip, the romantic frustrations, the class distinctions, the pitiful starvation, and the marriage that drained the very hope from the struggling Englishman. It demonstrates how all of this and more was replayed in the author's compassionate writings. Although the title alludes to Dickens's novel *Great Expectations*, this picture book is a fine introduction to "A Christmas Carol." Teachers can have students pick out the childhood events that might have given rise to elements of that classic. Homeschoolers of large families will find much to compare to their own homes. This is also a simple history lesson delivered through both the events and the clear, detailed drawings. This fits social studies units about nineteenth-century England, children's issues, and the literature of Charles Dickens. This book also has a bibliography of works about Dickens and a partial list of his titles.

Related read: For a shorter, more text-driven biography, try the Charles Dickens section in Kathleen Krull's *Lives of the Writers: Comedies, Tragedies (and What the Neighbors Thought)*.

 Dickens, Charles. *A Christmas Carol and Other Stories.* **Illustrated by Arthur Rackham, Robert Buchanan, and Barbara Buchanan. Reader's Digest Association, 1988. 287pp.**

Contains some of Dickens's most popular shorter works, including "A Christmas Carol," "The Chimes," "The Cricket on the Hearth," and the afterword adaptation of the 1923 essay "The Greatest Little Book Ever Published" by A. Edward Newton (1863–1940). The texts of these stories are the same as those in other copies. What makes this book worth checking out is the collection of ink drawings and colored prints. Here yet another set of artistic interpretations will delight the reader.

 Latrobe, Kathy. "A Tale of Two Cities." In *Readers Theatre for Young Adults,* **26–30. Teacher Ideas Press, 1989. 130pp.**

Support for *A Tale of Two Cities.* taken from chapter 4 of that book, "The Preparation." This skit has only three reader parts: the banker Mr. Jarvis Lorry, 17-year-old Miss Lucie Manette, and the Narrator. Each of the parts is about the same number of lines and level of difficulty. This passage jumps directly into the intrigue the characters face. Because of the roundabout way they speak, this skit is more challenging both to player and audience than others in this collection.

Dickens, Charles. *A Christmas Carol.* **Illustrated by William Geldart. The Whole Story. Viking, 1999. (1843) 107pp.**

His business partner Jacob Marley now dead, the miserly Scrooge is destined to conduct heartless business all day, every day, with no one to appreciate his efforts. Then, one Christmas eve, Marley's ghost appears to warn his old business partner of the importance of caring for others. Three spirits of Christmas—Past, Present, and Future—visit Scrooge. At the sight of the two children, Ignorance and Want, Scrooge is reminded of his own unkind words—suggesting that the needy go to workhouses or prisons. Richly colored, detailed illustrations are accompanied by images from historic publications and notes about the times and the life of the author. Details about the exploding population, stock speculations, and other indicators of London economics fill the margins of this delightful book. The historical information and the story illustrations combine to support the reader's comprehension of this edition.

 Dickens, Charles. *A Christmas Carol.* **Illustrated by Roberto Innocenti. Stewart, Tabori & Chang, 1990 (1843). 152pp.**

This is a wonderful book for introducing the classic tale. The contrasts between haves and have-nots are laid bare. Greed, poverty, debtor's prison, and Christmas icons stand out. This is the kind of book that is nice to have and to hold. The tall, elegant tome is one Dickens would probably have kept for himself. And every page of text is like a manuscript reproduction, with a holly sprig at the top of the frame holding tall, elegant print. The mood-capturing, detailed illustrations use perspective to propel the viewer into hidden corners and rooftop niches—and provide internal support for the reader. This edition is a fine small-group read-aloud.

 Dickens, Charles. *A Christmas Carol.* **Illustrated by Eric Kincaid. Birmax Books, 1992 (1843). 93pp.**

Here is the original, unabridged tale in large print with extra wide margins, filled top to bottom with large illustrations that propel the old Christmas classic into fairyland. Kincaid's use of contrast in subtle and dramatic colors and his powerful sense of facial expressions make this a picture book to view all year.

 Dickens, Charles. *A Christmas Carol.* **Illustrated by Arthur Rackham. Weathervane Books, 1977 (1843). 147pp.**

This is the famous morality tale, filled with ghosts that terrorize and teach—an old dog of a man who learns new tricks for finding happiness, and a little boy who gets a possible reprieve from an early grave. Scrooge, after meeting the ghost of his former business partner and the ghosts of Christmas past, present, and future, and making spectral visits to scenes that have been and may be, decides that money isn't everything. Yet he uses his money to make quite an impact on those around him. That's the tale.

Readers may feel slightly off-balance at first because this text uses all single quotation marks, rather than double, and the quotes are embedded in the paragraphs rather than set out as extracts, making the text slightly denser than it would appear otherwise. Nonetheless, it is not hard on the eyes. Arthur Rackham's 1915 illustrations are quite another set of scenes. Each has a caption that suggests a message, but Rackham takes poetic license and teases the viewer with contrasts at every turn. An ink drawing caption in all caps reading THERE WAS NOTHING VERY CHEERFUL IN THE CLIMATE appears below a windswept, snow-covered rooftop, from which chimney smoke swirls ominously over the heads of two little boys, presumably assigned to shovel the snow, who are going at it full-speed and smilingly in a snowball fight. The classic pictures and captions alone are worth the first reading of this book, offering internal support for the new reader.

Audio version: *A Christmas Carol.* Penguin AudioBooks, 2 cassettes, approximately 3.25 hours. Read by Geoffrey Palmer. Teachers who traditionally read this book aloud to their students may find this recording a welcome change that allows a different voice to read the tale of ghosts and morality. Variety can be added to the long reading by stopping the tape occasionally to change the pace or for discussion.

Video version: *Scrooge.* CRS/FOX, 1970. 1 cassette, 115 minutes. Starring Albert Finney, Dame Edith Eradis, and Kenneth More. A musical rendition, one of many available video versions of this story.

 Dickens, Charles. *A Christmas Carol in Prose, Being a Ghost Story of Christmas.* **Illustrated by John Groth. Afterword by Clifton Fadiman. Macmillan, 1963 (1843). 128pp.**

This book contains 14 color plates and numerous ink sketches. The tale is broken into five "staves": "Marley's Ghost," "The First of the Three Spirits," "The Second of the Three Spirits," "The Last of the Spirits," and "The End of It." Illustrations by John Groth call attention to seldom-remembered bits of the story. A sketch of Robinson Crusoe illuminates the references to other literature, and a sketch of Scrooge forcing an extinguisher-cap over the first spirit shows what such an instrument was. The font, though big enough for easy reading, does not propel the story as fonts in some other copies do. But it has the whole story as it was presented in 1843. Readers who want more support may listen to an audio edition or may want to begin with START HERE! and NEXT READ titles in this collection.

Dickens, Charles. *A Tale of Two Cities.* **Illustrations by "Phiz." Introduction by Sir John Schuckburgh. Oxford University Press, 1998 (1859). 358pp.**

This is Dickens's only historical novel and, according to Sir John Schuckburgh, it is the best constructed of all his books, reproduced here with the original 16 pen-and-ink illustrations. The Oxford edition is a pleasure to hold—a compact, cuddly little book. Though Dickens's description of the French Revolution is a compelling silent read, students are equally impressed when they hear it read aloud. Because the length can be tiring to a single reader, and some may need to have the character descriptions reviewed or details recalled from time to time, the educator may want to play the Richard Pasco reading annotated below, thereby introducing a different accent to the students as well as professional reading.

To engage students in reading short passages in an interesting way, small class teachers and homeschoolers may want to add the Latrobe skit annotated in this section. Because the skit is based on the fourth chapter of the book, students will get support from the early chapters and will have the practice of the dramatic scene to reinforce their familiarity with the characters. Students can also learn geography along with this classical literature and history when they are given notebook-sized maps for their reference and have large maps on the classroom walls.

Audio version: *A Tale of Two Cities.* The Audio Partners Publishing Corp., 1983. 11 cassettes, 14 hours, 35 minutes. Read by Richard Pasco. Pasco gives a dramatic persona to each character.

 Haining, Peter, ed. *The Complete Ghost Stories of Charles Dickens.* **Franklin Watts, 1983. 342pp.**

Twenty ghostly tales range from the very short, "The Lawyer and the Ghost" (pages 33–35) to the entire text of "A Christmas Carol." Original illustrations help set the mood and period and provide internal support for comprehension. These are good read-alouds for Halloween time, too.

Related reads: *A Christmas Carol, A Tale of Two Cities,* and *The Cricket on the Hearth and Other Stories* are available in AFFORDABLE formats through Dover Publications.

 Dickens, Charles. *Great Expectations.* **With an essay, "The Sense of Two Endings," by Anny Sadrin, and an 1861 critical review. Courage Classics, 1992 (1861). 532pp.**

Young Pip's chance encounter with the criminal Magwitch sets into motion events that will forever change Pip's expectations for his own future. Pip's efforts to understand the unseen forces that affect his good and bad fortunes come to very little for years. Close-up views of the disparity between the haves and have-nots in nineteenth-century England make this a social studies lesson within a fine tale. This volume delivers the epic as it is popularly known, and it also contains Dickens's original, more ambiguous ending. Teachers, tutors, and homeschoolers may want to read this book aloud to their students in segments, over time. Another way of acquainting students with Dickens's style and themes is to allow students to play out the *David Copperfield* skit cited on page 132. Students may then compare one long work with another, identifying themes.

Related reads: Other titles by Charles Dickens include *Hard Times; The Life and Adventures of Nicholas Nickelby; Oliver Twist, or, The Parish Boy's Progress;* and *The Posthumous Papers of the Pickwick Club.*

Nikolai Gogol (1809–1852) Collection

Son of a Ukrainian writer of puppet dramas, Nikolai Vasilievich Gogol was born in Mirgorod, Ukraine, in 1809. The sensitive lad enjoyed his father's estate but was forever plagued by insecurities and self-doubt. Young Gogol, planning to follow in his father's footsteps but writing in Russian, moved to St. Petersburg. Embarrassment at his failure to meet critical acclaim resulted in his running off to Europe. Returning from Europe in 1829 with plans to become an actor, Gogol again met defeat. Like many of his modern contemporaries, he was forced to accept a boring day job as a civil servant. There, unending bumbling of bureaucrats provided Gogol with the grist for his literary mill of later years. Before that happened, however, he embarked on a lackluster career as a writer of unappreciated prose. Yet he was establishing habits that would make his stories compelling and believable.

For example, on April 30, 1829, he wrote to his mother that he wanted her to tell him exactly what the most provincial Russian words were for the parts of a village deacon's costume—from his underwear out, and the same for the maids and matrons of the village. In 1831 and 1832, he published two volumes of short stories, written in the narrative style of Alexander Pushkin (whom Gogol met through a mutual friend), volumes that skyrocketed him into popularity. Such popularity qualified him to engage in a brief career as a university professor.

In 1835, Gogol began a return to his roots with *Mirgorod*, a collection of short stories about his boy home. In 1936, his comic play *The Inspector General* was produced, to rave reviews. But he felt misunderstood and again left the country, visiting Switzerland, Paris, and Rome. Over the next few years, he continued to write successfully, but a growing conservative religious conviction made him feel that writing fiction was fundamentally sinful. In 1840 he published *Selected Passages from a Correspondence with My Friends*, with was actually a didactic treatise using only letters written by Gogol, to Gogol, and answered by Gogol. Meanwhile Pushkin, a public admirer of Gogol's satirical wit and poetry, suggested Gogol use the vehicle of a soul-buying wanderer meeting many characters for his final great work, *Dead Souls* (part one of which was renamed *The Adventures of Chickikov* to appease religious censors), which remained unfinished in part because Gogol burned one nearly complete manuscript just days before his death. It may be noted that *Dead Souls* is believed to have been an inspiration for Joseph Heller's *Catch 22*.

Over time, Gogol also produced more short stories, his masterpiece being "The Overcoat," which is found in many editions including the collection of the same name below. "The Overcoat" was at the head of a trend of looking at, rather than overlooking, the poor and underclasses of nineteenth-century Russia. It is the tale of bedraggled Akaky, who saves his pennies to buy a new coat when the tailor tells him his old one cannot be repaired any more. Once he has his prized coat, which wins him an invitation to a party, Akaky becomes inebriated while celebrating, and he is robbed of the coat. But no official cares. No policeman investigates the crime. Akaky dies. A crime wave of coat thefts ensues, and those who might have made a difference are caught up in it.

Note: Readers may find some of Gogol's works online at The University of Adelaide Library, Australia, (http://etext.librryadelaide.edu.au/aut/gogol.html).

 Gogol, Nikolai. *The Collected Tales of Nikolai Gogol.* **Translated and annotated by Richard Pevear and Larissa Volokhonsky. Vintage Classics, 1999. 435pp.**

This book is divided into two geographic locations. There are seven Ukrainian tales and six Petersburg tales. The print is not large, but there is ample space between the lines. Words such as Cossacks, Petro, and Basavriuk may give the new reader pause, but the sentences are otherwise easy to read.

 Gogol, Nikolai. *Nikolai Gogol: Plays and Petersburg Tales.* **New translations by Christopher English. Oxford University Press, 1999. 400pp.**

This new translation has six of Gogol's most popular short stories, including "The Nose" and "The Overcoat." It also has two famous plays, *Marriage* and *The Government Inspector*. This book has notes on the translation, a bibliography, a Gogol chronology, and maps of St. Petersburg. The print is small, but not hard on the eyes. Groups may want to use these plays for readers theatre productions.

 Gogol, Nikolai. *The Overcoat and Other Short Stories.* **Dover Publications, 1992. 103pp.**

Ivan Yakovlevich, the barber, stuck his finger into the fresh bread his wife had served him and extracted a nose. So goes the tale "The Nose," in which the barber really doesn't know how it got into his bread.

The names of the characters in this and the other tales are long and unfamiliar to most American ears. The sentences are sometimes quite long. Even so, the stories are highly entertaining, making fine short reads. They are of particular interest to immigrants from the former Soviet Union (Russia, Ukraine, Belarus, etc.) and others who are eager to laugh at the absurdities of bureaucracy.

Other stories in this book include "Old-Fashioned Farmers," "The Tale of How Ivan Ivanovich Quarreled with Ivan Nikiforovich," and "The Overcoat."

O. Henry (1862–1910) Collection

William Sydney (also Sidney) Porter was born in North Carolina and later migrated to Texas to become the editor and publisher of *Rolling Stone.* At one point he was charged with embezzlement and fled to Central America, then returned to serve in a federal penitentiary, where, as he worked in the pharmacy, he lifted the ID of Etienne-Ossian Henry and began his career as O. Henry. Picking up bits and pieces of inmates' tales, he embellished incidents with flair and intrigue. In 1899 he published "Whistling Dick's Christmas Stocking" in *McClure's Magazine.* His tidbit collecting continued after his release. The sources of subsequent tales may be found in his term for New York, "Baghdad-on-the-Subway."

Twists of fate and clever interventions by altruistic heroes give O. Henry's stories an element of surprise—not necessarily happy surprise—at the end that has become his trademark. "The Last Leaf" deals with a girl who is counting down to her death by the numbers of leaves outside her window; "The Gift of the Magi" shows how the power of mutual concern can lead to an impossible resolution. O. Henry's most popular collection of short stories today is *The Four Million: The Voice of the City* (1908), in which the reader discovers that every person on the street or in the subway has a tale worth hearing.

 Henry, O. *The Four Million.* Project Gutenberg, 2001 (1906).

This is a collection of about 25 stories, available free online from Project Gutenberg (http://onlinebooks.upenn.edu/webbin/gutbook/).

Audio version: *The Four Million.* Books on Tape, 1982. 6 cassettes, approximately 6 hours. Read by various readers.

 Henry, O. *The Gift of the Magi and Other Short Stories.* Dover Publications, 1992 (1905). 96pp.

"The Gift of the Magi" is the story of a poverty-stricken young couple so much in love that each gives up something very precious in order to have a surprise Christmas gift for the other. He sells his heirloom pocket watch to buy her a comb for her beautiful, long hair, but she has sold it to buy him a chain for his watch. Surprise endings are the trademark of O. Henry's short stories, 16 of which are collected here from a variety of other books and periodicals in an inexpensive, easy to carry around edition. These might be called morality tales, but they are also just great storytelling. The language is too sophisticated for the new reader or new student of English, but for intermediate level readers and above, here is a glimpse of the writing that kept Americans glued to their reading chairs at the turn of the century. To build the vocabulary and sentence skills needed for O. Henry, readers may want to read John Steinbeck's *Of Mice and Men* or Willa Cather's collected stories.

Note: Many retellings of this classic story have been published, many without redeeming features. But Shari Lewis's retelling of "The Gift of the Magi" in her *One-Minute Christmas Stories* is not one of the latter.

Note: Text of "The Gift of the Magi" and many other O. Henry stories may be downloaded free at The Four Million—O Henry—Free Online Library (http://henry.thefreelibrary.com/The-Four-Million/2–1).

Related read: Now try Guy de Maupassant's *The Necklace and Other Short Stories,* annotated in this chapter.

 Henry, O. *The Ransom of Red Chief and Other Stories.* Random House Value Publishing, 1996. 209pp.

Told from the point of view of Sam, one of the kidnappers, the brilliant idea of taking a mortgage banker's son for ransom proves not to be as fruitful as expected. In short order, little Johnny, a holy terror, sets his captors' lives on end and gives them cause to understand why the bereaved parents refuse to take him back. This hilarious tale, which is republished every few years in various formats, may be found free online at The Literature Network (http://www/online-literature.com/o_henry/1041/).

Washington Irving (1783–1859) Collection

Born in New York City, Washington Irving was the youngest of 11 children born to a wealthy American merchant and an English clergyman's daughter. He studied law and traveled extensively before returning to the United States to join the family hardware business, which collapsed in 1918. During those years, he began his writing career, contributing to the *Morning Chronicle* and publishing *Salmagundi*. He took time out to serve as the New York governor's aide in the War of 1812. He also became engaged to Matilda Hoffman, a love affair that was cut short by her death in 1809 when she was only 17.

Irving's own scholarship as a researcher of histories was also budding. In 1809, readers were introduced to the character Dietrich Knickerbocker, a scholar who knew the town of New York inside and out, when *A History of New York* by the fictional Dutchman was published. Then came *The Sketch Book of Geoffrey Crayon, Gent.,* a collection of episodes published in 1819 and 1820, followed in 1822 by the sequel, *Bracebridge Hall*. These works put Irving in the full-time author category.

When his mother died, Irving began a 17-year sojourn in Europe, during which he wrote the Spanish histories *Columbus, Conquest of Granada*, and *The Companions of Columbus*, then moved to England, publishing *Alhambra*, about the legends and history of Moorish Spain. In 1832 he returned to America, began a tour of the country, and wrote *The Canyon Miscellany* and *A Tour of the Prairies*. Then he departed for Spain again, serving as ambassador from 1842 to 1845. He spent his final years in Tarrytown, New York, where he served as the president of the Astor Library (later New York Public Library) and continued to write, including *The Life of George Washington*. Despite all his scholarly work, however, he is best remembered for his two strange and whimsical stories, "The Legend of Sleepy Hollow," in which schoolmaster Ichabod Crane encounters a headless horseman, and "Rip Van Winkle," in which the title character went to sleep for 20 years. Washington Irving used several pseudonyms, including Jonathan Oldstyle, Gent. and Diedrich Knickerbocker.

 Barchers, Suzanne I., and Jennifer L. Kroll. "The Legend of Sleepy Hollow." In *Classic Readers Theatre for Young Adults*, 121–132. Libraries Unlimited, 2002. 243pp.

Five scenes adapted from the original story are ready to use in a classroom or homeschool dramatization. There is a mix of long and short reading parts, accompanied by other teaching ideas.

 Irving, Washington. *The Legend of Sleepy Hollow and Rip Van Winkle*. Illustrated by Thea Kliros. Dover Publications, 1995 (1819–1820). 75pp.

Although the scattered ink drawings are humorous and detailed, there are not enough of them to give the reader the much-needed support for "The Legend of Sleepy Hollow." Irving's language in the first story contains many archaic phrases and uses some very long sentences that make the reading slow going.

The second story, about Rip Van Winkle, a resident of the Catskill Mountains who awoke with a long grey beard after a 20-year nap, is easier reading. But both "The Legend of Sleepy Hollow" and "Rip Van Winkle" are classics everyone will want to become familiar with, and both are quite suitable as Halloween read-alouds. They were first published in *The Sketch Book of Geoffrey Crayon, Gent*. The print in this little book is very easy on the eyes, and there is ample space between the lines.

Irving, Washington. *The Legend of Sleepy Hollow, Found Among the Papers of the Late Diedrich Knickerbocher.* **Illustrated by Russ Flint. Biography of Washington Irving by Patricia A. Pingry. Candy Cane Press, 1999 (1819–1820). 64pp.**

This classic tale of a superstitious young man who thought he'd marry the beautiful daughter of the richest man in town is delivered in the original text. The plan was going very well until the young man heard about the vengeful headless horseman, who would ride through the town at midnight with his head under his arm. Just as the horrible night ride gripped the imagination of readers over 150 years ago, so it does today, perhaps even more. In this edition, the mysterious oil paintings of Russ Flint bring terror to new heights. The amply sized type has generous spacing between the lines.

This story was one of five first published in 1819 in a grey-brown paper covered pamphlet called *The Sketch Book of Geoffrey Crayon, Gent.* It was the two tales, "Rip Van Winkle" and "The Legend of Sleepy Hollow," that made Irving an overnight sensation. The inspiration for "Rip Van Winkle" was "The Goatherd," by George Webbe Dasent, published in *Popular Tales from Norse Mythology.* This can serve as an illustration of how one literary work inspires another. And it explains, in part, why readers are more successful writers than non-readers; they find other works that inspire them.

Tip: For additional support, see "Rip Van Winkle," a skit from the story, in *Readers' Theatre for Young Adults,* by Kathy Howard Latrobe and Mildred Knight Laughlin.

Henry James (1843–1916) Collection

The product of an affluent and prestigious New York family (his philosopher theologian father was among the country's first millionaires), Henry James dropped out of Harvard Law school in 1862 to become a writer. Two years later his first story appeared in print, and almost instantly his work became popular. He wrote for the *Nation* and *Atlantic* magazines from 1866 to 1869; was art critic for *Atlantic* from 1871 to 1872; moved to Paris, where he wrote for the *New York Tribune;* and was a volunteer for the displaced and wounded during World War I.

Some of James's most popular titles are *Portrait of a Lady, The Bostonians, The Tragic Muse,* and *The Sacred Fount.* His stories include "Daisy Miller: A Study" (1878, which he adapted into a three-act play in 1883) and "The Turn of the Screw" (1898, adapted into a play, *The Innocents,* in 1951). His autobiographical works include *A Small Boy and Others* (1913); *Notes of a Son and Brother* (1914); *The Middle Years* (1917); and *Henry James: Autobiography,* a collection of his autobiographical works (1956).

After James was publicly lambasted for his style in the H. G. Wells parody *Boon* (1915), Ezra Pound and Gertrude Stein responded with essays praising his work. His friendship with Edith Wharton is chronicled in their published letters. He also corresponded with Henry Adams.

"Daisy Miller" was rejected by an American magazine, and so first appeared in the British magazine *Cornhill* in 1878. Following its sudden success, it was published in book form, and then James revised and modified it into the play *Daisy Miller: A Comedy* in 1883.

James received the Order of Merit in 1915 and was commemorated by a James Memorial Stone in the Poet's Corner of Westminster Abbey, London.

James, Henry. *Daisy Miller*. Buccaneer Books, 1993 (1878). 83pp.
This is a hardcover reproduction of an out-of-print book. This edition has clear print, about 12 point. In this romantic tragedy, 27-year-old Frederick Winterbourne becomes smitten with one Miss Daisy Miller, a young American of a nouveau riche family, while she is on holiday in Switzerland. Later, when he is staying in Rome with his very socially astute and critical widowed aunt, Mrs. Costello, Winterbourne again meets up with the flirtatious Miss Miller, who is clueless about class etiquette. Mrs. Costello casts a negative shadow over the relationship between her nephew and the girl, setting in motion a series of events that leave the reader wondering about the class distinctions, pretensions at sophistication, and issues of courtship that continue to trouble the young and concern the old in both the Old and the New Worlds.

This classic tale is written in language so clear that if the print were bigger it would almost qualify as a START HERE! title. Long out of copyright, it can be found in single volumes and in collections of James's work.

Related read: For a slightly darker James tale, try *Turn of the Screw*.

James, Henry. *Daisy Miller*. Introduction by Henry James. Dover Thrift, 1995 (1878). 59pp.

In addition to the story text, this Dover edition has an introduction that James used for his New York presentations. The paper texture is rough and the print is small—note the difference between the number of pages here and elsewhere—but it is readable, and it is lightweight and easy to carry around.

James, Henry. *Daisy Miller and Other Stories*. Oxford World's Classics, 1998 (ca. 1878). 352pp.
"Daisy Miller" appears on pages 1–82 in this edition. Contents include acknowledgments, the introduction, a note on the texts, further reading, a chronology of Henry James, a preface by Henry James, "Daisy Miller" (1878), "Pandora" (1884), "The Patagonia" (1888), "Four Meetings" (1877), notes, and variant readings. The variant readings at the back

of the book neatly compare changes made between the first book editions and the New York editions for each of the works. For example, in "Daisy Miller" the first edition used the word "uncultivated," while the New York one used "uneducated" to describe her (some changes run more than 25 words). Examination of these editorial changes could raise consciousness about the writing process and many subtleties of the language. The pages in this edition feel very nice to the fingers.

 James, Henry. *The Turn of the Screw.* **Dover Thrift, 1991 (1898). 87pp.**

Two innocent orphans, a brother and sister, evolve into insidious liars in the presence of ghosts and an oppressive governess. For more on the story, see the next annotation. This is the original text as published in *The Two Magics* following its publication in serial form from January 27 to April 16 in 1898.

 James, Henry. *The Turn of the Screw and Other Short Fiction by Henry James.* **Introduction by R. W. B. Lewis. Bantam Books, 1981. 403pp.**

The contents include an introduction, "The Turn of the Screw," "Washington Square," "Daisy Miller: A Study," "The Beast in the Jungle," and "The Jolly Corner." In the introduction, R. W. B. Lewis reviews the situations in James's life that are parallel to those recounted in his fictional stories. For example, James began writing "Turn of the Screw" almost immediately after moving into Lamb House in the Village of Rye. In that house, James reported "a sort of terror," and in his letters one may find "expressions of fear."

"The Turn of the Screw" is about two young children, Miles and Flora, who, according to their new governess, Mrs. Gross, appear to be obsessed with the ghosts of former estate employees Peter Quint and Miss Jessel, who are bent on taking over the evil natures of the children. But is it the ghosts of the long-dead caretakers who haunt the minds of the children, or is the obsession with the children in the minds of the ghosts? A chilling atmosphere settles in as the reader is caught up in this psychodrama.

Note: There is written evidence that James did believe in his ghosts. Reading the introduction, which is conversational in tone, before attempting the stories, will support the reader with familiar words and ideas.

 James, Henry. *Henry James Novels 1871–1880: Watch and Ward, Roderick Hudson, The American, The Europeans, Confidence.* **Edited by William T. Stafford. The Library of America, 1983. 1,287pp.**

The five books listed in the title: *Watch and Ward, Roderick Hudson, The American, The Europeans,* and *Confidence;* an introduction and notes on the books; and a chronology will support the reader who has become interested in the work of Henry James. The chronology begins with James's birth in 1843 and is a year-period collection of events. The sections look like paragraphs, but mainly use only phrases. For example, 1843–1845 begins "Accompanied by mother's sister, Catherine Walsh, and servants, the James parents take infant children to England and later to France. Reside at Windsor, where father has nervous collapse ("vastation") and experiences spiritual illumination." Teachers or tutors may want to let students draw comparisons between some of James's life events and their own.

James, Henry. *Henry James Novels 1886–1890: The Princess Casamassima, The Reverberator, The Tragic Muse.* **Edited by Daniel Mark Fogel. The Library of America, 1989. 1,297pp.**

The three books listed in the title: *The Princess Casamassima, The Reverberator,* and *The Tragic Muse,* are followed by a chronology and notes. This volume will support the reader who has become interested in the work of Henry James. The chronology begins with James's birth in 1843 and is a year-by-year list of events. The sections look like paragraphs, but they consist only of phrases. For example, 1878 begins "Publishes first book in England, *French Poets and Novelists* (Macmillan). Appearance of 'Daisy Miller' in *Cornhill Magazine,* edited by Leslie Stephen, is international success, but by publishing it abroad loses American copyright and story is pirated in U.S. *Cornhill* also prints "An International Episode'." Teachers or tutors may want to use a passage such as this to begin discussions about plagiarism and copyright.

Rudyard Kipling (1865–1936) Collection

Born in India to British subjects, Rudyard Kipling spoke both English and Hindustani from an early age, an advantage that supported his writings later on, most notably his famous poem "Gunga Din" (1892). But at the age of six, when he was dumped on the unhappy doorstep of paid foster parents in England, and later, when he was sent to an equally unhappy boarding school, Kipling collected grist for his literary mill. At age 17, he returned to India to work as a journalist at the *Civil and Military Gazette,* a position secured by his father, who ran an art school. The *Gazette* position launched the writer into his career and an unending stream of letters, poems, articles, novels, and short stories, which earned him the Nobel Prize in 1907.

Kipling's short works were both enormously popular and hotly debated because of their political underpinnings. Given his upbringing and limited education, the author did show a significant degree of awe for the people the British had colonized. Today his social attitudes about the need to care for and train "heathens" is explained as a reflection of the times in which he lived, but his language and storytelling skills support his ongoing popularity. The window he provides into his times and the cultures he knew enriches today's readers.

Kipling, Rudyard. *Gunga Din.* **Illustrated by Robert Andrew Parker. Introduction by Kingsley Amis. Gulliver Books, Harcourt Brace Jovanovich, 1987 (1890). 32pp.**

Based on the story of a British army water carrier, an Indian national, this famous poem details heroic deeds of the loyal, reliable Gunga Din and episodes in Delhi during the Indian Mutiny of 1857. Spoken from the perspective of a rough-and-tumble British soldier, Kipling's poem reflects the racism common in that day, juxtaposed with the author's own deep respect for both the common infantry worker and the man who carried his water. In the end, Gunga Din catches a fatal bullet, causing the soldier to say the now-famous line, "You're a better man than I am, Gunga Din."

First published as poetry in magazines when Kipling was 24 years old, this poem was later part of a collection called *Barrack-Room Ballads* that contained many accounts by seldom-featured foot soldiers. The one-page Kingsley Amis introduction gives both biographical and historical information. Half the pages of this book are filled with informative, emotionally charged impressionistic paintings. Kipling's use of Indian phrases is discreetly compensated for by translations at the bottoms of the pages where they are used. The language of this poem is too complex for the new student of English, but native speakers at all reading levels will appreciate this brilliantly presented text, which has earned the Parents Choice Award. It is an excellent place to start reading the work of Kipling. Teachers and parents may want to take advantage of the geography lesson embedded in the map of India, including Afghanistan, Baluchistan, Kashmir, the Himalayas, Tibet, Bhutan, Burma, the Bay of Bengal, and the Arabian Sea.

 Kipling, Rudyard. *Kipling's Science Fiction.* **Tom Doherty Associates Book/TOR, 1992. 178pp.**

The 10 science fiction stories in this book are "A Matter of Fact," "The Ship That Found Herself," ."007," " 'Wireless'," "With the Night Mail," "As Easy as A.B.C.," "In the Same Boat," "The Eye of Allah," "Unprofessional," and "The Fairies' Siege." Nobel Prize Winner Rudyard Kipling wrote in many genres, always delivering rich detail and helping the reader be where the story was taking place. The print in this book is small, but it is very clear, and there is ample white space between the lines.

Kipling, Rudyard. *The Best Short Stories of Rudyard Kipling.* **Hanover House, 1961. 693pp.**

The stories in this book represent a range of genres. Among them are "At the Pits's Mouth," "A Wayside Comedy," "The Story of Muhamma Din," "A Bank Fraud," "Without Benefit of Clergy," "The Phantom Rickshaw," "Moti Guj—Mutineer," "The Man Who Would Be Kind," "The Children of the Zodiac," "The Maltese Cat," "The King's Ankus," "Red Dog," "Markalake Witches," "The Village That Voted the Earth Was Flat," and "The Eye of Allah." Each story is loaded with conversation, supporting comprehension and helping ESL readers learn the language in a high-interest format. The small print and narrow margins can be hard on the eyes. This volume, though quite old, is available on library shelves and at used bookstores. Using this as a way of identifying stories of interest, readers can then get support from illustrated and big print editions.

 Kipling, Rudyard. *The Haunting of Holmescroft*. (Originally published as *The House Surgeon*). Illustrated by Barbara Armata. <u>Classic Frights.</u> Books of Wonder, 1998 (1909). 56pp.

A night of ghost story telling ends with a pair of gentlemen discussing a real haunted house; not that anyone has died there, it's just that the magnificent house itself creates a pall over anyone who lives there. One of the storytellers sets out to uncover the source of the melancholy mansion. This story first appeared in a 1909 collection called *Actions and Reactions*. Other titles in that book include "An Habitation Enforced," "Garm—a Hostage," "The Mother Hive," "With the Night Mail," "A Deal in Cotton," "The Puzzler," "Little Foxes," and "The House Surgeon"—later called "The Haunting of Holmescroft." There are many fine ink illustrations, but not enough to make this a picture book. The print is large and the story compelling, making this a good introduction to one of the finest storytellers of the twentieth century. The format of a small book with big print is new reader, mature reader, and new language learner friendly. Because this edition is out of print, it is easiest to find in libraries and used book sources. Copies of this story show up in collections every few years, but the small, single volume is recommended. This is a perfect October read for any population.

 Kipling, Rudyard. *The Jungle Book*. Illustrated by Christian Broutin. <u>The Whole Story.</u> Viking, 1996 (1894). Illustrations copyright 1994. 210pp.

Mowgli, the main human character in these tales, was abandoned as a baby to be raised by wolves. Because of that upbringing, the tales here are full of inter-animal communications. Readers are privileged to listen to the conversation of the mother and father wolves as they discover the man cub in need of a warm place and something to eat.

This book is loaded with internal support. The same pages also have photographs of actual wolf-children who have been brought in from the wild. Historic photographs and illustrations, combined with information in the margins, provide the reader with far more than most editions of this work. As the story animals interact, the sidebars illustrate little-known facts related to the subject. The battle between a mongoose and a cobra, a magical display of the aurora borealis (northern lights), and a tiger surrounded by a swarm of bulls are but a few of the captioned illustrations that at once propel these classic poems and stories and provide the reader with scientific insights. There is a page-sized map of India after the contents. This is a fine read-aloud, read alone, and study book.

Related reads: Other Kipling titles include *Barrack-Room Ballads* and *Just So Stories*.

Abraham Lincoln (1809–1865) Collection

Born to carpenter/farmer Thomas and Nancy Hanks Lincoln in a log cabin in Hardin County, Kentucky, Abraham Lincoln grew up in rural homes in Kentucky and then Indiana, losing his mother when he was 10 and gaining a stepmother and three step-siblings the following year. He reached adulthood with very little formal education, but with all the benefits of being a voracious reader. When the family moved to Illinois, he earned the nickname "Honest Abe." "I could read, write, and cipher . . . but little else," he said. Yet he did manage a great deal of self-education, became a lawyer, and served eight years in the Illinois legislature. Some historians believe the stories of New Salem residents, who claim that in 1832 Lincoln and the angelic, beautiful, scholarly Ann Rutledge became unofficially engaged and that, but for her untimely death, believed to have been due to typhoid fever, she would have been his wife upon his completion of law school.

In 1842, after an extensive and tumultuous courtship, he married Mary Todd. In a letter on legal matters to friend Samuel D. Marshall, Lincoln closed with, "Nothing new here, except my marrying, which to me, is a matter of profound wonder." He and his wife, Mary Todd, had four boys, only one of whom, Robert, grew to adulthood. When Abraham Lincoln unsuccessfully ran for the Senate in 1858, his success in the debate against his opponent, William Douglas, won him national stature and a place on the Republican presidential candidate ticket in 1860, an election he won. One of his most famous works is the 1863 "Emancipation Proclamation," declaring freedom for all slaves in the Confederacy. Later that same year he delivered another of his oratorical feats, the now famous address consecrating the burial grounds at Gettysburg.

The "Gettysburg Address" is among the most read and recited passages in American literature. Lincoln's presidency was marked by the Civil War, during which he won a second term of office. His inaugural address was conciliatory in tone: "With malice toward none, with charity for all, with firmness in the right as God gives us to see the right, let us strive on to finish the work we are in." On Friday, April 14, 1865, Lincoln and his wife were attending a play at Ford's Theatre, when actor John Wilkes Booth shot the president, mortally wounding him.

Lincoln, Abraham. *The Gettysburg Address.* **Illustrated by Michael McCurdy. Foreword by Gary Wills. Houghton Mifflin, 1995 (1863). 46pp.**

Delivered during the throes of the American Civil War on November 19, 1863, this short and powerful message—which followed a two-hour oration by another speaker—continues to be used as memorization fare.

The historic consecration ceremony speech Lincoln delivered at the cemetery at the Soldiers' National Cemetery at Gettysburg is illustrated line-by-line with full-page scratchboard ink drawings. The sensuous, graphic images support comprehension. For more background on this speech, try *The Living Lincoln: The Man, His Mind, His Times, and The War He Fought, Reconstructed from His Own Writings,* edited by Paul M. Angle and Earl Schenck Miers (annotated below). This book is excellent support for units on the U.S. Civil War, citizenship, national monuments, rituals, and death.

 Angle, Paul M. and Earl Schenck Miers, ed. *The Living Lincoln: The Man, His Mind, His Times, and The War He Fought, Reconstructed from His Own Writings.* **Barnes & Noble, 1992. 673pp.**

Rare glimpses into one of the most important minds of America, indeed of the world, emerge from his profound diary entries, one-line letters on the field, and public speeches. Lincoln spoke to issues of the Civil War, racism, family matters, consolation, and his own grief. Support is internal. The difficulty of the texts is as diverse as the audiences he addressed. This is a shopping mall of history and of the man who delivered the consecration address at the cemetery at Gettysburg. The text of the "Gettysburg Address" is on page 591.

Jack London (1876–1916) Collection

Born out of wedlock in San Francisco on January 12, 1876, to Flora Wellman, John Griffith Chaney (renamed John Griffith London later that year when his mother married John London) was forever obsessed with the question of his parenthood. He looked a great deal like William Henry Chaney, a prominent man with a similar shock of dark hair and literary successes. But Chaney never acknowledged the lad. In 1879 Jack's stepfather moved the family to a truck farm in Oakland, then later to a 20-acre farm in Alameda, California. This no doubt began the writer's lifelong fascination with agriculture. It also began his lifelong involvement with alcohol.

One day, as the five-year-old Jack lugged a lard bucket of beer to his stepfather working in the field half a mile away, he began to investigate the brew reserved for adults; by day's end, he had collapsed into a hangover, the first of many.

It was Ouida's *Signa* and Irving's *Tales of the Alhambra* that sparked his love affair with books in 1885. In 1885, the nine-year-old Jack was enamored of his dog, Rollo, who may have been the model for the hero, Buck, in *Call of the Wild.*

In 1891 London purchased *Razzle Dazzle,* a sloop in which he began a romance with the sea that would manifest in an eight-month stint aboard a whaling schooner and, in 1907, an around-the-world sailing cruise aboard the *Snark*. In 1894 he marched to Washington, D.C., became a hobo, traveled the United States and Canada, and spent 30 days at hard labor in the Erie County Penitentiary for vagrancy—which manifested in *The Road* in 1907.

In 1899 he published 61 new works, including jokes, stories, and essays. London was engaged to report on the Mexican Revolution for *Colliers* in 1914, but the project was delayed when authorities suspected him of writing the antimilitary pamphlet "The Good Soldier." He denied it, and missed the war; even so, he wrote brilliant articles. Although he entered the University of California at Berkeley, he later dropped out for lack of funds. In 1897, he left for the Yukon and the Klondike gold rush. He became an active socialist, a political stance that would cost him some benefits in the years to come, and perhaps motivated him to promise all comers that they might stay at his ranch, The Beauty Ranch, as long as they pleased—without paying—which many did. Word of his generosity attracted hordes of friends, fans, and hangers-on. Seemingly, the famous author had limitless resources, but he didn't. And seemingly, he could dash off best sellers effortlessly, but he couldn't. London's finances raced from one end of the pole to the other and back. He could write on command, but with great effort; he worked at his writing very hard, devoting every morning to a thousand-word minimum.

London first married Bessie May Maddern, divorced her, and then married socialist Charmain Kittredge, a frivolous spendthrift who did not provide the much-wanted heir but remained with him to the end of his life.

The life of Jack London is reflected in his many stories, which mainly focus on three geographical areas—California ranchlands, the South Pacific, and the Klondike—all of which he had learned about first-hand. But critics observe a radical disparity in quality. This is not surprising. Some of his work was inspired from within; some was inspired by creditors. Some gestated for years; some was aborted half-done. Regardless of what he did not manage to do during his 40 action-packed years, Jack London did give us a wealth of imaginative and believable tales.

Latrobe, Kathy. "White Fang." In *Readers Theatre for Young Adults,* **49–52. Teacher Ideas Press, 1989. 130pp.**
    Three voices lead the reader into an introduction that tells how White Fang's mother came to be and how White Fang's destiny was determined.

Labor, Earle, Robert C. Leitz III, and I. Milo Shepard, ed. *Short Stories of Jack London: Authorized One-Volume Edition.* **Macmillan, 1990. 739pp.**

This is by no means a collection of all the stories ever written by Jack London. However, the editors say that there are certain ones that should be in every London collection. They are "To Build a Fire," "The Law of Life," "Love of Life," "All Gold Canyon," "The Apostate," "Koolau the Leper," "Samuel," "War," "A Piece of Steak," "The Mexican," "Told in the Drooling Ward," "The Red One," and "The Water Baby." Readers may want to start with these. The editors also explain that they have included some less well-known stories that "represent the astonishing scope both of his subject matter and of his creative genius." "Story of a Typhoon Off the Coast of Japan" is one of these, "The Water Baby" another. There are about 50 tales here of varying length. All make great read-alouds.

For support, a new reader may want to begin by reading *The Call of the Wild* (annotated below) or by listening to the audio recording of that work. That will help the reader acclimate to London's style. In addition to the stories, there is an extensive introduction and a chronology.

 London, Jack. *The Call of the Wild.* **Illustrated by Philippe Munch.** <u>The Whole Story.</u> **Viking, 1994 (1903). 126pp.**

Kidnapped. The stately king of his spacious California estate, Buck had been stealthily smuggled from home, forced into a train, beaten mercilessly, and sold in Alaska. The Klondike gold miners needed dogs to labor as the relentless search for riches moved at a furious rate. Such a service animal Buck became. But that was hardly the end of his adventures.

This is the original text as loved by thousands when it was first published in 1903. In this rendition, the text is nestled among many historical photographs, drawings, and descriptions that make the time of the gold rush and Alaska come alive. Beautiful color illustrations provide avenues for comprehension to any reader who loves the wilderness, dogs, or wolves. In the Dove Audio edition, Ethan Hawke reads this classic tale at a fairly fast clip, causing the reader to follow quickly.

Audio versions: There are a couple of audio versions of this book:

> *The Call of the Wild.* Dove Audio, 1993. 2 cassettes, approximately 3 hours. Read by Ethan Hawke.

> *The Call of the Wild and Other Stories.* Blackstone Audiobooks, 1979. 5 cassettes, 7 hours. Read by John Chatty.

London, Jack. *White Fang.* **Illustrated by Philippe Munch.** <u>The Whole Story.</u> **Viking, 1998 (1906). 237pp.**

White Fang is half dog, half wolf. As a pup he was forced to fight for his survival against much bigger animals. From the innocent pup emerged a feared and ferocious predator. This is his story as seen through his own eyes.

Jack London wrote this tale as a companion to his overwhelmingly popular *Call of the Wild*. His understanding and respect for Alaska, its occupants, and their history emerged through his fictional accounts. This edition provides the original, unabridged text and invites the reader into London's deeper knowledge by providing richly illustrated marginal notes that tell about the times and scientific implications behind London's words. (For example, there is a detail explaining the Alaskan migration, and there are diagrams showing how the foot of a wolf is designed to walk on snow and how the track of a she-wolf is different from that of a he-wolf.)

It is possible to spend an entire reading session examining just one page of this provocative book. Although information-intensive, the illustrations and sidebars make this classic accessible to most adult new readers. The 🎭 readers theatre introduction can open the door to this story. The audio recording is a pleasant listen, but does not compare to reading this edition with the internal support it provides.

Audio version: *White Fang.* Blackstone Audiobooks, 1981. 5 tapes, 7 hours. Read by John Chatty.

Related reads: A less challenging story of a wolf dog is *Jim Ugly* by Sid Fleischman. A good follow-up read is *Never Cry Wolf* by Farley Mowat. *White Fang, Call of the Wild*, and a collection of Jack London short stories are available in AFFORDABLE formats through Dover Publications.

Henry Wadsworth Longfellow (1807–1882) Collection

Born into a socially prominent New England family, Longfellow followed an academic path in his youth and in his career. Educated first at Bowdoin College in Maine, he then went to Europe to study languages (and over time he became a translator of poetry from many European languages, not the least of which was the *Divine Comedy* by Dante), returned to teach at his alma mater, and married Mary Potter, who died in Europe in 1835. He wrote about his travels in *Outre-Mer: A Pilgrimage Beyond the Sea* (1835). Longfellow then returned to America, accepting a professorship at Harvard. On December 30, 1839, he wrote in his diary about how he'd been inspired by the news account of the shipwreck of the *Hesperus*. He dashed off a full draft and went to bed, but could not sleep as more ideas came to him. He got up and added more. By three o'clock it was done.

"It did not come into my mind by lines, but by stanzas," he wrote. In 1841 "The Wreck of the Hesperus" was published in Park Benjamin's *The New World*, and it became one his most popular works. It is his storytelling poems about actual events that continue to enjoy a very high readership. He wrote the romantic novel *Hyperion,* featuring Mary Ashburn (modeled after his second wife), and *Voices of the Night,* a poetry collection, in 1839, and *Ballads and Other Poems* in 1842.

In 1843, Longfellow was remarried, this time to Frances Appleton, from an upper-class family. The wedding present from her father was a mansion called Craigie House. In rapid succession, Longfellow wrote "Evangeline," "Hiawatha," "The Courtship of Miles Standish," "Paul Revere's Ride," "Tales of a Wayside Inn," and "Kavanagh." In 1861 Frances Longfellow died, leaving Longfellow in a state of depression that temporarily stopped his work. In 1865 he translated *The Divine Comedy,* and he wrote "Christus" in 1872. Never acclaimed as a great poet, Longfellow's narrative story and historical elements have made his works appreciated and enduring. He was indeed a good storyteller.

 Longfellow, Henry Wadsworth. *Hiawatha.* **Illustrated by Susan Jeffers. A Puffin Pied Piper, 1996 (1983). 32pp.**

In "The Song of Hiawatha," an epic poem published in 1855, Longfellow recognized the traditions, myths, and values of the Ojibwa tribe of the Algonquins of Maine. He used Hiawatha, a composite figure, to reflect this civilization that was fast disappearing. In this book Susan Jeffers has chosen the portion of the poem that tells about the childhood of Hiawatha, a time spent with his beloved Nokomis. Through front and back illustrations, Jeffers suggests those parts of the poem not printed here. But the most famous verse, "By the shores of Gitche Gumee, By the shining Big-Sea-Water, Stood the wigwam of Nokomis, Daughter of the Moon, Nokomis," begins the text of this elegantly illustrated book.

Ideal for any new reader or English language learner, this edition has been honored by the *Booklist* Reviewers' Choice, the *School Library Journal* Best Book of the Year, and the Parents' Choice Award. This is a wonderful read-aloud in any setting and lends itself to readers theatre. It also is an excellent support for units on poetry, North American Indians, environmental issues, and intergenerational relationships.

Related read: If you liked this story, you may also want to read the picture book *Brother Eagle, Sister Sky* by Susan Jeffers.

 Doré, Gustave. *The Dore Illustrations for Dante's Divine Comedy.* **Translated by Henry Wadsworth Longfellow. Dover Publications, 1976 (as published in three volumes by Ticknor and Fields, Boston, in 1867). 135pp.**

An image of writhing bodies, each engaged in its own agony, is made clear as one reads: "FORGERS Every one was plying fast the bite/ Of nails upon himself, for the great rage/Of itching which no other succor had (Inf. XXIX, 79–81)" (page 61). The reader is compelled to revisit the scene and discovers that every suffering soul is indeed engaged in the act of scratching some dreadful itch. The full-page illustrations on 9¼-by-12-inch pages propel this book, but the one- and two-line captions hold it together, supplying readers at all levels with a breathtaking introduction to this famous work. Longfellow's translating skills add yet another dimension to the poet/storyteller who speaks so simply.

 Longfellow, Henry Wadsworth. *Paul Revere's Ride: The Landlord's Tale.* **Illustrated by Charles Santore. HarperCollins, 2003. 40pp.**

Here, the story of Paul Revere's ride is shared among nineteenth-century gentlemen by a fire at a wayside inn. Santore's brilliant acrylic paintings give immediacy to the words in the classic poem.

 Longfellow, Henry Wadsworth. *Paul Revere's Ride.* **Illustrated by Monica Vachula. Boyds Mills Press, 2003. 32pp.**

Realistic detail sketches complement full-page paintings that deliver the atmosphere and content of the night on which Paul Revere made his historic ride. This is a beautiful, thought-provoking, well-researched edition that will inform the reader well beyond the Longfellow text.

 Longfellow, Henry Wadsworth. *Poetry for Young People.* **Edited by Frances Schoonmaker. Illustrated by Chad Wallace. Sterling Publishing, 1998. 48pp.**

Twenty-eight entries include "Hiawatha's Childhood," "The Wreck of the Hesperus," "The Slave's Dream," and "The Children's Hour." "The Witnesses" (page 28) reveals the watching skeletons of a sunken slave ship. These ghostly monitors are quite different from those described by Coleridge's ancient mariner, so the two poems would make a stimulating pair for discussion and comparison. There are occasional notes to clarify obscure or archaic words and terms. The type is easy to look at.

 Applebaum, Stanley, ed. *Henry Wadsworth Longfellow.* **Dover Thrift, 1992. 81pp.**

Included in this little book are "Paul Revere's Ride," The Courtship of Miles Standish," "The Wreck of the Hesperus," and "The Children's Hour." There are alphabetical lists of titles and first lines.

Applebaum, Stanley, and Thomas Crofts, eds. *Evangeline and Other Poems.* **Dover Publications, 1995. 67pp.**

Here are poems from various collections, selected from *The Complete Poetical Works of Henry Wadsworth Longfellow: Cambridge Edition* (Houghton Mifflin, ca. 1914). The poems are in chronological order by first publication date. They include "The Skeleton in Armor" from *Ballads and Other Poems*; "Carillon," "The Belfry of Bruges," "The Arsenal at Springfield," and "Mezzo Cammin" from *The Belfry of Bruges and Other Poems*; "Evangeline"; six poems from *Flower-de-Luce*, excerpted from "Divina Commedia";

"Changed" and "Aftermath" from *Birds of Passage*; and "The Cross of Snow" written in homage to his dead wife, from *A Book of Sonnets*. The introduction contains an explanation of some of the odd patterns used by Longfellow. Having translated poetry from Spanish, German, French, Swedish, Danish, and Italian, he was inclined to adopt poetic forms intended for those languages, respectively. "Evangeline" is written in dactylic hexameter, typical of the "ancient Greek and Roman epic poetry." There are two indexes, one of titles and one of first lines.

 Fradin, Dennis Brindell. *Hiawatha: Messenger of Peace*. **Margaret K. McElderry Books, 1992. 42pp.**

There once was a mythological Indian named Manabozho, a god who could "take mile-long steps and also turn into a wolf." In the mid-1800s, Henry Schoolcraft wrote *The Myth of Hiawatha*, telling the Manabozho legend, but using the name Hiawatha. Inspired by the Schoolcraft tale, Henry Wordsworth Longfellow wrote a now very famous poem about Hiawatha, mixing legendary features with the popular theme of conversion to Christianity. Thus, the story of the real Hiawatha became convoluted.

Dennis Fradin sets the story straight in this book. The real Hiawatha was an Iroquois leader who lived in what is now New York State in the early 1400s. Although he came from a warring people, who believed in unending raids for revenge, the real Hiawatha struck upon the notion of peace and forgiveness. When Ododarhoh, an evil man from a different tribe, murdered Hiawatha's wife and all their daughters, Hiawatha refused to take revenge. Instead he left the longhouse of his wife's tribe and became a hermit in the woods, where he was approached by another peacemaker named Drgandawida, from a Canadian tribe. Together the two men talked about a program of restitution, payment in wampum for wrongdoings to displace the current program of unending bloodshed. This was the start of a plan that became the Iroquois Federation, a union of tribes ruled by laws. Some of those laws were adapted by the forefathers of the United States. It is his influence as a peacemaker that makes the real Hiawatha significant.

The language in this book is simple, and the story is told in a sequential manner, fostering comprehension. The book contains many historical drawings and photographs of the legendary figures, artifacts, and longhouse life, as well as a map of the Lake Ontario region where the five Iroquois tribes lived. There is a detailed index and a brief bibliography. Readers of the Longfellow poem will be interested to learn the real story.

Longfellow, Henry Wadsworth. *Paul Revere's Ride*. **Illustrated by Ted Rand. Dutton Children's Books, 1990. 46pp.**

This classic tale of the 1775 ride through the Boston countryside—by the future Revolutionary War hero Paul Revere (1735–1818)—which was written by Henry Wadsworth Longfellow, is now illuminated by the thrilling watercolors of Ted Rand. Although some of the language in this poem is archaic, the meaning and importance show on every page and are supported in this book by a one-page history of the circumstances of Paul Revere's ride. The book has dazzled students of all ages since it was printed and is well worth reading. The study units it serves well include Paul Revere, the American Revolution, the Battle of Lexington, colonial America, and civil disobedience.

Related read: *Paul Revere's Ride* by David Hackett Fischer is a lively, informing, 464-page exposé of the political motivations behind some of the misreported details in Longfellow's poem, a biography of Revere dating from before the immortalized incident, and historical background on the real events surrounding this now-famous ride. Also available on audiocassette.

 Monteiro, George, ed. *The Poetical Works of Longfellow.* **Introduction by George Monteiro. Houghton Mifflin, 1975. 689pp.**

"Time and again his most popular pieces have been offered as models of how not to write serious poetry," says Monteiro in his 11-page essay about the poet and his works. Yet the very need to publish this volume suggests that there is something compelling about Longfellow's legacy. Despite being a serious-looking volume, this book contains the full texts of works that are often published only in part. And they are presented in a two-column format that makes them very easy to follow. This is a good way to see the entire 22 verses of "The Song of Hiawatha," complete with an introduction that provides historical insights.

The same is true for "Evangeline: A Tale of Acadie," which also has a passage from Nathaniel Hawthorne's *American Note-Books* in which Hawthorne relates the true account of the French Canadian couple separated on their marriage day by the government, and how Evangeline spent her life in search of her beloved, only to find him on his deathbed, a discovery that killed her. Hawthorne was not interested in the history for a romantic book when a mutual friend told him about it, but Longfellow delighted in it as the subject of a poem. This collection is supported by multiple appendixes, a chronology of Longfellow's poems, an index of first lines, and an index of titles. This is the place to look for a good copy of the poems in text-only form.

Longfellow, Henry Wadsworth [1807–1882]. *Tales of a Wayside Inn.* **University Press of the Pacific, 2002. 268pp.**

Set in a Boston inn, where a group of travelers follow the tradition of the *Canterbury Tales*, each in turn sharing a story. This is a collection of tales related to actual events, current and historical, or to the lives of Longfellow's friends. Though not easy reading, the tales are compelling even today. Readers may get support from reading ⌐ and ⌐ books from the Chaucer collection (chapter 2).

Related reads: Other works by Longfellow include "Christus: A Mystery"; "Evangeline"; and "The Wreck of the Hesperus."

Herman Melville (1819–1891) Collection

Born in New York City, New York, the third of eight children, to Allan and Maria Gansevoort Melville (both of prosperous, families of good lineage), Herman Melville was considered by them to be slow-witted. When Melville was 12 his father died, leaving the responsibility of the family felt and fur business to Herman and his brother Gansevoort. But the insolvent business went bankrupt. Melville finished school in 1834 and entered the Albany Classical School, becoming an active member of the debating society.

He eventually worked as a bank clerk, a teacher, and a farm hand for his uncle, Thomas Melville. But it was no doubt his work in 1839 as a cabin boy on a New York to Liverpool merchant ship and then as a seaman that prepared for his career as a journalist and writer of some of the greatest seafaring novels of all time. In 1841, aboard the whaler *Acushnet*, Melville headed for the South Seas. In 1842, the ship weighed anchor in the Marquesas Islands, where Melville and a shipmate jumped ship.

Four years later, *Typee: A Peep at Polynesian Life* (1846), which told of Melville's capture by and life among the cannibals of Nuku Hiva, became an overnight success. In the following year the sequel, *Omoo: A Narrative of Adventures in the South Seas*, was published. Also in 1847, Melville married Elisabeth Shaw, daughter of the chief justice of Massachusetts. (The couple had two sons: Malcolm, who committed suicide in 1867, and Stanwix, who became a seaman and, following a long illness, died in a San Francisco hospital in 1886.) Melville had published three more books by the time he was 30: *Mardi: And a Voyage Thither* (1849); *Redburn: His First Voyage* (1849); and *White-Jacket: Or the World in a Man-of-War* (1850).

Drained by his relentless activity, Melville retired to the eighteenth-century farm, Arrowhead, that he had bought near the home of Nathaniel Hawthorne. The older Hawthorne, who for financial reasons had been obliged to work in the Salem custom house in 1842, was both a neighbor and for two years a close friend. Indeed, Hawthorne provided critical advice on Melville's now most famous work, and Hawthorne and other close members of his circle show up as characters in Melville's works. In the seclusion of Arrowhead, Melville continued to work on a book called *The Whale*.

Later titled *Moby-Dick* (at Hawthorne's suggestion), the book met with only mild acceptance when first published in 1851. In the next year *Pierre* was another financial and critical failure. By 1857 Melville had turned from prose to poetry. He found the lack of critical approval demoralizing, and he was further humiliated when, to make ends meet, in 1866 he had to take a job as a customs inspector on the New York docks, a position he kept until 1885. He continued to write, but published at less frequent intervals. In a state of depression, he began work on *Billy Budd*, which was on his desk when, at age 72, Melville died of a heart attack, on September 28, 1891. By then he was a virtual unknown. In 1924, more than 30 years after his death, *Billy Budd* was published for the first time. During a revival of his works, Herman Melville received spontaneous critical approval and was eventually identified as one of America's greats.

 Melville, Herman. *Moby Dick.* **Illustrated by Rockwell Kent. Modern Library, 1992 (1851). 822pp.**

    A reproduction of the 1930 Random House edition, this book is graced with illustrations by Rockwell Kent and is more than 200 pages longer than the Oxford University edition. Readers at all levels will revel in Kent's luxurious black-and-white illustrations. Libraries tend to keep this edition in the reference section. It is worth visiting. An index of literary allusions shows how Melville drew on sources of the past, including *The Fairie Queen*, *Hamlet*, *Pilgrim's Progress*, *Paradise Lost*, and many, many others. This reinforces the notion that we learn to write through what we read.

 Melville, Herman. *Moby-Dick Or, the Whale.* **Illustrated by Barry Moser. Arion Press, 1979 (1851). 594pp.**

    This limited edition of 265 copies measures 15 by 10 inches on hand-made paper, with 100 boxwood engravings by Barry Moser. It has first-letter illustrations at the start of each chapter; chapter I, starting with the letter "C", has the curve of a huge wave restating that letter. The book is out of print. In 1981, the University of California Press published it in two reduced formats. This is a print-lover's wonderland.

    Related read: For the true whale story that inspired *Moby Dick*, see *In the Heart of the Sea: The Tragedy of the Whaleship* Essex, by Nathaniel Philbrick.

 Melville, Herman. *Moby Dick.* **Introduction by Patrick McGrath. Oxford University Press, 1999. 605pp.**

    A common wanderer named Ishmael tells the story, which begins with his wish to get away from funerals, boredom, and depression in the way he is accustomed to do: by going off to sea. So it is that he is in the right place at the right time to board the whaling ship of the mentally ill Captain Ahab, a man possessed with the notion of doing battle with a great white whale, Moby Dick. The nightmare adventure redoubles as Ishmael comes to understand that the whale, too, has a vendetta.

    Considered Melville's masterpiece, this tale combines what the author has learned from his own seafaring days, the lore of the sea, and unparalleled storytelling ability. The language of Ishmael is not difficult to follow. Neither is the story line, except for its surreal elements. But the length of the book makes it challenging, and beautifully read, unabridged audio recordings are not readily available. Readers may want to find one of the many videos available to use as a foundation and then start reading it a few weeks later. No movie contains all that Melville has to offer, so the reader may still expect to be surprised as well as very much entertained.

Related read: Another Melville adventure title is *Billy Budd*.

Alfred Noyes (1880–1958)

Alfred Noyes was born on September 16, 1880, in Wolverhampton, England. His father, a grocer who became a teacher at Aberystwyth, taught his son Latin and Greek, and sent him to Exeter College in Oxford in 1898. Alfred Noyes proved excellent at rowing, but he was busy pursuing his poetry career and did not graduate. He did publish the critically praised *The Loom of Years*, the first of six volumes of poetry in as many years. Although his 12-book, 200-page epic poem in blank verse, "Drake: An English Epic," about life at sea and first seen in serial form in *Blackwoods* magazine, is evidence of his prowess and tenacity, it is "The Highwayman," published in 1907 in *Forty Singing Seamen and Other Poems*, that is his most time-honored poem. He became an instant popular success.

In 1907 he also married Garnett Daniels. Royalty checks allowed them to travel between the United States and England. In 1914, he began teaching modern English literature at Princeton University. A recognized Romantic, some criticized Noyes for failing to become a modernist. In 1916, while working as a wartime propagandist in the News Department of the Foreign Office, Noyes claimed to have read the Black Diaries, which incriminated Irish patriot Sir Roger Casement, who was executed for high treason. For 20 years Noyes would be haunted by his involvement in what he later admitted might have been a British intelligence plot. Meanwhile, caught between the evidence of science and the emotional pull of religion, Noyes was inspired by a look through a telescope at Mt. Wilson, California. From that experience emerged *The Torchbearers*, a three-volume epic published as *Watchers of the Sky* (1922), *The Book of Earth* (1925), and *The Last Voyage* (1930).

In 1926 his wife died, and in 1927 Noyes converted to Catholicism and married a widow, Mary Angela Mayne Weld-Blundell. He produced two works reflecting his search for spirituality, *The Unknown God* (1934) and an analytical biography of Voltaire, *Judgment Comes* (1941). Although at first approved, the Voltaire biography was censored via "suspension of approval" by the Vatican, a stigma that remained until 1939. Noyes moved to Lisle Combe, St. Lawrence, Isle of Wight, in 1929. He published a collection of poems and essays, *Orchard's Bay*, in 1939. During most of World War II Noyes lived in Canada and America, going back to England in 1949. During that period he produced his autobiography, *Two World's for Memory* (1953), which he had to dictate due to failing eyesight. *A Letter to Lucian* (1956) was followed by *The Accusing Ghost, or Justice for Casement* (1957). Alfred Noyes died on June 25, 1958, and is buried on the Isle of Wight.

Noyes, Alfred. *The Highwayman*. Illustrated by Charles Keeping. Oxford University Press, 2001 (1913). 32pp.

> The wind was a torrent of darkness among the gusty trees,
> The moon was a ghostly galleon tossed upon cloudy seas.
> The road was a ribbon of moonlight over the purple moor,
> And the highwayman came riding—
> Riding—riding—
> The highwayman came riding, up to the old inn-door.

So begins the sensuous depiction of a clandestine romance between the innkeeper's voluptuous daughter and the impeccably groomed outlaw, a romance that before the end of the night will cause the young woman to shoot herself and the highwayman to give up his life, both with such energy that the ghostly scene will continue to replay throughout eternity. The language is far from simple, but illustrations support the story.

This moralistic tale is hardly for the faint of heart. With only seven or eight large print lines per page, the 1913 work is further enhanced by modern yet timeless images that have won this book the Kate Greenaway Medal. Its uses are many. The homeschooler may use it as a family values discussion starter. The elementary teacher may offer this as a read-aloud treat on a rowdy Friday afternoon. The high school classroom teacher may find it a fine example of morality lessons in literature. The tutor–student pair could use it as a reading and vocabulary source through several sessions. No reader can put this book down, once begun.

Ouida (1839–1908) Collection

Marie Louise de la Ramee was born in Bury St. Edmunds, England, on January 7, 1839. The sound of her own babyish pronunciation of Louise became her pen name, Ouida. She is known for her popular romantic tales, such as the novels *Under Two Flags* (1867), the first of the Foreign Legion tales featuring a noble hero loved by two very different women; *Moths* (1880); *In Maremma* (1882); and children's books, including *Two Little Wooden Shoes* (1874), *Bimbi* (1882), and *The Dog of Flanders* (1872).

Although her stories reflect sweet and swashbuckling romanticism, she also contributed to progressive essays of the time, seeing women as something other than extensions of men and their homes. Her name appears with other notables in an 1890 booklet of letters calling for an end to vivisection in America. In spite of her success in publishing over 40 novels, she was a poor money manager and died in poverty in Italy on January 25, 1908.

Ouida. *A Dog of Flanders.* **Dover Publications, 1992 (1872). 68pp.**

Nello, a little boy, and Patrasche, a big dog, are both orphans; and that is the basis for their work together, when they had work. They lived with crippled old Jehan Daas, where all three were hungry every day and sometimes had nothing to eat at all, in the miserable little hut at the side of the hill in Flanders. Then one day matters took a turn for the worse. The steadfast old dog proved more faithful than anyone had imagined. Some may consider this a parable on the times, or on any time when the poor and helpless are disenfranchised. As an example of sentimental literature, this is a classic. Do not expect a dry eye at the end. Although the language is not simple, the story line is straightforward, making it accessible to intermediate readers of English.

Video version: *A Dog of Flanders.* Warner Bros. Family Entertainment, 2000. 1 cassette, 101 minutes. Producer: Frank Yablans. Starring Jack Warden, Jeremy James Kissner, and Cheryl Ladd.

Related read: Another touching tale about a boy and his dog is Wilson Rawls's *Where the Red Fern Grows.*

Note: Many of Ouida's titles are now available in downloadable editions.

Edgar Allan Poe (1809–1849) Collection

At once tragic and brilliant, the life of Edgar Allan Poe remains an enigma. Biographies of Poe offer up many details about his orphan status, rightful feelings of abandonment, unrequited love, addictions, and desperate financial straights. His attacks on Henry Wadsworth Longfellow were legion, with Poe accusing the poet of "didacticism." Conversely, Poe idolized the works of Nathaniel Hawthorne, and he published his sentiments about his contemporary in many journals of the time. Still, it is Poe's huge and powerful body of macabre works that has gripped the imagination of readers for all the generations since he was first published. The mind of Poe, when committed to paper, gives readers a chance to be thrilled by a man who could conjure words to do unto the language what no other dared. A master of the dark inner self, Poe pulls that self out for us to look at and shudder over.

Latrobe, Kathy. "The PurloinedLetter." In *Readers Theatre for Young Adults,* **53–58. Teacher Ideas Press, 1989. 130pp.**

This dramatization from the first half of the short story "The Purloined Letter" introduces the problem of a missing letter to the audience and to the famous Parisian sleuth C. Auguste Dupin. The range of difficulty among the five reader parts provides a chance for beginning readers to work with highly skilled public speakers. Some of the vocabulary is challenging, which is not a problem in this format and is very likely to yield both better readers and Poe fans. Tutors, homeschoolers, and traditional teachers may want to use this as an introduction either to the short story or to Poe.

Lewis, Shari, and Lan O'Kun, rewriters and adapters. *One-Minute Scary Stories.* **Illustrated by Pat DeWitt and Robin DeWitt. Dell Picture Yearling, 1991. 48pp.**

This little book contains retellings of "The Tell-Tale Heart" and "The Monkey's Paw," among others. It is a very useful tool for comparing the original classic with a retelling to ferret out what it is that makes the classic tale better.

Loewen, Nancy. *Poe, a Biography.* **Photographs by Tina Mucci. Creative Editions, 1993. 63pp.**

Ethereal, out-of-focus images of typewriter keys and tombstones fill the better part of each two-page spread. Yet the small columns of text reveal a life with more details than many traditional texts have about this brooding, unfortunate genius. Excerpts of the referenced work are comingled with background information that reveals the frame of mind of Edgar Allan Poe when he wrote. For example, recurring personal losses, including the death of his mother when Poe was less than three years old, the death of the beautiful mother of his best friend when Poe was only fifteen, and the death of his foster mother, may have left him unable to deal with the repeated brushes with death that his very young wife has as he watches, unable to deter the inevitable.

Having been jilted by his betrothed—in most part because her father intercepted their correspondence—Poe had eventually married his 13-year-old cousin, Virginia Clemm. The two found domestic tranquility that transcended their extreme poverty and the addictions that Poe used to obliterate his horrid memories, depression, and paranoia. As his beloved Virginia approached the grave, Poe began to labor over "The Raven." Though not sequential in presentation, the quotes and images in this book propel this dramatic life story along in a salient fashion. This is a fine introduction to one of literature's great minds.

Krull, Kathleen. *Lives of the Writers: Comedies, Tragedies (and What the Neighbors Thought).* **Illustrated by Kathryn Hewitt. Harcourt Brace, 1994. 96pp.**

In just a few pages you will learn intimate and important details about the lives of 20 famous writers, including Edgar Allan Poe. There is some overlap among the featured writers, which can provide scaffolding for more in-depth biography reading or reading the author's works. Of note is a literary terms list, an index of writers, and a "For Further Reading . . . and Writing" list.

 Poe, Edgar Allan (1809–1849). *The Raven.* **Illustrated by Gustave Doré (1832–1883). Dover Publications, 1996. 53pp.**

The publisher's note on the opening page of text gives background on the author, the illustrator, and times during which the works of the two were combined into this eerie and masterful creation. The complete text of Poe's poem fills three full pages and then is followed by page upon page of text and full-page engravings, text and full-page etchings. This is a grown-up's picture book, if ever there was one. The Dover reproduction of this work, which was first published in 1883, a year after the illustrator's death, provides a magical look at the classic. For the individual reader, it is a valuable find. As a small group vehicle, it provides a rich text for discussion. Tutors and homeschoolers may want to combine this edition of *The Raven* with Coleridge's *The Rime of the Ancient Mariner*, also illustrated by Gustave Doré, in a comparative study of symbolism of birds, grief, and death.

Streissguth, Thomas. *Edgar Allan Poe.* **Lerner Publications, 2001. 112pp.**

The huge, doll-like eyes of Eliza Poe, mother of the soon-to-be orphaned Edgar, greet the reader with stunning presence. Abandoned by his father before the birth of his younger sister, and then adopted by a childless, well-endowed couple, the author was destined to live a life of extremes and contradictions that no doubt provided grist for a tormented and very creative mill. This book delivers background details about the 1800s and is peppered with photographs, etchings, and reproductions of literary pieces that give the writer a recognizable place and time.

Strange incidents are also described, such as Poe's reading of "The Raven" to the publisher Graham and his entire staff. After refusing to publish the work, the party collected $15, which the humiliated but poverty-stricken poet was forced to accept. A list of sources, a bibliography, and an extensive index end the book. In addition to short chapters, with many subsections of less than a page, there are insets giving incidental information. For example, a one-page inset on "The Gothic Romance" gives the history of the genre in a nutshell and Poe's relationship to it. Another places him in juxtaposition to "Transcendentalism." These features make this a good choice for the homeschooler who has students at multiple grade levels. It is also a fine source of short read-aloud passages for the teacher or tutor.

 Poe, Edgar Allan. *The Gold-Bug and Other Tales.* **Dover Publications, 1991. 121pp.**

Here are nine chilling tales by the master of the macabre: "Ligeia" (1838), "The Fall of the House of Usher" (1839), "The Murders in the Rue Morgue (1841), "The Masque of the Red Death" (1842), "The Pit and the Pendulum" (1842), "The Tell-Tale Heart" (1843), "The Gold-Bug" (1843), "The Black Cat" (1843), and "The Cask of Amontillado" (1846). The print is very small, but clear, and the paper is newsprint quality. It is lightweight, making it a good carry-around candidate. This book is available in an economical cassette package called *Edgar Allan Poe's The Tell-Tale Heart and Other Stories*, in which three of the tales are read. The cassette package is a fine gift item for the Poe enthusiast.

Audio version: *Edgar Allan Poe's The Tell-Tale Heart and Other Stories.* Listen & Read, Dover, 1996. 1 hour, 1 cassette. Read by Earl Hammond. Contains "The Tell-Tale Heart," "The Cask of Amontillado," and "The Black Cat." The tape, accompanied by the three story texts, is ideal for a listening center in homeschool or public school.

 Poe, Edgar Allan. *The Pit and the Pendulum and Other Stories.* **Illustrated by Jame's Prunier.** <u>The Whole Story</u>. **Viking, illustrations copyright 1998. 153pp.**

Seven of Poe's most dreaded tales are here: "The Gold-Bug," "The Oval Portrait," "The Pit and the Pendulum," "The Cask of Amontillado," "Some Words with a Mummy," "The Tell-Tale Heart," and "The Murders in the Rue Morgue." Richly illustrated short tales of intrigue and horror are but the toe of the scarab in this beautifully presented collection. In the margins of each page are scientific details, illustrated and explained so that the reader can be as informed as the most sophisticated investigator of Poe's time. What makes a scarab gold? What is the significance of an orangutan's prehensile hands and feet? Why does it matter that they are vegetarians? The answers to these questions and more are in the sidelines for the reader of this fascinating book. Warning: This is not a fast read. Days will be spent in study of the more-than-marginal clues.

 Thomas, Dwight, and David K. Jackson. *The Poe Log: A Documentary Life of Edgar Allan Poe 1809–1849.* <u>American Authors Log.</u> **G. K. Hall, 1987. 919pp.**

Following the introduction to this book is a collection of biographies on all the people referenced throughout the book. These short passages are not only of interest in that they shed light on the many people with whom

Poe interacted, they help the reader connect to the ways of publishing during Poe's time.

Beyond that, this book, although entirely too long to tackle head-on, is also a treasure trove of short passages relating to the life of Edgar Allan Poe. Excerpts from letters to him and from his correspondents reveal a life that was not completely dark. For example, the second entry for 1837 is from Francis Lister Hawks, extending an offer to Poe and more than highly assuring him, "and I know well you have the ability" (page 237). The historic documents reproduced here, occasional scenes, and surprising pictures include a reproduction from a watercolor of Virginia Clemm Poe (page 238). Taken in parts, this book is accessible; it is challenging only when viewed as a 919-page tome. There are eleven chapters corresponding to the major periods in Poe's life, and an extensive index.

Aleksandr Sergeyvich Pushkin (1799–1837) Collection

Aleksandr Pushkin was born an aristocrat and the son of a Balto-German mother and an African general, Ibrahim Hannibal, during unsettled times. He died at the age of 38 in a dual of honor over his beautiful and flirtatious wife. Yet his literary works (poetry and Russian folktales, which he began putting to paper in poetic form) continued to inspire generations of creative souls, including the musicians Glinka, Tchaikovsky, and Rimski-Korsakov. Rimski-Korsakov created operas for the tale of Czar Saltan and Le Coq d'Or (or the Golden Cockerel). Modern illustrators have retold many Pushkin tales; American readers may recall hearing *The Magic Goldfish,* about a poor fisherman, his greedy wife, and an enchanted fish. Pushkin has been referred to as the Russian Lord Byron. Russian ESL students regard Pushkin as one of their great storytellers. That is no doubt why Karen Hesse chose a book of Pushkin stories as the base for Rifka's letters.

These titles will be immediately appreciated by literate Russian English-language students and will serve as consciousness-raising for others. The picture book will give a fine introduction to the author. Then the Hesse book will provide a contemporary take on how Pushkin is valued today.

Hesse, Karen. *Letters from Rifka.* **Puffin Books, 1992. 148pp.**

Because of the way in which Rifka and her cousin Tovah revered the Pushkin book used here, the contemporary reader comes to see the important role Pushkin plays in the Russian cultural identity.

Young Rifka is fleeing Russia and will never be able to send her letters to anyone. They serve only as a diary. Set immediately after World War I, with the first entry dated September 2, 1919, the journal-letters of Rifka to her cousin Tovah, who was left behind in Russia during the Bolshevik Revolution, are written directly on the pages of a book of Pushkin verses the two girls had shared. Just before an entry is made, a quote from Pushkin is presented, serving as a reminder of how similar human events remain throughout time. The language in the book of poems Rifka and Tovah had shared was perhaps on a more challenging level than the language of the the the picture book *The Tale of the Golden Cockerel* (annotated below). Yet the stories Rifka tells about her frightening and lonely journey are every bit as gripping as those of the famous Pushkin. This historical novel is a fascinating follow-up to an introduction through the Pushkin picture book. This book has won the National Jewish Book Award, IRA Children's Book Award, Christopher Award, Sydney Taylor Book Award, ALA Notable Book, ALA Best Book for Young Adults, *School Library Journal* Best Book of the Year, Horn Book Outstanding Book of the Year, and *Booklist* Editor's Choice.

 Pushkin, Alexander. *The Tale of the Golden Cockerel*. Illustrated by I. Bilibin [Ivan Iakovlevich Bilbin (1876–1942)]. Translated and retold by Patricia Tracy Lowe, translation copyright by Emme Edixioni, 1975. Thomas Y. Crowell, 1975. 20pp.

This is an ancient Russian folktale retold by the great Russian poet Alexander Pushkin many generations after it had begun as oral history. The powerful Czar Dadon, who once enjoyed fighting with his neighbors, now preferred to spend his life peacefully, but he cannot because of the many neighbors who have learned to be his enemy. When the Czar calls on an old sorcerer to give him relief, the sorcerer provides a magical cock that can foretell any danger, thereby making it impossible to take the Czar by surprise. As payment, he promises the sorcerer anything he wishes. When time to pay up comes around, the Czar reverts to the mindset of his youth. How this dilemma is resolved is the stuff of Russian literature. Long after Pushkin's death, the Russian artist Bilibin decided to illustrate some of Pushkin's work. This book is filled with reproductions of those hundred-year-old images. Special features include a summary of the book; a one-page biography of Pushkin.

Mary Shelley (1797–1851) Collection

Mary Godwin Shelley was born in London to radical writer William Godwin (author of *An Enquiry Concerning Political Justice*, 1793) and feminist Mary Wollstonecraft (author of *Vindication of the Rights of Woman*, 1792) on August 30, 1797. Within 10 days her mother was dead. .

Henceforth, Godwin lavished attention on his little girl, taking her everywhere, including into the company of intellectual adults, such as Charles and Mary Lamb and James Marshall. Then Godwin married Mary Jane Clairmont, a widow with a young daughter and son of her own, who proved not to be on the same intellectual or social page as the parents of Mary. Clairmont was immediately jealous of the child and began to limit her access to her father. Not only was Mary's informal education curtailed; she never received the formal education she might have expected. Reading from her father's extensive library and engaging in dialogue with the visitors he brought into their home (William Wordsworth, Charles Lamb, Samuel Taylor Coleridge, and Thomas Holcroft, for example) was her primary source of literary understanding.

In 1812, Godwin sent his daughter to spend the summer with the idyllic William Baxter family, where Mary became fast friends with the two Baxter girls. Upon her return home, she met her father's new young friend and political protégé, the author Percy Bysshe Shelley, and his wife, Harriet Shelley. Within a short time, Mary and Percy, with the complicity of Jane Clairmont, had developed a strong attraction to one another. On July 28, 1814, Mary, her half-sister Claire, and Percy ran away together, an adventure chronicled in Mary's journal of December 19, 1822, which documented poverty in France, baths in Switzerland, Marlow, Milan, Lucca, Venice, Rome, Naples, Florence, and so on. She soon wrote and published *History of a Six Weeks' Tour through a part of France, Switzerland, Germany, and Holland* (1817).

Sometimes with and sometimes without the company of Claire, Mary lived with Percy in Italy until his death. The two were married on December 30, 1816, three weeks after the body of Harriet was found in a London park lake. They were on holiday with Lord Byron and John Polidari on Lake Geneva in 1816, when Byron challenged each member of the party to make up a horror story. Mary had what she termed a "waking" nightmare. It was the image of the creature now known as Frankenstein, the inspiration of over 50 movies. She finished *Frankenstein: Or, The Modern Prometheus* in 1817 and published it in 1818. Her next book, *Mathilda*, is believed to be autobiographical, describing a woman who can see that she is becoming cold, suspicious, and unlovable.

In 1822, Percy and his friend Edward Williams drowned. Mary's next novel, *The Last Man* (1824), was a dark and gloomy tale that featured Adrian, Earl of Windsor, the idealized image of her husband, who had enjoyed a steady stream of other women.

Mary Shelley, finally reconciled with her father, continued to support him until his death. She left a vast legacy of her own works, but devoted her final years to nonfiction, the last of which was *Rambles in Germany and Italy in 1840, 1842, and 1843* (1844), a book about her travels with her only surviving child, Percy, and to editing Percy Shelley's works. She was diagnosed with a brain tumor in December 1850 and died on February 1, 1851.

Barchers, Suzanne I., and Jennifer L. Kroll. "Frankenstein." In *Classic Readers Theatre for Young Adults,* **179–198. Teacher Ideas Press, 2002. 243pp.**

Twelve scenes adapted from the original story are ready to use in a classroom or homeschool dramatization. There is a mix of long and short reading parts, accompanied by other teaching ideas.

 Latrobe, Kathy. "Frankenstein." In *Readers Theatre for Young Adults,* **59–62. Teacher Ideas Press, 1989. 130pp.**

This skit, based on chapter 15 of Mary Shelley's book, has three key players, the Narrator, the lonely Monster, and the blind DeLacey. Because DeLacey cannot see the creature, who is explaining his fugitive plight, the man is not repulsed by the monster, and the audience has an opportunity to understand the fugitive's perspective. Then the children return, providing ad lib bit parts as they fall into shock. This skit will work beautifully in a homeschool setting, with a small group of new readers or learners of English, or as a cooperative learning group in a traditional classroom. It provides the foundation for discussion about contemporary prejudice.

 Shelley, Mary. *Frankenstein.* **Illustrated by Philippe Munch. <u>The Whole Story</u>. Viking, 1997. 253pp.**

The young Frankenstein is a compassionate soul, a student who is driven by scientific insights and personal impulses to spend his study time creating, or re-creating, life. Inadvertently, he produces something unexpected and terrible. This is the story of Frankenstein's times. It treats the reader to a wealth of information about anatomy, electricity, seafaring, literature, mental illness, and history. First published in 1818 by 18-year-old Mary Shelley (wife of poet Percy Bysshe Shelley) in a response to a dare from her friends, *Frankenstein* proved one of the most gripping English-language romance novels ever written.

Beautiful illustrations bring the horrific monster to life. Pictures of historic whaling ventures and Knights of the Round Table are included in the extra sidebar messages of this edition. All the extra information will not only help the new reader understand better, it will leave all readers loaded with a wealth of information they might never have looked for independently. The print is big enough, and there is lots of space between the lines. The book is admittedly long, and the tale has many more complexities than movies on the same subject suggest, but the passages are broken into very clear parts, mostly letters, each with its own perspective, so the format offers internal support. This is a book worth reading or reading aloud and discussing.

Video version: *Frankenstein: The Man Who Made a Monster.* Universal Studios, 1931. 1 cassette, 1 hour, 11 minutes. BW. Starring Boris Karloff, Colin Clive, Mae Clarke, John Boles, Edward Van Sloan, and Dwight Frye. Director: James Whale. This is the all-time classic horror film.

Robert Louis Stevenson (1850–1894) Collection

Born in Scotland in 1850, Robert Louis Stevenson was a sickly child who suffered from tuberculosis throughout his life and eventually died of it. Yet he traveled extensively, acquiring experiences that were grist for a literary mill that produced numerous stories about strange and horrible situations. In 1880 he married Fanny Osbourne, with whom he eventually collaborated on plays (most unsuccessful).

A prolific writer for all audiences, within a two-year period Stevenson produced *A Child's Garden of Verses* (a book of poetry), *The Body Snatcher*, *Prince Otto*, and *Dr. Jekyll and Mr. Hyde*. In 1883 he wrote *Silverado Squatters*, a California memoir, and the book he is perhaps best known for, *Treasure Island*. During their travels, Stevenson and his wife met fascinating characters, such as Princess Ka'iulani of Hawaii, many of whom influenced his writing.

The Stevensons continued to travel for several years, often in search of a cure for tuberculosis, finally settling on the island of Samoa. The island mystics and folklore may have given Stevenson an elixir for the writer's mind, spiriting up the imp in the bottle.

 Barchers, Suzanne I., and Jennifer L. Kroll. "Dr. Jekyll and Mr. Hyde." In *Classic Readers Theatre for Young Adults*, 199–214. Teacher Ideas Press, 2002. 243pp.

These modern language readers theatre scripts will help new readers and ESL students develop an understanding of this classic story. Two narrators and ten other players provide the entire story line in 10 scenes.

 Lewis, Shari, and Lan O'Kun, rewriters and adapters. "Dr. Jekyll and Mr. Hyde." In *One-Minute Scary Stories*. Illustrated by Pat DeWitt and Robin DeWitt, xx. Dell Picture Yearling, 1991. 48pp.

Lewis is a master at fast, well-told tales. Though she has dropped many of the details that make these stories classics, she uses fine language and provides the liveliest of retellings of the story lines to be found. It is not easy to reduce a short story to a two-page bit of entertainment, harder still to do that to an entire novel. Yet Lewis has written many one-minute collections that are great reads. Because the stories in this collection are classics to be savored as much for the authors' style and voice as for the story lines, these Lewis retellings should NOT be considered replacements for or even be employed as the introduction of these stories.

That being said, this little book is a very useful tool for comparing the original classic with a retelling to ferret out what it is that makes the classic tale better. Readers who check out one of these Lewis books and one of the classics featured will find that they can appreciate literature much more than they might have imagined. That exercise will help bring home that it is the details as much as the plot that make these famous stories last. The

Lewis retellings also provide a fine refresher to the reader who has not read a particular tale in a long time. They fit into academic units such as regional legends, bipolar disorder, hysteria, and obsessive relationships.

 Stevenson, Robert Louis. *The Bottle Imp.* **Illustrated by Jacqueline Mair. Clarion Books, 1996 (1891). 60pp.**

So hideous was it, the men who saw the imp turned to stone for hours. The imp can deliver anything the mortal might wish. The catch to this ownership is that the bottle must be sold for less than was paid for it. And it must be sold, for anyone owning it at death will be damned forever. Written and first published in Samoan in 1891, the story is brought to life here through the vividly colorful illustrations that reflect Hawaii, where most of the story takes place. The twisted plot is not a fast read, and some pages are solid text, but the type is large and easy on the eyes.

Stevenson, Robert Louis. *The Strange Case of Dr. Jekyll and Mr. Hyde.* **Illustrated by François Place.** The Whole Story. **Viking, 1999 (1886). 105pp.**

The good Dr. Jekyll is eager to assist and experiment; Mr. Hyde is the epitome of wanton carnage. Yet they occupy the same body.

Although Stevenson was under the influence of the works of Edgar Allan Poe, and he may have been inspired by Oscar Wilde and Mary Shelley as well, this tale of dual personalities was the product of a sickbed nightmare Stevenson had. The popularity of the tale was immediate, and thousands of copies have since been produced, but this edition holds new promise for the reader. Indeed, it makes this classic highly accessible. While the text is easy to read, there is much more here to inform and entertain. Colorful illustrations of the text abound, historical pieces of information run along the margins and are also illustrated, the history of the author's circumstances is detailed front and back. In short, this is at once the text and the history of the text that has been the delight of millions of readers from Queen Victoria to you. This tale will serve well as a discussion starter about split personalities, dual personalities, crime, and good versus evil, and it is an excellent support text for study about nineteenth-century England.

Related read: See the three-player, two-page skit version of this tale in Kathy Latrobe's *Readers Theatre for Young Adults.* See also the Stevenson biographical sketch in Kathleen Krull, *Lives of the Writers: Comedies, Tragedies (and What the Neighbors Thought).*

Stevenson, Robert Louis. *Treasure Island.* **Illustrated by Francois Place.** <u>The Whole Story.</u> **Viking, 1996 (1886). 296pp.**

As he sets out to sea, young Jim Hawkins has a map to a hidden treasure. Before long, however, he learns that his fellow travelers are pirates and that Long John Silver is one mighty dangerous fellow. Written in 1881 as entertainment for Robert Louis Stevenson's stepson, this became one of the all-time famous adventure stories, with suspense, murder, mutiny, and glory on the high seas. Like the other <u>Whole Story</u> series books, this one has extraordinary illustrations on every page, and a wealth of information about seafarers, ships, pirates, and their weapons, too. One engraving shows Edward Teach (also known as Blackbeard) lying on the deck of a ship and attempting to fight off an attacker. A two-page spread displays rope work and knots used for many purposes.

This is an exciting read and a marvelous, open-anywhere fact book. The language is accessible. This is a fine book for those who enjoyed Sid Fleischman's *The Ghost in the Noonday Sun.*

Related reads: For more support, see *Pirate Queens,* by Jane Yolen and illustrated by David Shannon, a 32-page story about real women who worked as pirates on the high seas. Other Stevenson titles include *An Inland Voyage* (1858), *Travels with a Donkey in the Cevennes* (1879), and *Kidnapped* (1886). Other titles in <u>The Whole Story</u> series include *The Adventures of Tom Sawyer* by Mark Twain; *Around the World in Eighty Days* by Jules Verne; *The Call of the Wild* by Jack London; *Frankenstein* by Mary Shelley; *Heidi* by Johanna Spyri; *The Jungle Book* by Rudyard Kipling; *Little Women* by Louisa May Alcott; *The Pit and the Pendulum and Other Stories* by Edgar Allan Poe; *White Fang* by Jack London; and *The Picture of Dorian Gray* by Oscar Wilde.

Leo Tolstoy (1828–1910) Collection

It may seem odd that belief in the simple life, hard work, and class equity was embraced by the affluent Count Leo Tolstoy, especially when, because of his literary successes, he had been welcomed into and had enjoyed the high society of his time. He was one of the four sons of Count Nikolay Ilyich Tolstoy. His mother died before Leo's second birthday.. Before he was 10, just after the family moved to Moscow, his father also died, leaving the care of the Tolstoy boys to their adoring aunts. That time was recorded by Tolstoy in his autobiographies *Childhood* (1852), *Boyhood* (1854), and *Youth* (1857).

After a brief stint at the University of Kazan, he returned to the family estate of Yasnaya Polyana, where, after unsuccessful attempts to improve the lot of the serfs, with some guilt he joined the Moscow social circuit. In 1851 he joined the Russian army in the Caucasus and began writing short stories and his autobiographies. At the same time, he was keeping a diary in which he recorded his inner thoughts, frustrations, and feelings of social concern. It is from his diaries that we now can understand one of the world's great moral philosophers and his belief in the notion of nonviolent protest. His first excursion into Europe made a poor impression on him, as reflected in *Lucerne* (1857). He returned to the family estate and established a school for the peasant children.

At 34, he took the 18-year-old Sofya Andreyevna Behrs as his bride. He soon published *Cossacks* (1863), which had been inspired by his military service. Because of his diaries, we know that he changed the time period several times for his next big work, *War and Peace*, in which his attitudes about social justice and revolution are reflected. Then came the great love story *Anna Karenina*, which also drew on his military experience.

Tolstoy and Fyodor Dostoyevsky (1821–1881) gave the realistic novel its place among the classical genres. The *Death of Ivan Ilyich*, about the evolving thoughts of a common man who is dying of cancer, reflects Tolstoy's changing spiritual perceptions. Conventional beliefs of both his religion and the tsarist social system failed to prove reasonable in the face of the world he saw, and these inner struggles were further reported in essays of this period. They also manifested in his lifestyle, as he gave up his regal wardrobe and began to make his own shoes. In 1901, Leo Tolstoy was excommunicated from the Russian Church. He objected to government executions through scathing essays and moralistic stories. Being a man of action, he began to divest himself of all worldly possessions, including the royalties for his works, which his wife and children believed they needed to support the family. Estrangements followed. So it was that in 1910 Tolstoy left his estate for life in a monastery. He died en route.

Muth, Jon. *The Three Questions*. Scholastic, 2002. 32pp.

What is the best time for each deed? Who are the right people to be with? What is the most important thing to do? These are the questions a czar wishes to have answered in Tolstoy's famous *The Three Questions* (referenced in *An Introduction to Literature* under "The Three Hermits" in this collection). In this book, substituting the boy Nikolai for the czar; a wise turtle for the wise hermit in the original Tolstoy story; and a heron, a monkey, and a dog for the other characters, Muth presents the same philosophical themes and accompanies them with stunning, yet delicate, watercolor illustrations.

"What is the best time to do things? Who is the most important one? What is the right thing to do?" asks the boy. The answers are discovered by the boy, not given by the wise old turtle (or wise old hermit in the original). There are just a few lines of text per page. This is a very fine philosophical discussion starter and a good way of showing how one great writer has inspired creativity in another person.

"The Three Hermits." In *An Introduction to Literature,* **13th ed., 242–246. An old Volga District legend retold by Leo Tolstoy in 1886, translated by Aylmer Maude. Pearson/Longman, 2004.**

A bishop, sailing aboard a great vessel, heard about a small island on which three hermits worked to save their souls. The bishop, intent on teaching them a thing or two, persuaded the captain to detour close enough so that the bishop might take a lifeboat to the island. When he met the scruffy trio, they joined hands in a prayer, "Three are ye, three are we, have mercy upon us!" and all looked joyfully heavenward. The bishop spent the day teaching them to recite the Lord's Prayer, which they happily did. Then the bishop returned to his ship, which had barely weighed anchor when he saw a very bright thing upon the water moving at breakneck speed toward the ship. He blinked and saw that it was the three hermits, holding hands and running atop the waves to catch up with him. They'd already forgotten the prayer and wanted another lesson. This lesson in humility was also about Tolstoy's philosophy concerning prayer and his belief in the power of a simple lifestyle.

"The Three Hermits" has been rewritten as a church opera and is a delightful introduction to Tolstoy. Although the text (with many variations) can be found online, and there are numerous references to it in both secular and spiritual essays, there are few hard copies available. This anthology also contains "The Three Questions," "The Death of Ivan Ilych," and a very brief essay, "What Is Art?" Homeschoolers and ESL teachers may want to use "The Three Hermits" as a readers theatre activity. This translation has lots of dialogue in clear, modern English.

Note: This translation of "The Three Hermits" is also available in a Tolstoy collection from the Oxford University Press, *The Raid and Other Stories,* reprinted in 1999.

 Tolstoy, Leo. *The Death of Ivan Ilych and Other Stories.* **Translated by Aylmer Maude and J. D. Duff. Signet Classics, 2003. 301pp.**

This is a fine collection of Tolstoy's short stories. From two excellent translators come "Family Happiness " (1859), translated by J. D. Duff; and "The Death of Ivan Ilych" (1886), "The Kreutzer Sonata" (1889), and "Master and Man" (1895), all translated by Aylmer Maude. The modern English prose in these translations is very easy to understand. The longest, and perhaps most famous, is "The Death of Ivan Ilych" which is sometimes found as a stand-alone book. This is a good place to start with teacher readings of Tolstoy.

Tolstoy, Leo. *The Kreutzer Sonata and Other Short Stories*. <u>Master-</u>
<u>pieces of Russian Literature</u>. **Dover Thrift, 1993. 140pp.**

"How Much Land Does a Man Need?" (1886), translated by Louise and Aylmer Maude, is a parable designed to instruct about avarice and envy. It begins with a town sister and a country sister; the former begins by belittling the latter's food and mannerisms. Soon after, both the country husband (newly convinced of his need for more land) and the Devil (pleased that the husband has discovered a compelling want) emerge from their eavesdropping perches to enter a liaison.

"The Death of Ivan Ilych" (1886), annotated above, is also translated by Louise and Aylmer Maude. The translator of "The Kreutzer Sonata" (1891), which deals with adultery and the decadence so abhorred by Tolstoy, particularly after his conversion to radical beliefs, is unknown, but did a fine job for us. The 28 chapters range from one to five and a half pages. The print is small but clear. These thought-provoking stories would serve well as reada-louds or readers theatre presentations.

 Tolstoy, Leo. *War and Peace*. **Translated by Ann Dunnigan. Intro-**
duction by John Bayley. A Signet Classic, New American Library,
1983. 1,456pp.

This epic historical novel Takes place in the context of Napoleon's 1812 invasion of Russia and the Russian resistance. *Voini i mir* (a novel in six volumes) was first published in Moscow (1863–1869) and has been translated many times. It was published by Harper in 1886. Tolstoy takes the reader through mighty extremes of love and hate, fear and triumph, joy and terror. Romance drives the heart of this epic historical novel, as social roles shift and fortunes move like coins in a vending machine. Natasha and Pierre are hardly a match as the tale begins, but war makes some things better.

Although this book is too challenging for the new reader or the new speaker of English, it is a work that will support any reader in pursuit of literature in the English language , will give the history student an overview of the era, and will delight anyone who has encountered the book in another language. With audio support, Tolstoy comes alive, a positive experience even for the very new reader. To access this text, the new reader may want to check out this book and an audiocassette reading of the book, using the former as a subject reference, and the tape as the way to access the stories. Listening to a well-constructed work is not only pleasurable; it teaches organization in writing. Listening to fine reading puts the sound of good reading in the head. Readers at all levels benefit by listening to well-done audio presentations of good literature. The movie is also available on video. In this case, however, the process of listening to the elegant BBC production on tape is a literary experience that goes far beyond the thrilling historical record. Homeschoolers may want to link this to their world history units.

Audio version: *War and Peace.* BBC Radio, Bantam Doubleday Dell Audio Publishing, 1997. 10 cassettes, approximately 9 hours. This BBC dramatization has a full range of sound effects and characters.

Related reads: See also Tolstoy's plays, including *The Power of Darkness, Fruits of Enlightenment,* and *The Living Corpse.*

 Tolstoy, Leo. *Anna Karenina.* **Translated by Richard Pevear. Penguin Books, 2004 (1886). 838pp.**

The rebellious Anna Karenina is trapped in a loveless marriage when she encounters the exciting and amorous Russian officer, Aleksei Vronski. She abandons her husband and child to enter a liaison; it ends in her suicide. Contrasts between men and women, social conventions and human passions, and country and city life in the nineteenth century present a dashing drama, as a landowner works to improve the lives of his serfs. The ill-fated affair of Anna and Vronski make this romance one of the all-time great stories and one of Tolstoy's two finest works, the other being *War and Peace.* Originally published in 1873–1876, there are several translations in libraries and bookstores. This translation is praised for coming closest to Tolstoy's gutsy and powerful imagery. It is an Oprah's Book Club selection. The sheer length of this book might scare away a new reader. If, on the other hand, it were read aloud, section-by-section, and then discussed, it would provide an excellent introduction to this author and this period in history.

Note: This book is also available online through Project Gutenberg, but in an earlier translation.

Audio version: *Anna Karenina.* Books on Tape, 1984. 10 cassettes, approximately 15 hours. Read by Jill Masters. This is a reading of an older translation, which might be used as a listening-only device.

Mark Twain (1835–1910) Collection

Born Samuel Langhorne Clemens in Florida, Missouri, under the flame of Halley's Comet, Mark Twain lived on and learned from the Mississippi River, even working as a steamboat pilot in 1857. That career gave him insights he used when creating his most famous character, Huckleberry Finn, and the material for his book *Life on the Mississippi*, a life that ended abruptly when the Civil War ended, allowing commerce on the river. Twain was a traveling journalist and humorist who drew from his environment. While working as a roving correspondent in California, he produced his famous short story "The Celebrated Jumping Frog of Calaveras County."

The first American author to write in the American vernacular (rather than the formal British), Twain is known for his dry, deadpan satire and an unquenchable font of humor. Yet he also had a very serious scholarly side. In *Mark Twain Historical Romances* readers will find three historical novels that reflect intensive study. The notes in this book about the three volumes will provide readers with insights often overlooked. Anyone who is going to write about Mark Twain would do well to draw upon the research that is provided in this thousand-plus page volume.

 Barchers, Suzanne I., and Jennifer L. Kroll. "The Prince and the Pauper." *Classic Readers Theatre for Young Adults,* **223–240. Teacher Ideas Press, 2002. 243pp.**

Ten scenes from *The Prince and the Pauper* are ready to use in a classroom or homeschool dramatization. There is a mix of long and short reading parts. This book has sixteen classic stories summarized, retold in a dramatic script format, and accompanied by other teaching ideas. This is very high-level comprehension support for the books addressed and helps new readers get to know the authors well.

 Harness, Cheryl. *Mark Twain and the Queens of the Mississippi.* **Simon & Schuster Books for Young Readers, 1998. 38pp.**

This wonderful book is loaded with pictures that provide detail about the Mississippi, the Indians, the archaeological sites, the riverboats, the Civil War, and more. Read about the race between the *Rob't E. Lee* and the *Natchez*. Find out about those Calaveras County frogs. Search the heavens for comets seen in Samuel Clemens's time. Here are the roots of many of Twain's story ideas. Readers will learn about Twain's acquaintance with the Chippewa, Fox, Shawnee, and Choctaw. The book has maps of many kinds and time periods and a short bibliography. While the illustrations run off the edges of every page, the text is fast-moving, too. Open it at the beginning and spend hours enjoying the trip, or open it at random and just have a good time. This book supports U.S. history, transportation, and famous writers units.

Lasky, Kathryn. *A Brilliant Streak: The Making of Mark Twain.* **Illustrated by Barry Moser. Harcourt Brace, 1998. 41pp.**

Born under the streak of Haley's Comet on November 30, 1835, Samuel Clemens died when the Comet returned on April 20, 1910. In between, under the name of Mark Twain, he became one of America's most noted authors and funniest public speakers. But long before achieving that fame, young Clemens had a life not unlike the ones he wrote about, and this is the story of that life. Lasky can always be counted on to do her research well. Great illustrations, lots of information, and good reading, too. At the end there is a list of books about Mark Twain and a list of books by Mark Twain.

Latrobe, Kathy Howard, and Mildred Knight Laughlin. "A Connecticut Yankee in King Arthur's Court." *Readers Theatre for Young Adults,* **65–69. Libraries Unlimited, 1989, 130pp.**

This is a skit annotated in the King Arthur collection in chapter 2. See also the easy-to-read skit "The Adventures of Tom Sawyer," on pages 70–72 in the same book.

 Twain, Mark. *The Mysterious Stranger and Other Stories.* **Foreword by Edmund Reiss. Signet Classic, 1962. 256pp.**

Here are nine stories by Mark Twain. The novella *The Mysterious Stranger* was first published posthumously in 1916 and is one of his most controversial works, reflecting what is called his dark period. Other titles in this collection include "The Celebrated Jumping Frog of Calaveras County," "The Facts Concerning the Recent Carnival of Crime in Connecticutt," "The Stolen White Elephant," "Luck, the $1,000,000 Bank-Note," "The Man That Corrupted Hadleyburg," "The Five Boons of Life," and "Was It Heaven? Or Hell?"

The book also contains a bibliography showing when each story was originally published. In spite of the early copyright date, this collection is still in print, is listed on the Penguin Classics Web site, is available for sale in mainstream chain and independent bookstores, and can be found in many libraries. There are also Dover editions with many of the same stories. The language in these stories is not at all simplified, but the moving plots keep a high level of reader interest.

 Ross, Stewart. *Mark Twain and Huckleberry Finn.* **Illustrated by Ronald Himler. Penguin Putnam Books for Young Readers, 1999. 44pp.**

This is a nonfiction picture book to be read by any person who is interested in serious study of Mark Twain, especially the implications of his character Huckleberry Finn. Having come under fire for a variety of reasons, this character and the book of the same name have been both immensely popular and righteously attacked. There are pictures along with long pages of solid print. The pictures will give support both to the new reader and to the person who is preparing a research report. This book also has a chronology of the life of Sam Clemens/Mark Twain and a further reading list.

 Twain, Mark. *The Adventures of Tom Sawyer.* **Illustrated by Claude Lapointe.** <u>The Whole Story.</u> **Viking, 1995 (1876). 284pp.**

The simple life in a small town on the Mississippi afforded easy living to everyone—everyone except those who encountered the original trickster Tom Sawyer, whose entire life was spent working up ways to get out of work. And he was pretty good at it, too. After hearing how much fun he expected to have whitewashing his aunt's fence, Tom's friends were falling all over themselves to get in on the action.

This classic tale is here in the original text that entertained thousands of readers in 1876. It is enriched through marginal illustrations, historical photographs, and inside information not available to those first readers. For example, one of Tom Sawyer's friends, Joe Harper, was modeled after the author's real boyhood friend, John Briggs. And the sweet Becky Thatcher was Mark Twain's first love, Laura Hawkings. Photographs of Briggs and Hawkings are in the margins of this beautiful and informing book. So is a wealth of other information. There are copies of education-promoting picture cards, once distributed by religious and philanthropic groups, showing the destinies of good students and of scoundrels. And a picture of a steamship paddleboat details why this hull was ideal for the sometimes deep, sometimes shallow Mississippi River. This copy is so well presented that anyone who reads it will want to keep it. This edition supports units on small towns, rural life, nineteenth-century Middle America, and trickster tales.

Note: This story is also available in an (%) format from Dover Publications.

 Twain, Mark [1835–1910]. *The Adventures of Tom Sawyer.* **A Watermill Classic, 1980 (1876). 314pp.**

This complete, unabridged edition of *The Adventures of Tom Sawyer* above has no pictures. It was re-typeset in large print to make reading easier. The margins are quite small, but this paperback book is one the reader can carry along and read anywhere. Reading The Whole Story edition will give the reader a world of internal support for this tale.

Note: This story is also available in an (%) format from Dover Publications.

 Twain, Mark. *The Complete Short Stories of Mark Twain.* **Introduction by Charles Nieder. Hanover House, 1957. 676pp.**

Here are 60 short writings created over the course of Mark Twain's lifetime. Sixteen are essays. This collection reveals the humor, wit, and sarcasm that made this American icon so beloved. The print is quite small, making this a second-string choice for a reading copy; it is the print, not the language, that marks this edition . But it is readily available on library shelves and is certainly far better than no Twain at all. And for those who have already savored the best known of his tales, it is very nice to know where the others are.

Related reads: Dover Publications provides *The Mysterious Stranger and Other Stories* and *Humorous Stories and Sketches* in formats.

Twain, Mark. *Life on the Mississippi*. **Illustrated by Walter Stewart. Harper & Row, 1917 (1874). 527pp.**

"When I was a boy, there was but one permanent ambition among my comrades in our village on the west bank of the Mississippi River. That was, to be a steamboatman" (page 32). The village Twain refers to is Hannibal, Missouri. Life on the Mississippi River was exciting and adventurous, especially to the teenaged Samuel Clemens. Here are the author's recollections of the small town people, the river-wise travelers who had been to "St. Loois" and such, and a way of life that too soon disappeared in reality, but is remembered in the books of Mark Twain.

Twain's prose is down-home and conversational. He tells the reader what he's thinking as though the two were engaged in conversation on a front porch. There is plenty of space between the lines of this book, making the print not too tiresome to the eyes. The scattered full-page, black-and-white drawings are full of informing detail, but the thickness of this book makes it daunting. While almost any chapter would make a good place to start, a student of English as a second language might want to read along as the audio edition plays. A new reader might just enjoy hearing this tale as background support for Twain's other books.

Audio version: *Life on the Mississippi.* Books on Tape, 1977. 8 cassettes, 12 hours. Read by Michael Prichard.

 Twain, Mark. "Personal Recollections of Joan of Arc by The Sieur Louis De Conte (Her Page and Secretary)." *Mark Twain Historical Romances: The Prince and the Pauper; A Connecticut Yankee in Kin Arthur's Court; Personal Recollections of Joan of Arc, 541–970.* **Edited and with notes by Susan K. Harris. The Library of America, 1994. 1,036pp.**

Here is a rare look at the often-referenced book that Mark Twain wrote about Joan of Arc. In this monumental historical romance, Mark Twain employs a storyteller, Sieur Louis de Conte, born in 1410, two years before Joan of Arc, who became her childhood playmate and later her page and secretary. This man tells us: "[M]y hand was the last she touched in life." In extraordinary prose, Twain delivers a personal tribute to "the most noble life that was ever born into this world save only One." His sentences are often long and flowery, reflecting the mood of the 82-year-old man who is recalling the extraordinary life that ended so early.

Readers who lack familiarity with Saint Joan's story can easily acquire it by reading the 🕯 level stories *Joan of Arc, the Lily Maid* by Margaret Hodges and *Joan of Arc* by Diane Stanley. In *Lives of Extraordinary Women, Rulers, Rebels (and What the Neighbors Thought)*, Kathleen Krull also provides a powerful, brief summary, at the 🕯 level. The Twain story of Saint Joan is the least accessible in bookstores or libraries. The three historical romances in this volume show Twain to be a researcher—a scholar. But there is more. The chronology of the life of Samuel Langhorne Clemens (pages 973–1021) is written as a collection of annual essays. Each essay is a fascinating little bit of history unto itself. The "Notes on the Texts" (pages 1022–1025) give the publishing history of the three books in this volume. In that essay, Harris explains the laborious process Twain went through while writing the Saint Joan story for serialization in *Harper's Magazine* and later in book form. Letters suggest ongoing discrepancies between author and publisher, and works were often cut to suit publication requirements, so there are multiple options from which the editors of this volume could draw. This background information is very clearly written and may be appreciated by literature or composition teachers who want a coherent read-aloud that reveals this part of the writer's process.

Related reads: Other Twain titles include *The Adventures of Huckleberry Finn, The Prince and the Pauper,* and *A Connecticut Yankee in King Arthur's Court.* An overview of Twain's life an work can be found in Kathleen Krull's *Lives of the Writers: Comedies, Tragedies (and What the Neighbors Thought).*

Jules Verne (1828–1905) Collection

Born the son of a well-to-do lawyer in the center of maritime life, the port of Nantes, France, Jules Gabriel Verne was schooled in the traditional manner of the time and excelled in geography. After a childhood filled with waterfront adventures (including a sinking boat and being marooned on an island), Jules agreed to follow in his father's footsteps. He moved to Paris to study law, and he did begin earning a meager living as a stockbroker. But in the meantime, the Parisian social life led him to associations with Victor Hugo, Alexandre Dumas, and other notable members of literary circles. Under this influence, Jules Verne began to write plays. The first of 30 he would eventually write was *The Broken Straws*; it debuted before his twenty-third birthday. All was not completely well, however. In the midst of these successes and frivolity, Verne developed digestive problems that continued to plague him for the rest of his life.

Another important influence came into his life when he read the first French translations of works by the American Edgar Allan Poe, most specifically the balloon stories "The Balloon Hoax" and "The Unparalleled Adventures of One Hans Pfaall." In response, in 1851 he wrote "A Voyage in a Balloon," a science fiction tale that made literary history. Jules Verne and H. G. Wells were the acknowledged founding fathers of the genre now known as science fiction.

His association and lifelong friendship with children's author and publisher Pierre Jules Hetzel, which started in 1862, began his interest in writing for children. Hetzel became Verne's eager and welcomed critic. While his contemporary Lewis Carroll wrote fantasies such as *Alice in Wonderland,* and H. G. Wells wrote *The First Men in the Moon*, Verne struggled to ground his stories in a reality that could be believed. Although contemporaries may have argued about the practicality of some of his heroes' excursions, they were, for the time, quite possible. Soon after meeting Hetzel, Verne began writing a book each year, a pattern of production that lasted the rest of his life.

Hetzel also introduced Verne to the scientist Felix Nadar, who in turn introduced Verne to the scientific community. It was through these associations that Verne gathered much of the scientific data for his stories.

Already a socialist, Verne began to admire the radical revolutionary Prince Pyotr Kropotkin. Kropotkin may have been a model for later noble characters in Verne's works. Although Verne had married the widow Honorine de Viane, in 1857, in 1867 Verne traveled to America with his brother, Paul, leaving her behind, They visited Niagara Falls. He traveled to the Mediterranean and North Africa, and was honored in Rome by Pope Leo XIII, who blessed his books. It should be noted that there are numerous rumors about Verne, typically made up by journalists enlarging on facts. Some reports suggest that Verne was widely traveled. In truth the travel above is about all he actually did. He relied on research and interviews for the details about exotic lands that his characters get to see first-hand.

In 1871 Verne moved to Amiens, where an insane nephew later attempted to murder him. The gunshot only hit Verne's leg, but it did leave him permanently crippled. This event did have one positive outcome: his only child, Michel, who had been singularly rebellious and irresponsible, suddenly took some interest in his father.

In 1888 Verne was elected councilor of Amiens, where he died on March 24, 1905, leaving a legacy of 65 novels, 30 plays, 20 short stories, and countless essays, geographical works, and librettos. His works are now enjoyed in English translation, on tape, and on film.

Note: Readers are encouraged to look for the most recent translations available. That way the reading will have modern idioms and expressions. Also, some translators and movie scriptwriters reinterpret character names. If one runs into a name that sounds unfamiliar, it may be that the name has been adjusted to suit a script.

Krull, Kathleen. "Jules Verne." *They Saw the Future: Oracles, Psychics, Scientists, Great Thinkers, and Pretty Good Guessers,* **59–65. Illustrated by Kyrsten Brooker. Atheneum Books for Young Readers/Simon & Schuster Children's Publishing Division, 1999. 108pp.**

> Living in a time without electricity, Verne wrote about light as we enjoy it today; living in a cart and buggy time, he wrote about cars, now taken for granted; living in a time when soldiers used hand-held weapons, he wrote about the atomic bomb. Many of his prophesies may have been simple logical conclusions, or perhaps not. In seven and a half pages, the main points of Verne's entire, remarkable life are told in humorous detail.

This collection of clairvoyants and other prophesizing personalities offers a full-page illustration of each along with a biography. The print is ample, with lots of white space. This book has an excellent further reading list and an extensive index.

 Verne, Jules. *Around the World in Eighty Days.* **Illustrated by Jame's Prunier. <u>The Whole Story.</u> Viking, 1994. 296pp.**

Phileas Fogg makes a bet with the gentlemen at his club that he and his valet Passepartout can circle the globe in 80 days. While employing almost every known mode of transportation (in 1872), the pair encounters many cultures and customs.

This is the original 1873 text of the fantastic adventure, but more. From their London departure to their return, through historical photographs and carefully detailed renderings, the reader is given rich insights into such things as how one group of elephants varies from another; the intricacies of camel travel; what can happen when a tiger near the path gets hungry; the hazards of the *bares* or *eagres,* violent waves on the Ganges River; how a paddleboat runs; communication by telegraph; and much more. It is a storybook, a history book, and a book of science all in one.

This all-time favorite story will certainly delight the reader, but the trip through it may take more than 80 days this time. Hours may be spent on a single passage as the reader discovers more detail and reads it again for yet another layer of meaning. The sidebars of historical information and illustrations provide fascinating support for all readers. This beautifully researched classic is one to own.

Audio version: *Around the World in Eighty Days.* Books on Tape, 1993. 7 cassettes, 6 hours. Read by David Case.

 Verne, Jules. *Journey to the Center of the Earth.* **Translated by William Butcher. Oxford University Press, 1998 (1864). 234pp.**

This edition offers far more than a fine science fiction story. The contents read: "Introduction; Note on the Translation; Select Bibliography; JOURNEY TO THE CENTRE OF THE EARTH; Explanatory Notes; Appendix: Verne as Seen by the Critics." This indicates a story text from pages 1 to 218. The rest of the book will be of interest to the scientific and literary scholars who enjoy science fiction as well.

Within an ancient book is a parchment. Its runic message tells of a path to the center of the earth, a path found hundreds of years before. Axel/Harry, his uncle, and Hans, an Icelandic guide, are soon on a journey that leads through a dormant volcano to an underground sea. That is where the climate changes, and they encounter prehistoric creatures in the water and on the land. Little do they imagine that their port of entry will be blocked when they attempt to return to the surface.

As a pioneer in science fiction, Verne is revered for predicting many technological advances of the century that followed him. Here, however, is strong adventure. This book has been the inspiration of movies, theater interpretations, TV series, retellings, abridgments, adaptations, and complete convolutions. English-speaking readers are at the mercy of translators to tell them what Verne had in mind. This is not a simple story, nor is it simple language, but it is a lively bit of science fiction about a space not typically addressed. Because of the mismatch between most texts and most recordings, readers who want to listen for support are advised to do so at leisure and then to read a challenging translation copy of the book. Because of the award-winning pictures it has, readers who are new to Jules Verne may want to start with the edition of *20,000 Leagues Under the Sea* annotated below.

Note: The title of this book has also been translated as *Voyage to the Center of the Earth*. Readers should also note that translators and filmmakers have taken liberties with the names of the primary characters of *Journey to the Center of the Earth*. Hence, Professor Otto Lidenbrock is also represented as Oliver Lindenbrook and Professor Von Hartwigg. Axel is also called Harry or Henry. Although the language in this translation is not at all simple, it is a well-told tale.

 Verne, Jules. *Journey to the Center of the Earth*. Translated by Robert Baldick. Puffin Books, 1994 (1864). 291pp.

This is another respected translation.

Audio versions: There are many audio versions of the tales of Jules Verne, including:

> *Journey to the Center of the Earth*. Books on Tape, 2000. 8 tapes, 12 hours. Read by Tom Collette.

> *Journey to the Center of the Earth*. Blackstone Audiobooks, 2000. 7 cassettes, approximately 10 hours. Read by Frederick Davidson.

> *Journey to the Center of the Earth*. Recorded Books, 1988. 8 cassettes, 10 hours. Read by Norman Dietz.

Video versions:

> *Journey to the Center of the Earth*. 20th Century Fox Family Feature, 1959. 1 videocassette, 129 minutes. Closed-captioned for the hearing impaired. Starring James Mason, Pat Boone, and Arlene Dahl. Director: Henry Levin.

> *Journey to the Center of the Earth*. Hallmark Home Entertainment, 2000. 1 videocassette, 139 minutes. Closed-captioned for the hearing impaired. Director: George Miller.

Verne, Jules. *The Mysterious Island.* **Translated by Jordon Stump. Introduction by Caleb Carr. Illustrations from the original 1875 edition by Jules-Descartes Ferat. Modern Library, 2001 (1875). 629pp.**

During a northeastern tempest that raged for eight days in March 1865, five Union prisoners and a dog were hurled away at 90 miles per hour from Civil War Richmond in a balloon. Then suddenly they were dropped on an uncharted, seemingly uninhabited island. This sequel to *20,000 Leagues Under the Sea* found its beginnings in reports by Alexander Selkirk, who really was alone on an island in the South Pacific. Those who have seen the movie will delight at all the extra entertainment the book holds, though the movie will provide background knowledge for the reader.

Video version: *The Mysterious Island.* 2003 DVD release. 101 minutes. Starring Michael Craig, Joan Greenwood, Michael Callan, and Gary Merrill. Directed by Cy Endfield.

Related reads: See also *The Time Machine* and *War of the Worlds* by H. G. Wells, and *The Lost World* by Sir Arthur Conan Doyle.

 Verne, Jules. *20,000 Leagues Under the Sea.* **Illustrated by Diane Dillon and Leo Dillon. Translated by Anthony Bonner. Afterword by Peter Glassman. Books of Wonder. William Morrow, 2000 (1870). 384pp.**

First aboard a ship bent on investigation and then as a prisoner of the eccentric Captain Nemo, Professor Pierre Aronnax documents this round-the-world undersea adventure. He, his servant Conseil, and the volatile harpoonist Ned Land are unwittingly trapped aboard the incredible *Nautilus,* a submersible vehicle that looked like a giant fish or a whale. It takes them far away from the "civilized" world that is filled with injustice and hatred.

Although the language in this modern translation is easy to follow, the vocabulary is by no means simplified, and the sentences are sometimes long. But readers will find the compelling tale as gripping today as it was before such a technological achievement was reality. And the Caldecott-winning illustrators have filled this edition with dazzlingly clear, yet detailed and well-informed, color illustrations that propel this classic tale beyond any edition previously published. Because of differences between translations used and the modifications made for dramatization, which often greatly enhance the entertainment factor, readers are advised to just listen to audio editions and then read the book independently. Watching one of the many video editions can also be entertaining, but none can compare to the original tale for surprise and wonder.

Audio versions: There are many audio versions of this work, including

20,000 Leagues Under the Sea, Blackstone Audiobooks, 1998. 8 cassettes, approximately 11.5 hours. Read by Frederick Davidson.

20,000 Leagues Under the Sea. Books on Tape, 1993. 9 cassettes, 13.5 hours. Read by David Case.

20,000 Leagues Under the Sea. Recorded Books 1989. 10 cassettes, 14.5 hours. Read by Norman Dietz.

20,000 Leagues Under the Sea. Dove Audio, 1996. 4 cassettes, 6 hours. Read by Harlan Ellison.

Video version: *20,000 Leagues Under the Sea.* Walt Disney's Studio Film Collection, 1991. 1 cassette, 127 minutes. Starring Kirk Douglas, James Mason, Paul Lukas, and Peter Lorre. Director: Richard Fleischer.

Oscar Wilde (1854–1900) Collection

Born Oscar Fingal O'Flahertle Wills in Ireland, Oscar Wilde became one of the most notorious and most widely read poets, playwrights, and wits of his time. A member of the aesthetic movement supporting art for art's sake, Wilde was known for egotistical sarcasm and biting humor, giving anyone who had the urge to start a war of words with him plenty a lively time. He was known for his outlandish costumes, and he always held a flower while lecturing. Once tried for pedophilia, Wilde demonstrated that he was simply an ardent benefactor to the well-bred young boy in question. Later, less well-bred boys in significant numbers gave the courts no choice but to sentence him to two years of hard labor. Even then, he kept on writing.

Though he wrote for all ages, the titles listed here will serve adult readers very well, showing some of the range of this gifted writer. Both *Little Hans* and *The Selfish Giant* are morality stories, with twists of irony. The supernatural thriller about Dorian Gray has a story line that moves forward at a severe rate, until the reader discovers the supreme deception. The referenced readers theatre script is a good way to ease into the novel. This tale also became a movie that is still enjoyed by classic film connoisseurs. *Salomé* is a one-act play that was written exclusively for adult audiences, specifically those audiences that sought to see the famed Sarah Bernhardt in the buff. It can, however, also be used as a readers theatre performance in a group of 13 sophisticated readers. Reading these texts promises to create Wilde fans for life.

 Wilde, Oscar. *The Canterville Ghost.* Illustrated by Inga Moore. Candlewick Press, 1997 (1891). 127pp.

When the family of American minister Hiram B. Otis bought the ancient English manor Canterville Chase, they also purchased the ghost of Sir Simon, who in 1575 had murdered his wife and then disappeared under mysterious circumstances. Since then he'd done a horrid business, visiting terror on anyone who encroached on his turf, sending generations of victims into fits of insanity and occasionally death. But the minister and his family didn't believe in ghosts, even though every time eldest son Washington Otis cleaned up the bloodstain it would reappear by the following morning.

Though quite definitely a ghost story, this book is filled with Wilde asides. In describing Mrs. Otis he says, "Indeed, in many respects, she was quite English, and was an excellent example of the fact that we have really everything in common with America nowadays, except, of course, language." He also tosses in literary allusion. For example, when someone uttered a truly awful oath, a cock named Chanticleer responded. The finely detailed illustrations provide much information, and the story moves along at a surprising pace, with a surprising ending. Though Wilde's language is by no means simple, this little—it can be held in one hand—book with its large print and widely spaced lines is the ideal introduction to this author.

 Wilde, Oscar. *The Selfish Giant*. Illustrated by Gertraud Reiner and Walter Reiner. Harvey House, 1967 (1888). 76pp.

For seven years the children have been playing in the giant's garden and the birds have been singing in the trees. Now the giant has come home again, and he says that's the end of that. Winter, and all of Winter's cronies (Wind, Snow, etc.), decide to come and stay inside the big walled garden. The other seasons come and go outside the wall, but leave the selfish giant's turf to Winter. The giant begins to miss the other seasons. One day a linnet happens to land on the giant's windowsill and begins to sing, somewhat making him reform. Spring reappears, and so do children, who cause the flowers to bloom in trees they climb. But one sad little boy is too small to get into his snow-frozen tree, so the giant helps him. That's the last the giant sees of him until the end of his life, when the boy shows up, this time with wounds in his hands and feet, which the giant wants to avenge. No matter, the boy has come to return a favor—to redeem the giant by taking him to the boy's garden this time. Note that Wilde also employed a linnet in *Little Hans*. Lots of pictures and big print help readers get into this very clear spiritual tale. This introduction to Wilde, at his least sarcastic side, is appropriate for all levels of reader and English language learner.

Wilde, Oscar. *The Canterville Ghost and Other Stories*. Dover Publications, 2001. 69pp.

The print in this edition is smaller, and there are no strongly supportive illustrations such as those used in the *Canterville* annotated above. Still, this little book offers four Wilde tales: "The Canterville Ghost," "The Sphinx Without a Secret," "The Model Millionaire," and "Lord Arthur Saville's Crime." This easy-to-carry book makes a nice addition to a budding personal or homeschool library.

Wilde, Oscar. *The Canterville Ghost.* Illustrated by Lisbeth Zwerger. A Michael Neugebauer Book/North-South Books, 1996. (This illustrated edition first published in Switzerland under the title *Das Gespenst Von Canterville* in 1986 [1891].) 36pp.

Again, the full text of Wilde's misdirected ghost story is offered in a memorable format with heavy, glossy leaves that feel very nice to the touch. Filling many pages with solid print, the large font is not quite as easy to look at as might be expected. This vertical format edition has humor-filled, full-page illustrations on approximately every third page. It promises to become an edition used more for picture perusing than reading, but is a good addition to the homeschool or personal library.

Wilde, Oscar. *The Fairy Tales of Oscar Wilde.* Illustrated by Isabel Brent. Introduction by Neil Philip. Voking.1994. 141pp.

The contents include "The Happy Prince," "The Nightingale and the Rose," "The Selfish Giant," "The Devoted Friend," and "The Remarkable Rocket" (all 1888); and "The Young King," "The Birthday of the Infanta," "The Fisherman and His Soul," and "The Star-Child" (all 1891). Each page is framed in a floral design. These stories have the puzzling Wilde twists that are his trademark. The language, while far from simple, offers entertaining side-effects.
Note: For another telling of "The Fisherman and His Soul," see Neil Philip's *Fairy Tales of the Brothers Grimm.*

Wilde, Oscar. *The Happy Prince and Other Stories.* Illustrated by Charles Robinson. Afterword by Peter Glassman. <u>Books of Wonder</u>. William Morrow, 1991 (1888). 136pp.
The five stories here are "The Happy Prince," "The Nightingale and the Rose," "The Selfish Giant," "The Devoted Friend," and "The Remarkable Rocket." By the time Wilde was 28, he had published one collection of poems and some magazine pieces. It was the publication of this collection of sentimental tales, originally illustrated by Walter Crane, that jettisoned him into the world of the popular writer. Most of these tales were created by Wilde for his sons, Vyvyan and Cyril.
The pictures in this book by Charles Robinson (who first illustrated Robert Louis Stevenson's *A Child's Garden of Verses* in 1895) were done in 1913, 13 years after the author's death. They are romantic paintings and graphic, flourishing ink drawings that give tremendous mood to each story.
Related reads: Other titles in this series include *The Wonderful Wizard of Oz* by L. Frank Baum, illustrated by W. W. Denslow; *The White Company* by Sir Arthur Conan Doyle, illustrated by N. C. Wyeth; *A Connecticut Yankee in King Arthur's Court* by Mark Twain, illustrated by Trina Schart Hyman; and *Around the World in Eighty Days* by Jules Verne, illustrated by Barry Moser.

Wilde, Oscar. *An Ideal Husband.* **Dover Thrift, 2000 (1895). 78pp.**

There are 15 characters in this play, several of whom can be played by the same readers. Quick wit and repartee give this four-act drama of blackmail and social extremes a bouncing pace that will compel readers theatre participants to move through the lines with lively humor. Short sentences and clear language make it a natural for new readers and speakers of English.

 Wilde, Oscar. *The Importance of Being Earnest.* **Dover Thrift, 1990 (1899). 54pp.**

"If I ever get married, I'll certainly try to forget the fact," announces Algernon to Jack, who is known as Ernest in town. This whimsical three-act play is full of adult wit and innuendo that will delight listeners and entertain readers at all levels. The sentences are short and full of wit. This is an ideal group reading text that could accommodate 18 players.

 Wilde, Oscar. *Little Hans (The Devoted Friend).* **Illustrated by Robert Quackenbush. Bobbs-Merrill Company, 1969 (1888). 48pp.**

Linnet tells the water-rat the story of a "not very distinguished" gardener, Hans, and his friend, big Hugh the Miller. Hans is pleased to have a friend, even though the rich man never gives him anything as a show of friendship except talk of friendship, which is far more valuable than actions—says Hugh. But at last Hugh promises to give Hans his broken wheelbarrow, and based on that promise extracts all manner of flowers and services from the gardener, and finally his life. There is a moral in this story, but you will have to see the way Oscar Wilde put the tale together to grasp it.

Wilde, Oscar [1854–1900]. *The Picture of Dorian Gray.* **Illustrated by Tony Ross. The Whole Story. Viking, 2000 (1890). 269pp.**

Dorian Gray is first introduced through a painting that details the most attractive physical traits a young man of his time could exhibit. The artist vows never to show the picture publicly, however, and his friend finds this attitude most peculiar. It will be many years later and many pages into the book before the reader learns that this mystical portrait is, in fact, a cover for a man who is capable of the most evil of indiscretions, yet who never seems to age. Subtle horror creeps upon the reader as the secret is revealed.

The margins of this edition present a wealth of information about the times in which the author and his subject lived. There is an 1881 magazine cartoon with Wilde's head as the center of a flower. Other marginal notes are illustrated with drawings by Gustave Doré, photos of vintage furniture, and hospital and scientific laboratory scenes. The *Dorian Gray* story illustrations are loosely sketched ink drawings with colored washes. Although the language is not simple, the large print and generous illustrations support the reader very nicely. For further support and a chance to practice reading aloud, see the skit based on the chapter 2 discussion of the new portrait, "The Picture of Dorian Gray," in *Readers Theatre for Young Adults* by Kathy Latrobe and Mildred Laughlin. Also supportive, the audio recording of this book makes great entertainment, but there are so many details that readers will want a copy handy for reference and review. This is a fine morality and values discussion starter.

Audio version: *The Picture of Dorian Gray*. Recorded Books, 1997. 6 cassettes, 9 hours. Read by Steven Crossley.

 Wilde, Oscar [1854–1900]. *Salomé*. **Illustrated by Aubrey Beardsley. Dover Publications, 1967 (1893). 79pp.**

Here is a simple tale of incest, jealousy, a woman scorned, pride, and murder. First written in French by Oscar Wilde (Fingal O'Flahertie Wills; and finally in Paris as Sebastian Melmoth), this one-act play was in rehearsal at the Palace Theatre with the famed Madame Sarah Bernhardt in the title role when censors attacked it. Then Lord Alfred Douglas translated it into English, whereupon it was again censored. Having been chided in the press for his low tale, Wilde responded to the editor of the *Times* on Thursday, March 2, 1893, in a letter that at first condemns the critics' credentials and then denies that he, Wilde, had written the play for one artist, Bernhardt. "I have never written a play for any actor or actress, nor shall I ever do so. Such work is for the artisan in literature—not for the artist" (page xiv).

Oddly, the illustrator, Aubrey Beardsley, liked neither the author nor the play, but delivered what is considered one of his most successful collections. Richard Strauss wrote an opera by the same name based on the story line, reaffirming the power of one art form to inspire another. Beardsley's dramatic black-and-white ink illustrations, though elegant, show male and female frontal nudity that may offend some readers. The margins of this large format reproduction are wide, but the print is small. There are 13 speaking parts and two groups, making it a candidate for an adult class read-aloud or readers theatre production.

Related reads: Other Wilde titles include *Poems; The Happy Prince, and Other Tales* (fairy stories); *The House of Pomegranates* (fairy stories); *Lady Windermere's Fan* (a play); and *A Woman of No Importance*.

Chapter 5

Modernism

Modernism was a movement that began at the turn of the twentieth century and lasted until the last half of the century, taking its strongest cue from post–World War I discrepancies in society. According to T. S. Eliot, the ordered world of the nineteenth century was incongruent with "the immense paranormal of futility and anarchy which is contemporary history." Many radical political attitudes displaced the ordered and predictable patriotism of the prior generation. Fascists were chic, and speaking against the government was popular. But attitudes could not be contained within the cup of politics; literature, too, dipped into the realm of the iconoclast. Writers disavowed the straightforward cause and effect sequences of earlier novels. Philosophy and irony created moral and dramatic tensions as authors employed ambiguity, flashbacks, self-ridicule, and open disgust for the proper order of things past. Perfect endings didn't fit the known world. And stories didn't sound the same. The language used and the process of getting from place to place in the modernist story were more important than the content.

This chapter covers works written by authors from the early 1900s up through the 1950s. Authors in this chapter are listed alphabetically; titles within each section are grouped by reading levels:

 Start Here!

 Next Read

 Support Here

 Challenging Read

James Baldwin (1924–1987) Collection

Born into poverty to a soon-widowed, beautiful mother, James Baldwin had none of the outward makings of a great American author. Then his mother remarried and began to have children who were each, in turn, to become his charges. Never appreciated by his preacher stepfather, Baldwin was nonetheless encouraged to work at church, and he became an orator of some consequence while he was still a child. It was at the local library that Baldwin may have gotten most of his formal literary training, for he read every book in the place. It was his work as a child preacher that gave him the time and solitude away from his household commitments that he needed write his sermons, the time needed to practice.

Discovery of his homosexuality served only to complicate Baldwin's life. It was not an acceptable condition for anyone in the 1950s, least of all a poor black man. Yet he overcame many of the antisocial behaviors that most whites and many blacks slung his way. In part through time, in the more welcoming environment of Paris, James Baldwin developed an extraordinary philosophy of tolerance and love. He strove through his works to make this earth a better place. Baldwin said that we can all be better than we are.

Over time Baldwin's works earned both condemnation and praise. His book *The Fire Next Time* was believed by some to be an incitement to riots, though the work itself speaks clearly of tolerance. Among his moments of praise were honors including: a *Partisan Review* Fellowship, a National Institute of Arts and Letters Award, and a Guggenheim Fellowship. His novels could eventually be found in mainstream public libraries, and his short stories appeared in magazines such as *Playboy*. And what greater praise than to have a peer such as Maya Angelou write him a poem of dedication. Baldwin's stories resonate not only with minority readers, but with any reader interested in equality and justice. The themes of racism, pride, and freedom are as relevant today as when the books were written.

 Angelou, Maya. "Ailey, Baldwin, Floyd, Killens, and Mayfield."
In *I Shall Not Be Moved*, 47, 48. Random House, 1990. 48pp.

> In this poem, Angelou memorializes James Baldwin, his style of writing, and his philosophy of life. The serious themes are delivered in light turns of phrase, very short lines on pages with lots of white space. The print is not large, but the placement of the text is easy on the eyes.

Baldwin, James. *Little Man, Little Man.* **Illustrated by Yoran Cazac. Dial Press, 1976. 96pp.**

In comic book format, with loose, whimsical cartoon figures; the games, fears, terrors, and secrets of Harlem life are revealed through two boys, WT and TJ. From frivolous events to menacing elements, using a dialect of primarily present-tense singular, Baldwin tells how it is. (Anyone who is overly sensitive to "ain't" should pass this book up.) The flap reads "A children's story for adults, an adult story for children . . ."

 Baldwin, James. *Go Tell It on the Mountain.* **Laureleaf, 1985 (1952). 221pp.**

Confronting racism, poverty, and life of the unloved child, Baldwin reveals Harlem family life and the powerful impact of religion through this fiction that seems far more autobiographical than is reported. The book is organized into three sections: "The Seventh Day," "The Prayers of the Saints," and "The Threshing Floor." In lively condemnation of his motherland, Baldwin lays out each little flaw in absolutely stunning, very personal situations. The format of the book and Baldwin's conversational approach support comprehension.

 Baldwin, James. *Early Novels and Stories.* **Selected by Toni Morrison. The Library of America, 1998. 970pp.**

More than a collection of Baldwin works, this is a tribute to one of America's most inspired authors. The works have been published elsewhere in individual book form and most can usually be found in libraries. *Giovanni's Room* was Baldwin's first attempt at writing about homosexuality, and the subject was way ahead of the times. It remains a title that is not always on library shelves. Included in this one volume are three novels and a short story collection—*Go Tell It on the Mountain, Giovanni's Room, Another Country,* and *Going to Meet the Man*—followed by Chronology 1924–1987," "Notes on Texts," and "Notes."

Anyone doing research on James Baldwin or his works will be well served by this anthology. The chronology contains dates and full-paragraph biographical discussions that are full of easy-to-understand language. The onionskin-thin pages make the book weigh less than it might. Even so, this is a book to read in the library or at a table, not on the bus.

 Baldwin, James. *The Fire Next Time.* **Vintage Books, 1993 (1963). 106pp.**

Starting with a letter to his nephew and namesake, son of his half-brother, Baldwin urges the angry, apparently self-loathing lad to become a better person than he may believe possible. He begins by giving the youth a sense of personal history, tracing the nephew's face to his father's face and back to the face of his grandfather (Baldwin's stepfather). Then, in simple reporting, Baldwin tells how important the nephew's day of birth was, who was there, and how the family drew hope from his arrival. Through very clear, uncomplicated language, Baldwin suggests that we can all improve upon who we are. This nonfiction book is an excellent introduction to one of the great American authors.

 Baldwin, James. *Just Above My Head.* **Dial Press, 1978, 1979. 597pp. Parts first appeared as "Have Mercy,"** *Penthouse* **(July 1978).**

A story of the power of religion over the individual and the force of the unconventional individual on his universe reads like Baldwin's own life experience. This novel jumps with gospel music, the Holy Spirit, homosexuality, old time religion, and Harlem, and is sprinkled throughout with lyrics from spirituals. It is not for the meek or the prudish. It is a powerful document, written in accessible, though often blasphemous, language.

Related reads: A few of the many other books by James Baldwin (not illustrated) are *The Amen Corner, Another Country, Blues for Mister Charlie, The Devil Finds Work, Giovanni's Room, Going to Meet the Man, If Beale Street Could Talk, One Day, When I Was Lost,* and *Tell Me How Long the Train's Been Gone.*

Willa Sibert Cather (1873–1947) Collection

The life of Willa Cather appears to have been a model for how to have a life that will produce one of the most influential writers of her time. Most of her books draw on the rugged experiences of her own childhood, and her education provided both formal and informal means to achieve literary success. She and twin brother William were born to Sheriff Charles Cather and Mary Virginia Boak Cather, in the farming community of Black Creek Valley, Virginia, near the Blue Ridge Mountains. Then the entire family—Willa, her two brothers, sister Jessica, her maternal grandmother, and Willa's parents—moved to become homesteaders with Willa's paternal grandparents in Webster County, Nebraska, where they stayed for one year. Then they moved to Red Cloud, Nebraska, where her father opened a minimally successful insurance and loan business.

Meanwhile, Mrs. Cather attempted to make ladies of her daughters, a plan that proved futile with the willful Willa, who cut her hair, wore boy's clothing, and loved horseback riding. Willa also met Annie Sadilek, the model for the lead character in the book *My Antonia*. After her graduation from Red Cloud High in 1890, Willa moved to Lincoln and soon entered the University of Nebraska, where she fell in love with the school athlete, Louise Pound. She also became active in journalism, published articles in local papers, and wrote short stories. Her 1892 story "Peter" was destined to become part of *My Antonia* (1918). Though eventually she would hold doctoral degrees in literature from the University of Nebraska, University of Michigan, University of California, Columbia, Princeton, and Yale, in 1895 she graduated from the University of Nebraska, ready to conquer the world, but she returned to Red Cloud.

When she was offered an editing position at *Home Monthly* in Pittsburgh, she went, calling Pittsburgh the birthplace of her writing career. In 1903 she published a book of poems, *April Twilights*. And she wrote stories for the magazine, which later became her 1905 book of short stories, *Troll Garden*. In 1906 she moved to New York and eventually became managing editor of *McClure's Magazine*, leaving there in 1912, on the advice of writer Sarah Orne, to begin her career as a full-time novelist. *Alexander's Bridge* (1912) was her first work as a career novelist. That same year she became entranced by the Anasazi cliff dwellings. *O Pioneers* was published the following year.

Then an unending font of literary works poured forth. *A Lost Lady* (1923), a modernist feminine story set in a prairie frame, is considered by many critics to be one of her two best works. The other is a story of two saints, *Death Comes for the Archbishop* (1927). *One of Ours*, about a Western lad in World War I, won the 1922 Pulitzer Prize. In 1931 Cather's mother died, and in the same year she published *Shadows on the Rock*. In 1933 she won the Prix Femina Americaine for her literary accomplishments. She published *Lucy Gayheart* in 1935 and *Sapphira and the Slave Girl* in 1940. In 1944 she was awarded the Gold Medal by the National Institute of Arts.

Although she never wrote directly about gender issues because such writing would not have been accepted by publishers or most readers of the day, her longtime love was Edith Lewis. They lived together in New York for 40 years. Willa Cather died at home on April 24, 1947, leaving behind the stipulation that her letters be burned. *The Old Beauty and Others*, a short story collection, was published posthumously in 1948.

Cather, Willa Sibert. *Alexander's Bridge.* **Introduction by Hermione Lee. Virago, 2002 (1912). Dial Books, 1997. 176pp.**

When respected, successful, and successfully married Boston bridge architect Bartley Alexander is engaged on a job in London, he unexpectedly becomes involved with a now-celebrated Irish actress and old flame. The affair propels Alexander into a double life that creates turmoil in his inner self and his work. The metaphorical bridge is the one between Alexander's past and his future. This is a mid-life crisis story, first published in serial form in *McClure's* magazine in 1912, before the term had been coined or the problem identified. The print is easy on the eyes. This is a good reference text for those interested in sociology, psychology, or turn-of-the-century (nineteenth-century) mores.

Audio version: *Alexander's Bridge.* Blackstone Audiobooks, 2000. 2 cassettes; 3 hours. Read by Marguerite Gavin.

Related read: A good follow-up read is *Uncle Valentine and Other Stories: Willa Cather's Uncollected Short Fiction 1915–1929.*

 Cather, Willa Sibert. *Alexander's Bridge.* **Sun Hill Rose and Briar Books, 2000 (1912). 208**pp.

 Cather, Willa. *Uncle Valentine and Other Stories: Willa Cather's Uncollected Short Fiction 1915–1929.* **Edited by Bernice Slote. University of Nebraska Press, 1973. 183pp.**

These stories are grouped into two sections: Pittsburgh stories ("Uncle Valentine" and "Double Birthday") and New York stories ("Consequences," "The Bookkeeper's Wife," "Ardessa," "Her Boss," "Coming, Eden Bower!"). Cather's even style is very easy to follow, and there is lots of dialogue.

 Cather, Willa. *Willa Cather: Early Novels and Stories: The Troll Garden, O Pioneers! The Song of the Lark, My Ántonia, One of Ours.* **Edited by Sharon O'Brien. The Library of America, 1989. 1,337pp.**

The titles in this volume are each very readable in their own right. After reading *Alexander's Bridge,* readers will be used to Willa Cather's style. The collection ends with a chronology and two sets of notes. The chronology looks like paragraphs but is mainly key point phrases. For example, midway through the 1911 marker it says, "Over the summer begins *Alexander's Bridge,* novel portraying a Western-born engineer's discomfort with his upper class Eastern World." The note on the texts contains valuable information about how the editing process modified the works. This three-page discussion is a great writing process discussion starter. Readers may want to begin with *Alexander's Bridge* or *Uncle Valentine and Other Stories: Willa Cather's Uncollected Short Fiction 1915–1929* (both annotated above).

Related reads: Other Cather titles include *O Pioneers, One of Ours* (Pulitzer Prize Winner), *Song of the Lark, My Antonia, The Troll Garden* (short stories), *Old Beauty and Others* (short stories), *Death Comes for the Archbishop, Shadows in the Rock, Lucy Gayheart,* and *Sapphira and the Slave Girl.*

William Faulkner (1897–1962) Collection

Born into an established New Albany, Mississippi, family in 1897, with a colorful great-grandfather who had served as a Confederate colonel and then as a politician, as well as writing fiction himself, and a lawyer grandfather who owned a railroad, William Faulkner enjoyed a secure early childhood, although the family moved to Oxford, Mississippi, when he was five. He hated school, dropping out of high school, but he did take some university classes later on. It is apparent that his voracious reading habit was his primary source of education. Critics recognize the stream of consciousness influence of James Joyce in *The Sound and the Fury.*

It could be said that Faulkner's literary career began in childhood, as the boy seemed always to be writing. As a boy, he also had aspirations to be an artist. He contemplated a graphic arts career, and at the age of 14 attempted to get his drawings published, illustrated his letters, and kept sketchbooks. He also became contributing illustrator to the University of Mississippi annuals. In addition, he also created small hand-made, hand-lettered, sometimes illustrated books, which he either gave away or sold. In 1920 he gave such a book, called *Lilacs,* to his friend Phil Stone. That same year, he produced a handful of copies of *Marionettes,* a play (a copy of which sold for $35,000 in 1975). He self-published *The Marble Faun,* a book of poems, in 1924. And two years later, he gave two gift books to his love interest, Helen Baird: *Mayday,* annotated below, and *Helen: A Courtship.* That same year, he gave the keepsake book of his poems, *Royal Street,* to Estelle Oldham Franklin, whom he married 10 years later. Although the recipients of these books clearly understood Faulkner and valued his work, most of the copies have been lost or destroyed in house fires.

He published his first novel, *Soldiers' Pay,* in 1926, followed by *Flags in the Dust (Sartoris).* Readers will see that Faulkner drew on family history, most especially the violent death of his great-grandfather, and the strong Mississippi traditions and attitudes about race, for the characters and details of his works. He wrote *As I Lay Dying* in the same year that he married Estelle Oldham. In 1950 he received the Nobel Prize for Literature. On July 6, 1962, he died of a heart attack.

The books in this collection give a view of the range of Faulkner's gifts. Readers can easily find copies of many of his books in print and on audiocassette in public libraries.

Faulkner, William. *Mayday.* **Introduction by Carvel Collins. University of Notre Dame Press, 1976 (1926). 88pp.**

The object of the author's affections, Helen Baird, received the only copy of the first edition, dated January 27, 1926, of this hand-written allegory that Faulkner also illustrated. He wanted to marry Ms. Baird and twice proposed. She didn't accept his offer, but she did appreciate the little bound book that tells of the trials of Sir Galwyn, a young knight who is off in search of the perfect woman. After encountering Hunger and Pain, who became his constant companions, Sir Galwyn does have three trysts that seem less exciting to him after the fact. As he travels, he has many a satirical thought and conversations that deliver his philosophy of life . . . or at least philosophy of the heart. Hunger remarks on the abysmal outcomes of the knight's encounters with the three females, each of whom had much to recommend her, including prospects for providing good employment opportunities to the knight:

> I remember to have remarked once that man is a buzzing insect blundering through a strange world, seeking something he can neither name nor recognize, and probably will not want. I think now that I shall refine this aphorism to: Man is a buzzing fly beneath the inverted glass tumbler of his illusions.

With such a topical story, it is not difficult to imagine how Helen Baird managed to ignore Faulkner. The first 41 pages of this little book provide a wealth of background on the author's views of romance, Faulkner's career, and how the single copy came to be in a university collection (which has yielded the book discussed here). Faulkner produced a number of hand-written gift books, most of which are lost. This trade book edition is well worth finding at a public library and reading slowly. The first part of the story takes a bit of getting used to, but then the author's metaphors and turns of phrase mix with an ever-present sense of humor. Collins, in the introduction to this book, spells out how literary devices and content in *Mayday* appear to have served as cornerstones for Faulkner's novels.

 Faulkner, William. *As I Lay Dying*. The corrected text. The Modern Library, 2000 (1930). 261pp.

Addie Bundren just watches as her various family members come forward to tell parts of their stories and how they manage to get through life on their Mississippi backwater farm. Addie Bundren is lying abed. She is dying. Her dying wish is to be taken back to Jefferson, Mississippi, for burial—far away from this place. The occasion of her dying, when she dies, and her distant burial trip have different meanings for the various members of the household who speak their interests in turn, chapter by chapter.

The simple folk in this poignant tale speak in a Southern dialect, using turns of phrase that Faulkner (1897–1962) knew well as a Mississippi native son. The paragraphs in this book are very short, some just a couple of sentences, some just a sentence. This format, and the easy-on-the-eyes print of the Modern Library edition, make the book accessible to the new reader. Internal support may also be found in the three-page introductory biography of the Nobel Prize winner. As a read-aloud, it could promote dialogue about high school dropouts and the power of reading for the success of the writer, two points that cannot be overlooked in this essay. The other obvious discussion topics are death, dying, and relationships.

Audio version: *As I Lay Dying.* Books On Tape, 1994. 8 cassettes; 12 hours. Read by Wolfram Kandinsky.

Related reads: Other Faulkner novels include *The Sound and the Fury, Light in August, Pylon, The Unvanquished, The Wild Palms, Intruder in the Dust, Requiem for a*

Nun, A Fable, The Town, The Mansion, and *The Reivers* (1962 Pulitzer Prize). Faulkner screenplays include *To Have and Have Not, The Big Sleep,* and *Land of the Pharaohs.*

Faulkner, William. *The Sound and the Fury.* **The Corrected Text. (Vintage International), Random House Trade, 1991 (1929). 336pp.**

After the Civil War, the demise of the old and powerful Compson family begins. The main character, Caddy, is described from the points of view of her three brothers:the "idiot" Benjy; neurotic Quentin, who is obsessed with his own shortcomings regarding the family holdings and the loss of his sister's virginity and with it the family honor; and Jason, the evil and insolent harborer of hatred for all categories of people.

Faulkner addresses issues of prejudice and the destructiveness of internalized bigotry. In this book, considered his most powerful work, he employs the multiple perspectives technique to give the reader the full picture. The emotional content, combined with carefully crafted sentences, make this a work of art. The recorded book will support new readers. Selected passages also serve well as read-aloud and discussion topics.

Audio version: *The Sound and the Fury.* Books On Tape, 1995. 6 cassettes, 9 hours. Read by Grover Gardner.

F. Scott Fitzgerald (1896–1940) Collection

Born in Saint Paul, Minnesota, on September 24, 1896, and having attended Princeton University (although he withdrew due to poor grades), Francis Scott Key Fitzgerald was destined to make an indelible impact on the literary scene. Dead of a heart attack at the age of 44, the golden boy of the flapper era had lived the extremes of happiness and misery with his beautiful wife, the artist, dancer, and writer Zelda Sayer. The popularity of *This Side of Paradise* (1920) and *The Great Gatsby* in 1925, and the tragedy of Zelda's mental breakdown in 1930, exacerbated by Fitzgerald's excesses in his personal life and his alcohol consumption. His literary career went on the skids, making life miserable. Furthermore, critics failed to give him his due. Yet he was paid a great compliment by Ernest Hemingway, when that author cited Fitzgerald in the now-famous *Esquire* magazine story "The Snows of Kilimanjaro." Fitzgerald was less complimentary to himself. Describing his 15 months' service in World War I, which began in October 1917, he later claimed he was "the army's worst aide-de-camp" ("Early Success," 1937).

Prolific during the early years, Fitzgerald wrote *This Side of Paradise* (1921), *The Beautiful and the Damned* (published serially in *Metropolitan Magazine* from September 1921 to March 1922 and then in book form in 1922); *The Great Gatsby* (1925); *Tender Is the Night: A Romance* (1934, and with revisions as *Tender Is the Night* in 1960); *The Last Tycoon: An Unfinished Novel,* which was published together with "The Great Gatsby" and

Selected Stories (1941); and numerous short stories, plays, media adaptations, and extensive correspondence. In 1939, he worked on the scripts of *Winter Carnival, The Women,* and *Gone With the Wind.* His easy-to-follow writing style makes the complex plots and tumultuous themes of the flapper era accessible.

 Turnbull, Andrew, ed. *F. Scott Fitzgerald: Letters to His Daughter.* Introduction by Frances Fitzgerald Lanahan. Charles Scribner's Sons, 1963. 172pp.

In the opening letter to his daughter, on August 8, 1933, F. Scott Fitzgerald lists things to worry about, starting with "Worry about courage," and he lists things not to worry about, starting with "Don't worry about popular opinion." He closes with an admonishment for her having called him *Pappy.* In her introduction to this book, Frances Fitzgerald Lanahan, or Scottie, describes the inherent loneliness in the writer's life. Lanahan concludes that had he not been her father, and had she been able to follow his advice, she would have been an extraordinary woman. She's right. These letters carry at once the sting of a dictator's lash and the wisdom of an artist who does not want his progeny repeating the mistakes of *his* youth.

In Turnbull's editor's note (page xvii), he notes Fitzgerald's propensity for misspelling. Then he gives several examples of the inconsistencies between Fitzgerald's spellings and the standard spellings of those words. Such a revelation will come as no surprise to the new reader who holds close a great novel that is yet to be put to paper. These short passages are by no means simplified, and there are no pictures. But they are loaded with examples of emotionally charged writing by one of the finest writers of his time. We would all do well to learn from his example—at writing, if not parenting. This book has an index.

Related reads: Other books of Fitzgerald letters include *The Letters of F. Scott Fitzgerald* and *Dear Scott/Dear Max.*

 Fitzgerald, F. Scott. *The Great Gatsby.* Charles Scribner's Sons, 1925. 182pp.

Nick Carraway is mesmerized by the dynamism of the lifestyle and persona of his mysterious neighbor, Jay Gatsby, the man who can buy it all. Little does he understand that everything the Great Gatsby accomplished has been for the love of Daisy Buchanan, a Louisville beauty on the other side of Long Island Sound, who caught the eye of the young Gatsby when he was too poor to keep her attention. Even though Daisy marries the wealthy, philandering thug Tom Buchanan, the Great Gatsby continues to feed his infatuation for her. He becomes a man consumed.

Carraway is the intrigued recorder of all that makes up this godlike persona, who indulges his guests with all the heavenly delights of the Jazz Age, and of all that ultimately brings Gatsby back to earth, where tragedy awaits. The language in this gut-wrenching story is not difficult. Only the print size and number of pages will make it a challenge. Some readers will want to open it at random, reading and then backing through to read a different spot. Every section is so compellingly written that there are no bad reads. It has been recorded by many gifted voices over the decades, but listening to this book is not the same as reading it slowly and savoring the elegant way Fitzgerald put pen to paper. A new reader may want to listen to a recording and then revisit the book at random from time to time. The video versions add yet a different dimension to this classic work.

Audio version: There are a number of audio versions, including:

> *The Great Gatsby.* Audio Partners Publishing, 2002. Read by Alexander Scourby

> *The Great Gatsby.* Recorded Books Steady Reader, 2001. 6 cassettes, 5 hours. Read by Frank Muller. The Steady Reader edition is simply read at a slower pace to facilitate following along. Beginner-level ESL students may appreciate being able to hear words spoken more distinctly.

> *The Great Gatsby.* Recorded Books, 1989. 3 cassettes, 4.5 hours, Read by Frank Muller.

Video versions:

> *The Great Gatsby.* A&E Network, 2001. 1 videocassette, 100 minutes. Starring Mira Sorvino, Toby Stephens, Paul Rudd, and Martin Donovan.

> *The Great Gatsby.* Paramount Pictures, 1997. 1 videocassette, 146 minutes. Produced by David Merrick. Directed by Jack Clayton Starring Robert Redford, Mia Farrow, Karen Black, Scott Wilson, Sam Waterston, Lois Chiles, and Bruce Dern.

Fitzgerald, F. Scott. *Trimalchio: An Early Version of* **The Great Gatsby. Edited by James L. W. West III. Cambridge University Press, 2000 (ca. 1921). 192**pp.

The manuscript F. Scott Fitzgerald submitted to his editor, Max Perkins, in 1924 was vastly different from the final product, which finally had a change of title. Until now, only a handful of scholars have had access to this pre-revision edition. This is a scholarly work about the scholarly process of editing. It shows the record of variants—how a finished book went from a very fine idea to a great one. One hundred forty-one pages of the book are the actual text of Fitzgerald's first attempt at this story. Appendix 2 is a note on *Trimalchio*, explaining that Trimalchio was a freed slave who had grown wealthy and hosted a banquet in the *Satyricon* by Petronius (ca. A.D. 27–66), and discussing the literary import of the banquet scene. There are copies of letters from Max Perkins in one appendix. The Cambridge University Press edition shows the wide margins and the way in which Fitzgerald made his numerous corrections. Even so, the text is quite readable and is a pleasure to read. Educators may want to select passages from this book to illustrate that the struggle to hone written language is not unique to the new reader.

Related reads: Other novels by Fitzgerald include *Tender Is the Night, The Beautiful and Damned,* and *This Side of Paradise.* Short story collections by Fitzgerald include *The Basil and Josephine Stories; The Pat Hobby Stories; Taps at Reveille; Six Tales of the Jazz Age and Other Stories; Flappers and Philosophers; Stories of F. Scott Fitzgerald; Babylon Revisited and Other Stories;* and *Bits of Paradise, Uncollected Stories by Scott and Zelda Fitzgerald.*

Fitzgerald, F. Scott. *Trimalchio: A Facsimile Edition of the Original Galley Proofs for* **The Great Gatsby [box set]. Afterword by Matthew J. Bruccoli. University of South Carolina Press, 2000 (1924). 64pp.**

The original text, *Trimalchio,* written by Fitzgerald while he was in France, is a complete and satisfying story, in many ways quite different from the final *Great Gatsby.* This is a facsimile of the only known set of 1924 galley proofs, complete with Fitzgerald's notorious hand-written misspellings and request for a title change. These unbound pages are about 24 inches long and are reportedly difficult to handle. The original can be found in the Fitzgerald collection of the Cooper Library at the University of South Carolina. The famous Fitzgerald spelling may give license to the would-be author-in-development.

E. M. Forster (1879–1970) Collection

Born in London on New Year's Day, 1879, to Edward Morgan Llewellyn and Alice Clara Forster, E. M. Forster was educated at King's College and Cambridge University. He held memberships in the American Academy of Arts and Letters, the Bavarian Academy of Fine Arts, and the Reform Club, and was president of the Cambridge Humanists. After receiving his master's degree in 1901, Forster traveled to Greece and Italy. *Where Angels Fear to Tread* first appeared in 1905. In 1912 the author arrived in India, where his literary efforts began to blossom, although *A Passage to India* did not emerge until 1924. A four-year stint as a Red Cross volunteer in Alexandria (1915–1919) also provided grist for his fiction and nonfiction mills. *Pharos and Pharillon,* a history, was published by Knopf in 1924. *Aspects of the Novel* (Clark Lecture, 1927), published by Harcourt, is still in print and serves as a guide to those who are studying the craft of novel writing.

Forster, E. M. *The Hill of Devi*. Harcourt on Demand, 1971 (1953). 267pp.

This autobiography includes details about Edward Morgan Forster's year as personal secretary to an Indian maharajah. The reader learns about the culture, customs, rituals, and politics in 1912, which are linked directly to the characters in *A Passage to India*. Letters that have some unfamiliar references give an insider's opinion of a thrilling life. Historic photographs give a clear impression of relationships.

Audio version: *The Hill of Devi*. Books On Tape, Inc., 1995. 6 cassettes, 6 hours. Read by David Case.

Forster, E. M. *A Passage to India*. A Harvest/HBJ Book, Harcourt Brace Jovanovich, 1924 and 1952. 322pp.

Traveling with her prospective mother-in-law in search of her city magistrate fiancé, Adela imagines she has been accosted by the gentle and accommodating Dr. Aziz. The story sets in motion an almost unstoppable chain of repercussions that show how difficult it is for people to become friends in the face of political, social, and religious differences.

As personal secretary to a maharajah in 1921 (detailed in his autobiography *The Hill of Devi*), Forster learned much about the country and culture that informs this novel. For the sociology student, this classic study in British–Indian race relations of the 1920s could easily be compared to those in the American South of the 1950s or anywhere there are fixed lines of demarcation between groups. For the ESL student there is lots of dialogue in what is now considered Forster's greatest work of fiction. This is not a simple tale, but it is clearly told and can be savored slowly, especially in a discussion group. Listening to some of the audio recording can boost the reader into this text.

Audio version: *A Passage to India*. Newman Books-on-Cassette, 1984. 2 cassettes, 2 hours, 56 minutes. Read by Ben Kingsley. This abridged performance by Academy Award winner Ben Kingsley reveals one of the truly great readers of our time. Any literary group would benefit from hearing his recording.

Video version: *A Passage to India*. Columbia Pictures Home Video, 1985. 1 videocassette, 163 minutes. Starring Peggy Ashcroft, Judy Davis, James Fox, Alec Guinness, Nigel Havers, and Victor Banerjee.

Forster, E. M. *A Room with a View*. Alfred A. Knopf, 1989 (1908). 242pp.

Lucy Honeychurch is imprisoned by the social customs of her guardians, who engage in snobbery that prevents the young woman from engaging in any strong relationships. While on holiday with a friend in Italy, she complains that her room has no view. The lower-class expatriate, Mr. Emerson, offers his own room and that of his son. This sets in motion a flurry of inner conflicts, social discord, and a view of life as Lucy has never understood it before. On her return to England, her engagement to a shallow young man of her own class proves a stark contrast to the glimpse of that other reality. To find out who she marries, you have to read the book. Or in your library you may find a video of the 1986 movie based on this story.

Audio versions:

> *A Room with a View.* Recorded Books, 1993. 6 cassettes, 8.25 hours. Read by John Franklyn-Robbins.

> *A Room with a View.* Blackstone Audiobooks, 1992. 5 cassettes, 7.5 hours. Read by Frederick Davidson.

Related reads: Other E. M. Forster titles include *Where Angels Fear to Tread; Howard's End; The Longest Journey; Abinger Harvest; Life to Come and Other Short Stories; The Last Nine Days of the "Bismarck"*; and the *Hornblower* saga, starting with *Mr. Midshipman Hornblower* and ending with *Admiral Hornblower in the West Indies*

Ernest Hemingway (1899–1961) Collection

A quintessentially American storyteller, Ernest Hemingway began his writing career as a journalist, then writing about his adventures in novels and short stories. During World War I he served as a volunteer ambulance driver. In 1921 he met Gertrude Stein, F. Scott Fitzgerald, Ezra Pound, and other literary figures in Paris. He won the Pulitzer Prize for *The Old Man and the Sea* and the Nobel Prize for Literature in 1954.

Because of the way Hemingway reveals details about those locales and because of his sensitivity to history and culture, he is highly appreciated and often studied in Mexico and South America. A victim of disabling diabetes, he killed himself in 1961. The unpublished works he left behind continued to be introduced for another 20 years.

 Hemingway, Ernest [1899–1961]. *The Old Man and the Sea.*. **Illustrated by C. F. Tunnicliffe and Raymond Sheppard. Introduction by Charles Scribner Jr. Scribner Classics, 1996 (1952). 93pp.**

The old Cuban fisherman, his need to make one prize catch, and the respect bestowed upon him by the young boy who looks after him provide universal themes. The old man's days on the sea as he battles the great marlin in the Gulf Stream—talking with it, coaxing it, and finally defending it against the savage sharks—is at once an emotional roller coaster ride and a spiritual experience. It earned Ernest Hemingway the Nobel Prize for literature in 1953, and was the last Hemingway novel published before his death. Initially a story published in *Life* magazine, this very thin book is a gold mine for the reader who is unsure of venturing past short stories. With sensational ink illustrations throughout this slim, hardbound edition, this copy is a joy to hold, to peruse, and to read.

Related reads: See the struggle of a man against a sea beast also in *The Black Pearl* by Scott O'Dell, and in *Moby Dick* by Herman Melville (annotated in chapter 4).

Hemingway, Ernest. *A Farewell to Arms.* **Charles Scribner's Sons, 1995 (1929). 332pp.**

Set in the Italy of World War I, this tale of an American lieutenant ambulance driver and an English nurse bears the everlasting features of romance, wartime love, and the inevitable tragedies that befall young lovers again and again throughout history. The unabridged reading by Alexander Adams (below) is unrelentingly strong, the voice of the reader methodically marching through sunshine, rain, and snow to deliver the voice of one of America's greatest short story writers and novelists. Hemingway's simple language and repetitive use of words make this long book an easy read for all but the beginner in reading or English. Listening to the audio book will be a very fine experience for anyone.

Audio version: *A Farewell to Arms.* Books on Tape, 1999. 6 tapes, 1.5 hours each or 9 hours listening time. Read by Alexander Adams.

 Hemingway, Hilary, and Jeffry P. Lindsay. *Hunting with Hemingway, Based on the Stories of Leicester Hemingway.* **Riverhead Books, 2000. 317pp.**

Ernest Hemingway's younger brother, Leicester, ended his life in what Hilary Hemingway calls the family tradition—by suicide. Fifteen years later Leicester's wife died and left their daughter Hilary an audio recording, on which the voices of her father, her famous uncle, and others revisited hunting trips—unbelievably tall tales of Hemingway proportions of hunting, exotic game, diabetes, and drinking—that were later corroborated by a little bundle of artifacts. Through this reporting of the post mortem audio message, Hilary Hemingway came to grips with her own grief and her father's humanity and began to let go of her own resentment at what had seemed the ultimate cowardice. This simply written text is filled with both the definitive exotic game hunters' yarns and the emotional roller coaster of a daughter who had never gotten to bid her gregarious, diabetic father farewell. The audio recording will provide support for the new reader.

Audio version: *Hunting With Hemingway.* Abridged. HighBridge Company, 2000. 2 cassettes, approximately 3 hours. Read by Hilary Hemingway, whose tale of compassionate, personal discovery propels this unique insight into the lives of her father and his famous brother.

 Hemingway, Ernest. "The Snows of Kilimanjaro." In *The Snows of Kilimanjaro and Other Stories,* **3–28. Charles Scribner and Sons, 1964 (1924). 154pp.**

"The Snows of Kilimanjaro" reveals a loveless couple who have searched for adventure in the mountains overlooking the elusive Kilimanjaro. Harry, injured beyond repair, drifts in and out of consciousness and memories of the follies that have made up his life and stories he has never written, as he is tended by the affluent, supportive woman he will never come to love. Meanwhile, the snows fall on Kilimanjaro. These 10 short reads provide a gripping introduction to Hemingway. Charlton Heston is a powerful, convincing reader in the audio edition.

Audio version: *The Snows of Kilimanjaro.* Classic Literature Caedmon Audio, recorded in 1977, remastered in 1998, digitally mastered in 1989. 1 cassette, approximately 47 minutes. Read by Charlton Heston.

 Hemingway, Ernest. *The Sun Also Rises.* Charles Scribner's Sons, 1954 (1924). 247pp.

American expatriates drinking in Spain, drinking in France, changing partners, and drinking more—the Hemingway trademark of alcohol every few pages has a familiar ring. He opens the book with a biblical quote from Ecclesiastes:

> One generation passeth away, and another generation cometh; but the earth abideth forever. . . . The sun also ariseth, and the sun goeth down, and hasteth to the place where he arose. . . . The wind goeth toward the south, and turneth about unto the north; it whirleth about continually, and the wind returneth again according to his circuits. . . . All the rivers run into the sea; yet the sea is not full; unto the place from whence the rivers come, thither they return again.

So it is with the characters as they cycle through the story: rising, setting, rising again. This book is loaded with first-person reporting and dialogue. Simple, direct conversation as people talk about the bull fights and day-to-day events: travel, going to Paris, coming from California, going to New York, coming to Spain, falling in love, leaving a lover, rejoining a lover. It is through this kind of language that the entire tale is delivered, making it a very fine source of conversational English for high beginners and up. For a much less challenging bullfight story, try *Miracle in Seville* by James Michener, annotated in this chapter.

Audio version: *The Sun Also Rises.* Books on Tape, Inc., 1988. 7 cassettes, approximately 7 hours. Read by Alexander Adams.

Related read: *Mexico,* an epic tale of bulls by James Michener, is annotated in this chapter.

 Hemingway, Ernest. *True at First Light: A Fictional Memoir.* Edited and with an introduction by Patrick Hemingway. Scribner, 1999. 320pp.

In his introduction to this book, Ernest Hemingway's son Patrick, who completed the work after his father's death, explains the political mood in Kenya during the winter of 1953–1954 (Patrick lived half his adult life there). He explains who the Mau Mau were and how they might have altered the course of life for Hemingway and his wife Mary. Told from a first-person perspective, this autobiographical novel of Hemingway, his wife, and Debba, an African woman who might become the author's second wife draws on life as the author struggles with his attachments to two cultures, two women, and lifestyles that are so unrelated that it is difficult to imagine them outside this book. Readers will learn much about the political situations that are the foundations of current conditions in Africa. This is at once a look into the personal mind of this dashing author, a view of life as understood by a white minority in the middle of the twentieth century, and an exciting work of fiction.

A cast of characters with full-paragraph descriptions at the back is a very helpful guide. A Swahili glossary is likewise. The small print has lots of white space between the lines and ample margins.

Audio version: *True at First Light*. Simon & Schuster Audio, 1999. 8 cassettes, 11 hours. Read by Brian Dennehy.

Related reads: Other Hemingway titles include *The Complete Short Stories; Dateline: Toronto; Across the River and into the Trees; Green Hill of Africa; In Our Time; The Torrents of Spring; Death in the Afternoon; The Fifth Column and Four Stories of the Spanish Civil War; For Whom the Bell Tolls; Green Hills of Africa; Men Without Women; A Moveable Feast; To Have and Have Not;* and *Winner Take Nothing*.

Langston Hughes (1902–1967) Collection

Perhaps best known as the Poet Laureate of Harlem, James Mercer Langston Hughes was born in Joplin, Missouri, on February 1, 1902. Soon after, his parents divorced and his father moved to Mexico to start a ranch. By 1907, Hughes and his mother were living in a Topeka tenement; she took him to the public library and enrolled him in an all-white school. When a teacher remarked that a Negro child did not belong there, Hughes experienced overt racism for the first time in his life. Mother and son quickly accepted Mr. Hughes's invitation to live in Mexico, far from racial strife. But upon their arrival, there was an earthquake, marking the end of his mother's interest in Mexico. They returned to the United States, and Langston was sent to live in Lawrence, Kansas, with his grandmother Langston, who told him stories about his family that instilled in him a kind of pride he had not experienced previously.

He was part Cherokee. He was the great-great-grandson of Charles Henry Langston, brother of John Mercer Langston, who in 1855 was the first black American elected to public office, had been appointed U.S. minister to Haiti, and had been a university dean. His grandmother's own father had helped escaping slaves on the Underground Railroad. Her first husband had joined John Brown at Harper's Ferry. She took him to hear Booker T. Washington to speak. By the time she died, Langston Hughes had become an avid reader, a critical part of his literary preparation. He was very much influenced by Walt Whitman and Carl Sandburg, the latter causing him to appreciate free verse. He was very much a lover of jazz. He was also greatly depressed by his parents' neglect.

In 1921 he graduated from high school and published his poem, "The Negro Speaks of Rivers" in *Brownie's Book* and later in the NAACP magazine *Crisis*. He entered Columbia University that same year as an engineering major (a major his father considered more secure than poetry), but dropped out the following year. He worked his way to Africa on a freighter and traveled down the coast. Then he spent several months in Paris and Rome, finally returning to the United States in 1924.

In 1925, he got a job as a busboy in a hotel in Washington, D.C., where he met Vachel Lindsay, who arranged for the publication of some of his work and a scholarship to Lincoln University in Pennsylvania. In 1926 he published the poem "The Weary Blues," and his controversial essay, "The Negro Artist and the Racial Mountain." He also received the Witter Bynner Undergraduate Poetry Award. In 1927, with the support of his patron, Mrs. Charlotte Mason, he published *Fine Clothes to the Jew*, now a highly-collectible volume of poetry that opens windows into the worlds of brown-skinned girls and handsome elevator boys. His graduation in 1929 from Lincoln University was followed in the next year by publication of his first novel, *Not Without Laughter*. He spent the year 1932–1933 in the Soviet Union, where he continued to move to the political left. Then he moved to Carmel, California, and in 1934 produced a volume of short stories, *The Ways of White Folks*, which revealed his depressed feelings about race relations. So did his 1935 play *Mulatto*, which dealt with miscegenation and parental abandonment. With the advent of World War II, his politics began to move nearer the center again. He published several collections of poetry: *The Dream Keeper* (1932), *Scottsboro Limited* (1932), *Shakespeare in Harlem* (1942), and *Fields of Wonder* (1947). His autobiographical *The Big Sea* was published in 1940.

He produced dramas, song-plays, novels, and newspaper columns in the *New York Post* and the *Chicago Defender* (through which he introduced and chronicled his fictional character, Jesse B. Semple/Simple). Collections of those articles were published as *Simple Speaks His Mind* (1950) and *Simple Stakes a Claim* (1957), among others. He also edited anthologies, wrote about noteworthy blacks, and produced a body of children's books. But he had begun to fall out of the mainstream of radical black culture and so received less acclaim than he had known in the past. He died of cancer in New York City on May 22, 1967. Having produced two novels, three short story collections, 16 volumes of poetry, 20 plays, and countless other works, Langston Hughes was among the most prolific writers of his time.

Cooper, Floyd. *Coming Home: From the Life of Langston Hughes.* **Philomel Books, 1994. 32pp.**

Powerful and sensitive storytelling through pictures and words make up one of the most insightful biographies ever written about Langston Hughes. This book deals with tough issues like loneliness, hunger, and racism in a context that makes the incomprehensible meaningful. The author's note gives a brief summary of Hughes's life; there is also a brief bibliography.

Hughes, Langston. *Good Morning Revolution: Uncollected Social Protest Writings by Langston Hughes.* **Edited and with an introduction by Faith Berry. Foreword by Saunders Redding. Lawrence Hill & Co., 1973. 145pp.**

"Johannesburg Mines," "Merry Christmas China," "The Soviet Union and Women," and "God to Hungry Child" are among the gut-exposing cuts Hughes makes into the social bodies of oppression at home and around the world. The poet exposes the parallels between rank and color through undeniable illustrations.

This collection of revolutionary essays and poems provides a look at the 1940s and 1950s through the eyes of one of its most profound and prolific authors. Although many of the poems appear quite brief, they require considerable digestion time and re-readings. They lend themselves to small group discussions. Some readers may want to get one of the Langston Hughes commemorative stamp pages to keep with his poetry.

Related read: Tom Feelings, *Soul Looks Back in Wonder.*

Hughes, Langston. *The Sweet and Sour Animal Book.* **Illustrated by the students from the Harlem School of the Arts. Introduction by Ben Vereen. Afterword by George P. Cunningham. Oxford University Press, 1994. 48pp.**

"There once was an ape/Who bought a cape/To wear when he went/Downtown.\The other apes\Who had no capes,\Said, "Look at that stuck-up clown!" Discovered and published posthumously, these humorous and jabbing joking rhymes are more adult than children's fare. Each of the innocent illustrations is as sophisticated as a Picasso or a Chagall.

Hughes, Langston. *Famous American Negroes.* **Dodd, Mead, 1954. 148pp.**

Now out of print, this collection of 17 biographies offers a master writer's view of the world through the experiences of Fredrick Douglass, Marian Anderson, Booker T. Washington, Jackie Robinson, Harriet Tubman, and some less well-known figures on the American horizon. These brief, easy to understand, and compellingly written biographies can still be found on library shelves, in used bookstores, and online. They are

excellent examples of short research papers. The clearly presented anecdotes lend themselves to readers theatre interpretation.

Related read: *Famous American Music Makers* is out of print, but is available online.

 Hughes, Langston, and Arna Bontemps, eds. *Book of Negro Folk-Lore.* **Dodd, Mead, 1983 (1958). 624pp.**

Poetry, ballads, animal stories, animal rhymes, folktales, spirituals,
sermons, and many other collections of short passages are in this volume.
Of special interest to users of this guide will be the very short "Slave Memories" and slightly longer "On the Levee." A reader may just enjoy opening the book and reading whatever turns up. This rich collection is full of
thought-provoking literature, with a vast supply of good stories (three
pages and under), humor, and history. There are ways of learning about
America that can't be found in traditional textbooks; for example,
Hughes's brief essay on Depression-era house rent parties, complete with
copies of some of the invitations, reveals the ingenuity of people who still
needed a good time in a time when hard times were all around. It is an excellent reference tome for report writers. Some of the fiction dialogue is in
a Southern dialect that the ESL student may not want to study until later,
but essays and introductions by the authors offer very rich, traditional
English. Although out of print, it is readily available online.

 Hughes, Langston, and Zora Neale Hurston. *Mule Bone: A Comedy of Negro Life.* **Edited and with introductions by George Houston Bass and Henry Louis Gates, Jr., and the Complete Story of the** *Mule Bone* **Controversy. HarperPerennial, 1991 (1931). 282pp.**

In 1930, two of the leading literary minds of the day—no, of the
century—Langston Hughes and Zora Neale Hurston, wrote a play, a
comedy, about Negro life. What happened after that was a tragedy for Negro literary genius and American theater. The authors had a falling out,
and the play was not seen onstage during their lives. It was claimed that
Hurston told the original story to Hughes and then the two wrote the play,
whereupon Hurston rewrote it and tried to peddle it elsewhere, and
Hughes caught wind of the attempt. This book contains "The Bone of Con-
tention," a short story in three parts by Hurston (which contains strong di-
alects), the historic play (also in dialect), opinions about what actually
happened from many sources, and the remarkable correspondence that
reveals the intrigue guaranteed to grip readers' minds and keep them
looking for clues. This book can be found in libraries, used bookstores, and
online.

Note: A current revival of *Their Eyes Were Watching God* provides a
look at Zora Neal Hurston as a novelist. Available as an unabridged recording. See also *The Complete Stories* by Hurston.

Related read: *Black Boy*, an autobiography by Richard Wright.

Franz Kafka (1883–1924) Collection

Named for Emperor Franz Joseph of Austria-Hungary, Franz Kafka (a Czech-born Austrian), the first child of the upwardly mobile Hermann and Julie Lowy Kafka, was born on July 3, 1883. His childhood was marked by the deaths of two brothers (which he later believed were caused by physician error), being cared for mainly by Czech nannies (representing parental neglect), and writing plays for his little sisters (which they enjoyed). He was reportedly quiet and withdrawn, mostly a reader. He later reported that his very limited religious training was meaningless. Because his father wanted him to have the power language of the time, Kafka was sent to German schools, even though he spoke only Czech, the language of his nannies. But his language acquisition ability is apparent from his surviving writing. He had been writing since 1898, but the severe self-critic burned most of his early works.

In 1901 he graduated from Altstadter Gymnasium and entered Charles Ferdinand University to study chemistry. After changing majors several times, he settled on law, which would not interfere with his mental life. "German literature—may it roast in hell," he wrote in a letter in 1902. But he did master German, using it as the language of his literary achievements. At the university he met and established a very strong bond with Max Brod, a writer who would be his friend forever. In 1906 he graduated with a doctorate in law and began his insurance company career. His first job did not go well, being an interruption to his thinking, but he was eventually put on partial early retirement, which allowed him to work from 8:00 A.M. to 2:00 P.M. and think the rest of the time. This worked well until 1911.

In 1911, he and Max Brod made a trip to Paris, Italy, and Switzerland, during which Kafka discovered his own interest in Yiddish theater and, much to his father's chagrin, formed an association with Yiddish actor Isaac Lowy. Meanwhile, Brod convinced Kafka to start publishing his literary works. Also in 1911, his father insisted that he take over the running of his brother-in-law's asbestos factory, a situation which lasted until it nearly drove Kafka to suicide and ended in the closing of the establishment in 1917. Thanks to Brod, *Meditation*, a collection of short stories, had been published in January 1913.

In 1917, Kafka proposed, not for the first time, to Felice Bauer, as they traveled to Marienbad and then Budapest. But following this emotional commitment, Kafka began to spit up blood, which ended in the diagnosis of tuberculosis, and he took refuge at the home of his sister, Ottla, in Zurau. It was quiet there, and this offered Kafka a refuge from one of his greatest adversaries—noise. *The Blue Octavo Notebooks* resulted. Then he returned to Prague.

Milena Jesenska-Pollak, the wife of one of Kafka's friends, was at offended by her husband's unfaithfulness but enchanted by Kafka's talents. They became lovers. He could, and did, talk to her about his fear of sex, his inhibitions, etc. When she and her estranged husband reunited, Kafka broke off the affair. After Kafka's death, she became his translator.

There were others; Dora Diamant/Dymant must be mentioned. Kafka had a bond with her about Zionism and Hebrew. They shared a low-cost apartment, perhaps only as roommates. With Dora he was the happiest he had ever been. They wanted to marry, but on learning the news that he was desperately ill, her rabbi refused to perform the ceremony. In 1924, Kafka's health worsened, and he moved from one sanatorium to another. On June 3, 1924, he died, leaving a woe-begotten Dora. (Many years later, many of Kafka's relatives, including his dear sister Ottla, and friends were taken to Nazi camps, never to be heard from again.)

It was Max Brod, refusing to burn his friend's writings, who took Kafka's manuscripts to Tel Aviv to be published. Kafka's three novels *The Trial*, *The Castle*, and *Amerika*, published posthumously by Max Brod (1884–1968), were landmarks in the existentialist movement.

 Kafka, Franz. *The Trial*. Introduction by George Steiner. Definitive edition. Schocken, 1995 (originally published in German, 1925). 312pp.

> First his breakfast has not arrived at his bedside. Soon after ringing for service, Joseph K. is s arrested, for reasons he cannot discover. He has done nothing wrong. Then he is released, but must continue to report to court. The stress of trying to untangle the madness is complicated by the strange absences of his landlady, her cook, and his next-door neighbor. It is also affecting his bank job. This psychodrama draws the reader into a vacuum of suspicion and strange behavior. The dialogue, although puzzling in the mind of Joseph K., is very easy to follow, and the events follow one-by-one, like drips from a faucet. This edition has an appendix of passages deleted by the author and an appendix of Kafka diary excerpts.

 Kafka, Franz. *The Complete Stories*, 1995 (1937). 512pp.

> This book has all of Kafka's fictional works except his novels. His trademark, "The Metamorphosis," is surrounded by less well-known tales, some of which were only published posthumously.

 Kafka, Franz. *The Metamorphosis and Other Stories*. Translated and edited by Stanley Corngold. Bantam Books, 1972. 201pp.

> The classic "Metamorphosis" (first published in 1915) is the cornerstone of Kafka's tongue-in-cheek portraits of fantastic but almost believable tales. Gregor Samsa awakens one morning unable to get up from his bed to get ready for work, not that he ever really wanted to do such a thing

before. It comes quickly to his attention and then to the attention of his entire family that overnight he has become a beetle. His real metamorphosis does not begin until after this transformation has taken place. His family also undergoes changes as Gregor goes from self-pity to defiance to resentment to resignation. Each page reveals a bit more of the human qualities we all possess, and Gregor's story builds right up to the very surprising ending.

Note: The first 58 pages of this edition are the story text. Pages 59–201 are critical analysis, biographies, and a selected bibliography. This translation is based on the 1915 German edition in *Die Verwandlung*. There have been other German editions, but the translator chose this one as most likely to reflect the author's intentions. After reading "The Metamorphosis," the reader may want to venture into the other stories in this book: "The Judgment" (better translation of title: "The Sentence") , "In the Penal Colony," "A Country Doctor," and "A Report to an Academy." The book has two bibliographies: one of works by Kafka in English and German, and one of works about "Metamorphosis." The print is small in this edition, so don't be fooled by the small number of pages. The stories are lively and so full of the obvious that they take the reader by surprise. This is not simple reading. Kafka must be read again and again, but his stories are highly thought-provoking and make great discussion starters. For support readers may want to read *The Elizabeth Stories* by Isabel Huggan.

Related read: See also the Stanley Corngold translation of *The Metamorphosis*.

D. H. Lawrence (1885–1930) Collection

D. H. Lawrence was among the most colorful of modern authors, born David Herbert Richards Lawrence on September 11, 1885, in Eastwood, England, the fourth son of a hard-drinking coal miner, Arthur Lawrence, and a middle-class woman, Lydia Beardsall Lawrence—a bad mix for family harmony. She wanted upward mobility for her children. He believed his way of life was good enough. They fought, providing early grist for the mill of their son's most famous—some call it Freudian—clearly autobiographical work, *Sons and Lovers*. Young Lawrence suffered from bronchitis from the first few days of his life until its end. Perhaps because of his physical weakness, in stark contrast to his robust, athletic brothers, Ernest and George, he was more often found playing with girls than boys. As a result, he was the object of relentless bullying.

At age 13, in 1898, Lawrence won a scholarship to Nottingham High School and graduated at age 15. Then he went to work in a factory in Nottingham, where his physical condition worsened, and he was unable to establish a social life. In 1901 he met Jessie Chambers, who eventually became his collaborator and critic and submitted his works for competition (under her name) and publication. She is believed to be the model for Miriam in *Sons and Lovers*. Also in 1901, his 23-year-old brother, Ernest, died of pneumonia, causing his mother, already Lawrence's greatest emotional support, to become overly protective.

Lawrence began working as a pupil-teacher, writing secretly. Having come in first in the King's Scholarship Exam of 1904, in 1906 he was able to get a scholarship to Nottingham University College, where he earned a teaching certificate, then moved to Davidson Road School in south London.

Lawrence's *The White Peacock* was published on January 19, 1911, just after is mother's death. Through this work, Lawrence met Ezra Pound, H. G. Wells, William Butler Yeats, and other mainstream literary figures.

In February 1912 he published *The Trespasser*, about adultery. In March 1912 he met Frieda Weakley, the wife of his former languages professor, who was six years his senior. In May Lawrence and Frieda (abandoning her husband and three children) ran away to Germany, her homeland. Then came *Sons and Lovers* (1913) and *The Prussian Officer and Other Stories* (1914). Lawrenced married Frieda Weakley after she was divorced, intending to live with her in Italy, and eventually they would live in Italy, Germany, Ceylon, Australia, New Zealand, Tahiti, the French Riviera, Mexico, and Taos, New Mexico, where he planned a utopian artists' colony. But the newlyweds had a difficult time. World War I broke out, preventing a move to Italy. His book *The Rainbow* was banned. Much intrigue followed the couple, and Lawrence was arrested as a spy, obtaining release through his aristocratic father-in-law's connections.

In 1917, two collection of poems, *Look! We Have Come Through* and *Twilight in Italy*, were published, and the couple moved across the continent making many influential friends. Lawrence resumed his old hobby of painting in 1926, and his London showing was raided. A book of poems, including a dirty ditty about book banning, was censored.

Though deeply spiritual, Lawrence did not care for the simplistic and rigid institutes of his day, and said so. His iconoclastic notions about puritanism, sexual mores, and mediocrity proved to be the very fiber of his writing and served to keep the author at the center of controversy. Sexuality and mysticism were to him natural outlets for human beings oppressed by an industrialized society, perhaps reflecting his friendships with Aldous Huxley (who edited Lawrence's book of letters in 1932) and Katherine Mansfield. Philosophy, however, was not an accepted excuse for obscenity, and his work was occasionally banned.

At the age of 44, wracked with tuberculosis, and with Aldous and Maria Huxley by his side, Lawrence died on March 2, 1930. Drama and dissention followed him beyond the grave. Several of his followers and admirers wrote conflicting memoirs about him. *Lady Chatterly's Lover* (1928), banned in the United Kingdom until 1960, caused the publisher

Penguin to be prosecuted (but acquitted) under the Obscene Publications Act of 1959. *Lady* was used in the 1960s as a test case regarding what was literature and what was obscenity. The color and intrigue of Lawrence's own life at least equaled, if it did not overshadow, the situations in his ever-controversial works.

Note: Lawrence's works are available in many formats in public libraries, small independent bookstores, and mainstream bookstores. The Dover Thrift editions use smaller print and narrower margins than many, but now offer many AFFORDABLE Lawrence titles, including *Lady Chatterley's Lover, Sons and Lovers,; Selected Short Stories,* and *Snake and Other Poems.* New audio editions appear frequently. Just be sure to demand an unabridged version.

 Lawrence, D. H. *The Selected Letters of D. H. Lawrence.* **Edited by James T. Boulton. Cambridge University Press, 2000. 566pp.**

Here is a rich collection of short passages, perfect for short reading times and discussion starters. The letters selected by Boulton are sorted into seven sections: "The Formative Years, 1885–1913"; "*The Rainbow* and *Women in Love*, 1913–1916"; "Cornwall and Italy, 1916–1921"; "Eastwards to the New World, 1921–1924"; "New Mexico, Mexico and Italy, 1914–1927"; "Europe and *Lady Chatterley's Lover,* 1927–1928"; "Decline and Death, 1928–1930." The first section opens with a one-page chronology of Lawrence's life during the period. The letters include a very formal solicitation for employment as a junior clerk; a letter to Louise Burrows requesting help in getting around some submission rules; and a thank you note to the Reverend Robert Reid, in which Lawrence launches into a very serious discussion about religion. Footnotes provide the reader with topic insights and follow-up on what happened next. An index allows the reader to scan for topics and titles of interest or particular recipient names. Historic illustrations are clustered. This is a great little book for learning letter etiquette and conversational language.

 Lawrence, D. H. *Selected Short Stories.* **Dover Thrift Editions, 1993. 128pp.**

These seven stories focus on erotic notions that riled the sensitivities of censors in Lawrence's time. "The Prussian Officer," "Daughters of the Vicar," "Second Best," "The Shadow in the Rose Garden," "The White Stocking," "The Christening," and "Odour of Chrysanthemums" reveal a captain's unspeakable imaginings about his young orderly and the humiliation of illegitimate birth. These clearly written views of early twentieth-century mores are not appropriate for the faint of heart.

Blaisdell, Bob, ed. *Snake and Other Poems.* **Dover Thrift Editions, 1999. 64pp.**

This collection includes "A Collier's Wife," "Humiliation," and "Fireflies in the Corn." These easy-to-follow statements about physical attraction and emotion offer a smooth introduction to poetry for the mature adult.

 Lawrence, D. H. *Lady Chatterley's Lover.* **Grove Press, 1959 (1928). 368pp.**

The insecurities and indifference of Sir Clifford Chatterley, Lady Constance Chatterley's affluent husband who was left crippled by World War I, drive his young wife into the cottage of Oliver Mellors, their gamekeeper. Mellors is estranged from his insane wife.

This is a reprint of the book first published in Florence in 1928. The book was almost immediately put on banned book lists on several continents (including this one), and was available in pirated counterfeits. In reply to his censors Lawrence wrote, "I always labor at the same thing, to make the sex relation valid and precious, instead of shameful. And this novel is the furthest I've gone. To me it is beautiful and tender and frail as the naked self is." In response to the pirate editions, Lawrence described one such copy with his forged signature in *A Propos of Lady Chatterley's Lover.* Ironically, that description is now used to prove authenticity by collectors of the Lawrence counterfeits. Today Lawrence's novel is acclaimed as a literary triumph. This beautifully written story remains a gripping tale of tormented relationships. The reader who starts it will finish it. Listening to the unabridged audio is also an enriching entertainment experience that can certainly support comprehension, but reading the book slowly is even better. The language of Lawrence is not difficult, and there are many editions available to choose from. The book can be used for discussion starters about romance, physical disabilities, psychological disabilities, adultery, eroticism, and censorship in literature.

Note: After having read *Lady Chatterley's Lover*, readers will find other Lawrence works easier to follow. Advisors will want to alert readers that Lawrence uses mature themes that have been considered erotic.

Audio version: *Lady Chatterley's Lover.* Books On Tape, 1987. 9 cassettes, 13.5 hours. Read by Richard Brown.

Related reads: Other Lawrence titles include *Aaron's Rod, Twilight in Italy, Women in Love, Sons and Lovers*, and *The Rainbows.*

Lawrence, D. H. *Lady Chatterley's Lover.* **Modern Library, 2001 (1928). 496pp.**

The content is the same as above, with bigger print that is easier on the eyes.

James A. Michener (1907–1997) Collection

Raised by a desperately poor Quaker widow, Mabel Michener, who took in laundry and sewing and stray children in Doylestown, Pennsylvania, James Michener was, by his own account, a foundling who may have been born in New York, on an unknown date, probably in 1907. Although he always had straight As in school, he reported that he'd been suspended from every school he ever attended and twice from college. The reading of Dickens in his home and an aunt's gift of a complete set of the translated works of Honoré de Balzac were the strong literary influences in his life. By the age of 15, he was writing a sports column in a local paper.

Early on, Michener loved classical music and art and Japanese woodblock prints. While still in high school, he began to travel on his thumb, hitchhiking all over the United States, and continued to travel throughout most of his life. During the Korean War, he served as a reporter, and he continued his military connections in Russia and Afghanistan. Exempt from military service as a Quaker, he chose to join the U.S. Navy, becoming a naval historian, work that moved him back and forth across the ocean and led to his first collection, *Tales of the South Pacific* (1947), which in 1948 won him a Pulitzer Prize and became a hit as the Richard Rodgers and Oscar Hammerstein musical *South Pacific*. In 1949, he moved to Hawaii, the source of his first historical novel, *Hawaii* (1959). *The Fires of Spring* (1949), *Return to Paradise* (1950), and *The Bridges of Toko-Ri* (1953) were popular successes. Other historical works include *Caravans* (1963), *The Source* (1965), *Kent State* (1971), *The Covenant* (1980), *Poland* (1983), *Texas* (1985), and *Mexico* (1992). The fictional *Space* (1982) focused on the U.S. space program and exploration.

Michener also became politically active, running unsuccessfully for the House of Representatives in 1962. He did win numerous appointments, and accompanied President Richard Nixon on diplomatic missions.

One of his final works was his autobiography, *The World Is My Home* (1998; 1991). Suffering greatly, he announced that his dialysis treatments were too difficult for him to continue. He died at the age of 90 on October 16, 1997. He had married three times, the last wife being married Mari Yoriko, to whom he was married for 39 years, until her death in 1994. He published more 40 books and contributed over $100 million to universities, libraries, and charitable causes.

Michener, James A. *Miracle in Seville*. Illustrated by John Fulton. Random House, 1995. 109pp.

Magdalena Lopez, the Gypsy fortune-teller from Triana, is dedicated to keeping safe her lackluster but beloved bullfighter brother Lazaro Lopez. The Virgin Mary is determined to assist the rancher Don Cayetano

Mota in his spiritual quest to restore a line of bulls to glory. The American reporter Shenstone has come to Seville, Spain to document the story of the Mota bulls. He reveals the conflicts and the threats and the unbelievable, unreportable miracle that he barely understands. The graphic brown ink illustrations by American *matador de toros* John Fulton give details about the cathedral, the cross-eyed Virgin, and bullfighting that words could not. This beautiful book is one to have. The smooth, round Old Goudy Style typeface is large and very easy on the eyes. Here is the bullfighting story to start with.

 Michener, James A. *Mexico*. Random House, 1992. 625pp.

Through the family lines of American journalist Norman Clay, the history of Mexico from 500 to 1961 C.E. is told within the drama of the bullfight the American has been sent to cover. It is not until the end of the book that the reader discovers Michener has yet another theme up his sleeve.

Three pages of chronology in three columns help the reader keep up with the Palafox and Clay family trees and with the actual historic events that are key to all of Michener's novels. There are also maps on the front and back endpapers. Solid text on every page may be intimidating to new readers. Though clearly this book is a work of fiction, this saga will inform and inspire the ESL student from Mexico, regardless of ancestry. Its length may give new readers pause, but the language is not difficult. For support start with Michener's *Miracle in Seville,* annotated above.

Related reads: Other Michener titles include *Alaska, The Bridge at Andau, Chesapeake, Hawaii, Iberia, Sayonara*, and *Journey*. For another bullfight novel try *The Sun Also Rises* by Ernest Hemingway.

Arthur Miller (1915–2005) Collection

Born in Manhattan in 1915 to middle-class Jewish parents, Arthur Miller did not experience the throes of the Depression in the way that many Americans did. But when the time came, his parents could not put him through college. So he got a warehouse job as a loader and shipping clerk, and negotiated his way into the university, where he did very well. He also wrote plays, one of which won him $1,250. Literary successes followed, until *The Man Who Had All the Luck,* which didn't have any.

In 1956 Miller was obliged to appear before the House Un-American Activities Committee, where he refused to tell who had been at a party where Communists had reportedly been. He was convicted of contempt of Congress. The conviction was reversed in 1958. In 1965 he became president of P.E.N. (Poets, Playwrights, Essayists, and Novelists) and then won a second term. Meanwhile his works were a mix of the political and the personal, with increasingly complex themes. He is best known for his plays, which include *That They May Win* (1943), *The Man*

Who Had All the Luck (1944), *All My Sons* (1947), *Death of a Salesman* (1947), *An Enemy of the People* (1950), *The Crucible* (1953), *A Memory of Two Mondays* (1955), *A View from the Bridge* (1955 and revised in 1956), *After the Fall* (1964), *Incident at Vichy* (1964), and *The Price* (1968). He also wrote short stories and articles. He received numerous honors for his work, including the William Inge Festival Award for distinguished achievement in American theater (1995), the Edward Albee Last Frontier Playwright Award (1996), two Tony awards (1998) for *A View from the Bridge*, a Tony for Best Revival of a Play (1999), and the Jerusalem Prize (2003).

 Miller, Arthur, and Serge Toubiana. *The Misfits: Story of a Shoot.* **Phaidon, 2000. 192pp.**

This is a book for readers interested in filmmaking, scriptwriting, movies, movie stars, Marilyn Monroe, or *The Misfits*. It is cinematic history told from the inside through the pen of a literary great. It contains three sections: "Something Burning Up," an interview with Arthur Miller by Serge Toubiana, brief questions with answers from the heart in simple, straightforward answers; "Black Desert, White Desert," an essay by Serge Toubiana; and "The Shoot," a picture essay by Magnum Photographers. Small, but very clear, print is double spaced throughout, telling about the making of the movie *The Misfits*, the script Arthur Miller wrote as a gift for his then wife, actress Marilyn Monroe. He intended it as a gift for her, giving her the director of her dreams, John Huston, and a chance for her to have a dramatic role, but by the time the film was finished, their marriage had disintegrated.

Black-and-white photographs of Marilyn Monroe, Clark Gable, Montgomery Clift, Elliott Erwitt, Ernst Haas, John Huston, Thelma Ritter, and Arthur Miller at the Quail Canyon Ranch appear on almost every other page. Scenes of the horses and the shooting of the horse parts used for close-ups reveal secrets of the silver screen. The one- or two-sentence captions are a book unto themselves. But this text is also very easy to follow as the cast and crew suffer in the desert and on the set.

Clurman, Harold, ed. *The Portable Arthur Miller.* **Viking Press, 1971. 566pp.**

Following biographical notes on Arthur Miller's writings and an introduction are two main sections. Part I, "Plays," includes *Death of a Salesman, The Crucible, Incident at Vichy,* and *The Price*. Part II, "Other Works," includes *The Misfits* [1] (the original story), From *The Misfits* [II] (a cinema novel), "Fame" (a story), "Fitter's Night" (a story), From *In Russia,* and "Lines from California" (a poem). The book concludes with a bibliography of works by Arthur Miller.

In the biographical notes, Clurman says, "In his boyhood Arthur was neither particularly bright nor very well read. He was a baseball fan. He is probably the only man who ever read through *War and Peace* entirely on the subway, standing up. At college he also began to write—plays." This quote makes the reading-begets-writing point. Of special interest to readers here are the two editions of *The Misfits*. The original story is 34 pages long, much of it conversation. The cinema novel excerpt is nearly all dialogue. The original story (pages 447–480) is a compelling read, written in very clear, straightforward sentences. But for support, the reader and tutor may want to begin with the cinema story excerpt (pages 481–494). It is nearly all dialogue and gives the reader a chance to be in the moment with the characters the way he or she would be while watching a movie. This kind of comparison may help the new reader discover how one kind of literature informs another. It also provides a look at the writing process from a seldom observable perspective—the writer shifting audiences.

 Miller, Arthur. *The Misfits*. Viking Press, 1961 (1957). 132pp.

Roslyn, in Reno to get a divorce, is a comely woman who is cast among a group of well-intentioned, round-up and rodeo losers (Gay, Guido, and Perce) who each, in turn, reveals the ways in which circumstances and his own decisions have prevented him from fitting into the lackluster society of the time. This story was conceived as a film and is punctuated much like a play, giving it unpretentious language, lots of conversation, and clear action indicators. The dedication reads "Dedicated to Clark Gable, who did not know how to hate." The Pulitzer Prize–winning work evolved from a short story published in *Esquire* in 1957. Some readers may recall the movie starring the author's second wife, Marilyn Monroe.

Related reads: Arthur Miller's plays include *Death of a Salesman, All My Sons, The Crucible,* and *A View from the Bridge.*

Miller, Arthur. *The Misfits: And Other Stories*. Scribner Signature Edition, Mac Millan, 1987. 240pp.

The title story, annotated above, is available in multiple formats.

 Miller, Arthur. *Timebends: A Life*. Penguin Books, 1987. 614pp.

"Some ten years ago—when I was merely seventy—a certain number of biographers' proposals arrived" and that, Miller explains, gave him cause to contemplate his mortality. So he began to work on this monumental account of his life and much of the history of the United States during the twentieth century. His stories of growing up in Harlem and Brooklyn, the Great Depression, a Jewish perspective on World War II, Hollywood, and censorship of the darkest kind as he testified before the House Un-American Activities Committee are delivered philosophically and with wit. This autobiography gives the reader a broad range of first-hand views on the evolution of a writer, his craft, and his nation. Although the book is an easy read, the abridged audio version, read aloud by the author, provides the listener with a three-hour fireside chat that cannot be over-rated. Looking at the above annotated movie book will give more support than is required, but is still recommended for its enriching experience. The clear and detailed index can be used as a guide to topic sorting and index use. Of particular interest to readers of the *Misfits* texts may be the many places in the book where both *Misfits* and Marilyn Monroe appear.

Audio version: *Timebends: A Life*. Abridged. Penguin Audio, 1995. 2 cassettes, 3 hours. Read by the author.

Pablo Neruda (1904–1973) Collection

Neftali Ricardo Reyes Basoalto was born on July 12, 1904, in Parral, Chile, to Jose del Carmen Reyes Morales, a railway worker, and Rosa Basoalto de Reyes, a teacher. His mother died of tuberculosis shortly thereafter, and his father moved to Temuco, where Neruda spent most of his childhood. His father later married Trinidad Candia Malverde. At 10, the boy began to write poetry. Years later, during a Nobel acceptance speech, he would credit the works of Walt Whitman as his greatest influence. It was in Temuco that the 13-year-old met Gabriela Mistral, who fostered his writing ambitions. In honor of the Czechoslovak poet Jan Neruda (1834–1891), the young writer adopted the pen name Pablo Neruda when he published his first poem, "Entusiasmo y Perseverancia." His first book, *Crepusculario* (1923), was quickly followed by *Veinte poemas de amor y una cancion desesperada*, his most widely read work. At the University of Chile at Santiago he studied French and pedagogy. At 23, he was appointed Chilean consul to Burma, followed by diplomatic assignments throughout Asia and Europe. During this time, he wrote for literary magazines and befriended the Spanish poet-playwright-musician Federigo García Lorca (1898–1936).

Neruda began a series of volatile affairs and insalubrious marriages (which ended only with his romantic encounter with the Chilean singer Matilde Urrutia, whom he married in 1966). And his works took on a political charge when, after the assassination of García Lorca and during the Spanish Civil War, he went to Spain and then France to be part of the Republican movement. *España en el Corazon* (1937) appeared during the same year he returned to Chile. Two years later, Neruda was sent to Paris, first as the Spanish consul of immigration, and then to Mexico as consul general. It was there that he undertook the cumbersome job of rewriting his *Canto General de Chile* into an epic political and historical work, a compilation of 250 poems. It appeared in the underground press in Chile and was soon translated into many languages. In 1943 he returned to Chile, became a Communist, and was elected senator of the Republic two years later. But his protests against the actions of President Gonzalez Videla against striking miners forced him underground and then into European exile. *Las Uvas y el Viento* (1954) is considered an autobiographical account of that time. *Obras Completas*, a compilation of poems, grew with each republication, from 459 pages in 1951 to 3,237 pages in 1968. His permanent home base was at Isla Negra, but his travels continued. *Cien sonetos de amor* (1959, [*One Hundred Love Sonnets,* 1960]) is an homage to his wife, Matilde Urrutia. In 1970 President Salvador Allende appointed Neruda ambassador to France (1970–1972). In 1971, Neruda was awarded the Nobel Prize in Literature, and he is recognized as one of the major poets of the twentieth century. Pablo Neruda died of leukemia in Santiago on September 23, 1973. His poems, essays, and political lectures continue to be published around the world.

 Poirot, Luis. *Pablo Neruda: Absence and Presence.* **Translations by Alastair Reid. W.W. Norton, 1990. 189pp.**

This is a photo-illustrated collection of Neruda poems and memories of friends of Pablo Neruda. Stunning black-and-white 10-by-10-inch images of his home in Isla Negra, work areas, and living areas overlooking the Pacific Ocean, showing many of his beloved artifacts and reflecting the rustic environment in which he chose to spend his time, along with many lines from his poems in English and Spanish, fill the first part of the book—but without pictures of the poet-philosopher. Equally stunning images of many of his friends in their respective spaces, with translations of their memories of Neruda, show the enduring presence of a man who was an icon for social change in his beloved Chile.

In the book, Rafael Alberti recalls a party held in his honor at Neruda's home in 1946. As gate-crashers cooked themselves great quantities of eggs in the kitchen, Neruda took Alberti aside and privately read to him a new poem, "The Heights of Macchu Picchu." The book ends with a section called "Presence," which contains photographs of Neruda in many guises and his poems in English and Spanish as text. There is no contents page and no index, so the reader must wander through, back and forth, discovering gems. However, it is a treasure hunt for the mind. This historic commemorative volume is one to have and to keep.

Related read: *Memoirs,* a 384-page volume by Pablo Neruda, translated by Hardie St. Martin. Farrar, Straus & Giroux, 2001.

 Goodnough, David. *Pablo Neruda: Nobel Prize-Winning Poet.* <u>Hispanic Biographies.</u> **Enslow Publishers, 1998. 128pp.**

Pablo Neruda was a poet early on and became a diplomat of international repute, a personal friend of President Salvador Allende. Then he was forced to go underground, exiled as a Communist. (A fictionalization of his exile to an Italian fishing village is in the film *The Postman,* in which Neruda guided a postman in the art of metaphors and in which Neruda's poetry is used.) In 1971 he received the Nobel Prize in Literature, but the political tide turned in 1973, as General Augusto Pinochet assumed control and Allende was murdered. The poet died shortly thereafter. Now, Neruda is once again revered; his home (which was boarded up and remained so for many years) is open. The volume of his work is equaled only by its simplicity. His connections with such luminaries as Henry

Kissinger, Richard Nixon, and Salvador Allende are touched on in this book. The language is quite clear. Although the story may be a bit too simple for the reader who has come to know Neruda's work, it is a good introductory overview of this writer's life. The language is easy to follow. Historic photos, while not professional-looking, give an additional dimension to the experience. This biography has a chronology, chapter notes, and a reading list.

Related read: Now try Neruda's *Love*, a book of poems in Spanish and English.

 Neruda, Pablo. *Love: Ten Poems from* The Postman. Translated by Stephen Tapscott, W. S. Merwin, Alastair Reid, Nathaniel Tarn, Ken Krabbenhoft, and Donald D. Walsh. Compiled by Francesca Gonshaw. Miramax Books, Hyperion, (1969–1973) 1995. 48pp.

Ten love poems from the 1995 film *The Postman* (a simple postman who asks the great Neruda to teach him how to be a poet) are offered here in both the original Spanish, on the left, and the English translation, on the right. They compel the non-Spanish speaker to try reading that language. Titles include "Morning XXVII/Mañana XXVII," "XV I Like for You to Be Still/XV Me Gustas cuando callas," "Poetry/Poesia," "Walking Around/Walking Around," "VII Leaning into the afternoons/Inclinado en las tardes," "Adonic Angela/Angel Adonica," "Fable of the mermaid and the drunks/Fabula de la serina y los borrachos," "Ode to a beautiful nude/Oda a la bella desnuda," "XX Tonight I can write . . . /XX Puedo Escribir Los Versos . . . . ,"; "Ode to the sea/Oda del mar." These are timeless. A one-page biography begins with his birth in Chile in 1904. Neruda was an accomplished poet by the age of 17, became at once a social activist and exile, and won the Nobel Prize for Poetry in 1971. Two years later he died.

Neruda, Pablo. *Residence on Earth*. Translated by Donald D. Walsh. A New Direction Book, 1973 (1946 as *Residencia en la Tierra*). 359pp.

This collection of poems has the original Spanish on the left-hand pages and the English translations on the right. It is organized into chronological sections with a bilingual table of contents to guide the reader of either language or the learner of each. The English describing commonplace events, the death of a loved one, the rains of May, political events, the destruction of war, and the death of a soldier, is simple, clear, and compelling. This is a book for the serious reader who wants to think and who is willing to shed a tear upon doing so. Not recommended for the very young.

Skarmeta, Antonio. *The Postman*. Translated from the Spanish by Katherine Silver. Miramax Books, Hyperion, 1993 (1985). 118pp.

When the shy son of a village fisherman, Mario Jimenez, gets a job as the Isla Negra postal carrier, his only client is the famous poet Pablo Neruda. The young man hatches a plan to become the apprentice to the man whose mail must come from adoring women and whose love poems suggest a worldliness that Mario would like to emulate, a plan that would win Mario the heart of the sensuous barmaid Beatrice. The naïve young man does catch the interest of the poet and soon has enlisted him as advisor and confidant. Metaphor and poetry fill the pages as the old man and the young, and unexpected others, produce lines that dance. This fictional story, originally called *Ardiente Paciencia* or *Burning Patience* (reflecting on a Rimbaud line), has burning romance, political intrigue, compassion, joy, and heartbreak.

The concept of two men, one a powerful, gifted, accomplished man of the world who becomes unwelcome in his beloved homeland, the other a humble, simple peasant who becomes a solid citizen providing an essential service, coming together in the names of poetry and humanity is refreshing. It inspired the movie, which the new reader may want to watch, too. The equally intriguing real-life meeting of Skarmeta (who himself fled Chile in 1973 for political reasons) and Neruda is told in the four-page prologue, a short story that aspiring writers, lovers, and romantics may want to read for its own sake.

Video version: *The Postman (Il Postino).* Based on the Antonio Skarmeta novel *Burning Patience* (Methuen Publishing, 1988, out of print). U.S. distributor: Miramax Films, 1995. In Italian with subtitles, 1 videocassette, 105 minutes. Director: Michael Radford. Starring Massimo Troisi, Philippe Noiret, Maria Grazia Cucinotta, Linda Moretti. When the exiled poet Pablo Neruda begins to engage the postman of his Italian fishing village in stimulating dialogues, he unwittingly begins a collaboration that fosters the postman's wish to become a poet. This film is enriching in itself. Though fictional, it is an elegant introduction to the famous man's life and work.

Related reads: Other Skarmeta titles include *Chileno, The Insurrection,* and *I Dreamt the Snow Was Burning.*

Octavio Paz (1914–1998) Collection

As a member of the Mexican diplomatic corps, Octavio Paz was privileged to travel extensively, tasting some of the world's richest cultural brews. Always knowing he wanted to write, he did not struggle to climb the ladder of success. He was content to be where the intellectual stimulus seemed great. Then, in 1951, he was assigned to India, and his writing pallet opened up a rainbow never before imagined. He is now a Nobel Laureate. His original works are in Spanish, but there is such demand for translations that we can also enjoy them in English now. Spanish-speaking patrons may already be familiar with his work, which makes it a great choice for presentation in English.

Cowan, Catherine. *My Life with the Wave.* **Illustrated by Mark Buehner. Based on the story by Octavio Paz. Lothrop, Lee & Shepard Books, Morrow, 1997. 32pp.**

Inspired by Paz's poem of the same name, Cowan has created a picture book. While the adult poem contains adult themes, Cowan has written for and about a small boy who discovers a lovely wave and takes it home as a pet. There is trouble from the start. While there are definitely parallels between the two tales, this story is for children. It can be introduced to the adult student just as an example of one literary work inspiring another. It may even become a prompt for writing.

 Paz, Octavio, and Eliot Weinberger. "My Life with the Wave." In *Eagle or Sun?* **A New Directions Book, Fondo de Cultura Economica, 1960. 121pp.**

In Nobel Laureate Paz's story, a man falls in love with a wave that is trouble from the start, requiring special transportation in a water cooler on the train and then protection against those who get thirsty. The tale is awash with parallels to human relationships and with sensuous interpretation. A dual delight. Left-hand pages are in Spanish, with translations on the right. The intellectually charged blank verse will inspire in any language and, as may be seen in Catherine Cowan's work (above), may cause significant variations on the themes as other writers respond.

 Paz, Octavio. *In Light of India.* **Translated from the Spanish by Eliot Weinberger. Harcourt Brace, 1995. 209pp.**

For Mexican readers, this is a journey into the past; for Indian readers, this is a trip into Paradise; for the reader who is neither, a fascinating voyage is in store. Through these pages you will become a Mexican sojourner and an Indian spirit . . . forever and ever. This is the record of two journeys of Octavio Paz as he is led by his position with the Mexican consulate first briefly from Paris and later back for six years to India, where he became what he had been waiting to become as a poet. The language of this mystical pilgrimage is at once very easy to follow and marvelous to hear. Laced with poetic verses from Paz and others who express what he has in mind, it is a fine read-aloud work and presents a vision of India that will cause the reader to long for a ticket and a departure date. It explains much about how this Nobel Prize–winning poet came into his own. This is a memoir, nonfiction.

Related reads: Other works by Octavio Paz include *The Collected Poems of Octavio Paz 1957–1987; Configurations; A Draft of Shadows; Early Poems 1935–1955; Selected Poems; Sunstone; A Tale of Two Gardens; A Tree Within; Alternating Current; The Bow and the Lyre; Children of the Mire; Conjunctions and Disjunctions; Convergences; The*

Double Flame; Essays on Mexican Art; The Labyrinth of Solitude; One Earth, Four or Five Worlds; The Other Mexico; The Other Voice; and *In Search of the Present*

John Steinbeck (1902–1968) Collection

Born in Salinas, California, in 1902, John Steinbeck always drew on the history and people of his immediate surroundings for plots and characters. He sympathized with the downtrodden, the oppressed, and the unsung heroes who did not share his own advantages. Having studied marine biology at Stanford University (without earning a degree), he used his case log for the basis of two books about the Sea of Cortez.

Steinbeck worked as a farm laborer, ranch hand, factory worker, and construction worker. Traces of those experiences can be found in many of his works. *Cup of Gold*, his first book and only historical novel, was published in 1928. He became a war correspondent during World War II. A cross-country trip with his poodle, Charlie, also became a book. In 1940 he was awarded the Pulitzer Prize for *The Grapes of Wrath*; in 1962, the Nobel Prize in literature, and in 1964, the United States Medal of Freedom. Seventeen of his books have been made into movies. When he died in 1968, Steinbeck left behind an unfinished reinterpretation of Thomas Malory's *The Acts of King Arthur and His Noble Knights*. It was published in 1976 with some of his letters concerning the monumental project.

Steinbeck, John. *Of Mice and Men.* **Penguin Books, 1978 (1937). 185pp.**

Two men, dependable, good-natured George and his simple-minded charge Lenny, struggle endlessly to make enough money to buy a home of their own in Salinas Valley. But each time they get what should be steady employment, the eager-to-love Lenny gets into trouble. This time is no different, except that there is a beautiful young woman who took a shine to Lenny . . . and now she's dead. Very easy reading for native speakers of English, more difficult for ESL readers because of colloquialisms.

Audio version: *Of Mice and Men.* Penguin High-Bridge Audio, 1992. 2 cassettes, 3 hours. Read by Gary Sinise.

Steinbeck, John. *The Red Pony.* **Bantam Pathfinder Editions, 1938. (1937) 120pp.**

Robbie's father was a strong believer in responsibility. Robbie had wanted a pony of his very own. The weight of responsibility takes an enormous toll on the boy, and on his father, as the whole town sits in judgment. This short book is full of dialogue and is accessible, even as it brings the reader to tears. This is an excellent discussion starter for topics such as father–son relationships, child responsibilities, parenting, and values.

Related read: Now try Steinbeck's *The Pearl.*

Steinbeck, John. *The Acts of King Arthur and His Noble Knights: From the Winchester Manuscripts of Thomas Malory and Other Sources.* **Ballantine, 1976. 451pp.**

Here is the story of the legendary King Arthur, the background on his wizard guardian Merlin, the tale of the beautiful maiden Guenivere, and stories of many other people who were documented in Sir Thomas Malory's epic *Le Morte d'Arthur.*

Steinbeck tells about his early discovery of the magical spellings in Malory's tale and the profound affect the morality lessons had on his life. "For a long time I have wanted to bring to present-day usage the stories of King Arthur and the Knights of the Round Table. . . . I wanted to set them down in plain present-day speech for my own young sons and for other sons not so young—to set the stories down in meaning as they were written, leaving out nothing and adding nothing." And that is what John Steinbeck did.

This edition includes chapters ranging from 10 to 20 pages or more and selections from letters Steinbeck wrote as he pushed to get this project in order. Even with Steinbeck's clear prose, these fantasies may be too confusing to a new reader who is unfamiliar with the legends. For the new reader and new speaker of English who is just learning about King Arthur, a picture book on the topic from the King Arthur collection in chapter 2 may be a better place to get started.

 Steinbeck, John. *Grapes of Wrath.* **Introduction by Studs Terkel. Viking, 1989 (1939). 619pp.**

The introduction by Studs Terkel gives an insightful dimension to both this book and the author. For the story annotation see the 1940 edition (below).

 Steinbeck, John. *Grapes of Wrath.* **Illustrated with lithographs by Thomas Hart Benton [1889–1975]. The Heritage Press, 1940 (1939). 559pp.**

The wrath of God against the victims of one of the most famous droughts of all time follows one family from the Dust Bowl of Oklahoma down Route 66 and into the labor camps of California, where each temporary job for a grape picker is sought by 30 or more starving migrants. This is a tale of poverty and dignity, human sacrifice and survival, during the time known as the Great Depression. Conversation fills many pages, and the descriptions offer an omnipotent view of the land where no rain would fall. There are many editions of this monumental work. This one is notable for the bone-chilling lithographs that show up every few pages. Although there are not enough to qualify this as an illustrated text, it has images that will stay with the reader for a very long time. The audio edition (listed below) will also support the very new reader.

Steinbeck, John. *Grapes of Wrath: John Steinbeck Centennial Edition (1902–2002).* **Penguin, 2002 (1939). 455pp.**

See the 1940 edition (above) for the story line. This quality paperback edition has a very clear, easy-on-the-eyes font with plenty of space between the lines.

 Steinbeck, John. *The Grapes of Wrath and Other Writings 1936–1941.* **Penguin Books, 1996. 1,065pp.**

Three books—*The Long Valley*, a collection of short stories; *The Grapes of Wrath*, a novel about the Dust Bowl and Depression (NOT a short read); and *The Log from the Sea of Cortez*, a scientific expedition Steinbeck took with Ed Ricketts around the Gulf of California—are presented here along with other writings by Steinbeck in a new, improved form with corrections to the old typed manuscripts taken directly from Steinbeck's own originals. By surface description this is a daunting body of text. It could be. It is also, however, a fine assemblage of short reads (and the paper is quite thin, making it weigh less than other volumes of 1,065 pages). The many short stories provide easy access to read-alouds that are time-tested to be of high interest to the adult audience. Yet Steinbeck is not graphic or gratuitous; he reports the facts and lets the reader interpret the information. This allows sensuous and austere realities to emerge from the reading process. The short stories support longer readings, as does the audio recording. The stories are fine small group discussion starters. Steinbeck's log provides short nonfiction reads for the person with an interest in science. Any reader building a personal library would do well to add this book to the collection.

Titles included in *The Long Valley* part are "The Chrysanthemums," "The White Quail," "Flight," "The Snake," "Breakfast," "The Raid," "The Harness," "The Vigilante," "Johnny Bear," "The Murder," "St. Katy the Virgin," "Red Pony: I," "The Gift, II," "The Great Mountains, III," "The Promise," and "The Leader of the People." Also included in the volume are "The Harvest Gypsies" (the preliminary study for *The Grapes of Wrath*) and "Starvation Under the Orange Trees."

Audio version: *The Grapes of Wrath.* Penguin Audiobooks, 1998. 12 cassettes, 21 hours. Read by Dylan Baker.

 Steinbeck, John. *The Moon Is Down.* **Introduction by Donald V. Coers. Penguin Books, 1995 (1942). 112pp.**

First written as World War II propaganda against the Nazis, this tale describes how occupying soldiers are influenced by the citizens of the unidentified town they occupy. As the moon goes down, the young men's identity as soldiers is less compelling than the call of youth. Romance and war exchange places. Donald V. Coers wrote a new introduction to this book in 1995. It is a remarkable look into the psyche of the conqueror and the conquered and presents a tale of how the best laid plans cannot predict human realities.

Though not a simple story, this is a work that will drive the reader onward. For the ESL student there is a good deal of conversation, but there are many words that are in fact uncommon, making this a great vocabulary builder. Although there is an audio edition of this book, it is difficult to find. For support, readers may want to start with *Grapes of Wrath* or *Of Mice and Men*, or *Under the Blood-Red Sun* by Graham Salisbury. *Moon* also has a list of readings and a list of texts about Steinbeck.

 Steinbeck, John. *The Pearl*. Bantam Books, 1974 (1945). 118pp.

Kino is a poor Mexican fisherman who reveres his beloved Juana, the woman who rises before him each morning to make his meager corn breakfast, the same breakfast that is prepared in every grass hut in his village every morning of the year. And Kino is proud indeed of his infant son Coyotito, his first-born. The family is content—until a scorpion stings the child and the poor family goes begging to a world that doesn't recognize the needs of beggars, medical or otherwise. Kino knows he must provide for his wife and son in an extraordinary way. So on the day when he finds the greatest oyster with the greatest pearl in all the world, he begins to envision an education for his child and a new dress for his wife, unaware that his entire universe has just begun to swirl in an uncharted sea. This classic tale can be found in libraries everywhere, in large print and in keepsake editions. Readers are encouraged to go through the available copies at the local library or bookstore to see which copy feels easiest on the eyes. The simply told story is easy reading, but is best when read aloud well. For support consider the Hector Elizondo audio book interpretation below.

Audio version: *The Pearl*. Penguin-HighBridge Audio, 1994. 2 cassettes, 3 hours. Read by Hector Elizondo.

 Steinbeck, John. *The Pearl: John Steinbeck Centennial Edition (1902–2002)*. Penguin Books, 2002 (1945). 87pp.

For the story line, see the 1974 Bantam edition (above). This centennial edition is printed on a non-slick paper in an easy-on-the-eyes font. If you have a choice, read this one.

 Steinbeck, John. *Travels with Charlie: In Search of America*. Penguin Books, 1962. 277pp.

Having spent a lifetime writing about various parts of his homeland, John Steinbeck came to the realization that he did not really know it. So he configured a truck into a camper (named Rocinante in remembrance of Cervantes's steed), grabbed his beloved poodle Charlie, kissed his wife good-bye, and set out to see America, from an anonymous citizen's perspective.

Elegantly organized, this book is full of great characters and conversations. It shows how the author thought and what kind of man he was. This book is for all Americans, people who want to become Americans, and those who are just curious about Americans. This insightful travelogue is made even more accessible by the unabridged recording. Reading the book and listening to the tape is an excellent small group discussion starter.

Audio version: *Travels with Charlie: In Search of America*. Classics on Cassette, Penguin High-Bridge Audio, 1994. 6 cassettes, 8 hours. Read by Gary Sinise. Actor Gary Sinise has a clear, understandable voice.

 Steinbeck, John. *The Winter of Our Discontent*. **Penguin Books, 1961. 276pp.**

Ethan Allen Hawley, aka Eth, is an unremarkable man. Although Harvard educated, because of a dishonest partner he is now an employee in a grocery store he used to own—and the boss calls him Kid. And although his wife Mary is accommodating, his kids don't respect him. Day-by-day he discovers that honesty has not been a beneficial policy for him. Then he has a chance to make some money: a bribe. He will have to cheat his boss. When one part of his set of values slides, everything else must compensate accordingly, which is Steinbeck's point. A matter of plagiarism involving his son's essay, "Why I Love America," further clouds the black-and-white issues of a once-simple life. Reading Steinbeck's *The Pearl* or *The Red Pony* will provide background knowledge that will make this text accessible. Discussion topics supported by this book include plagiarism and family time.

 Steinbeck, Elaine A., and Robert Wallsten, eds. *Steinbeck: A Life In Letters*. **Viking Press, 1975. 906pp.**

Because he was uncomfortable talking on the telephone, John Steinbeck chose to write to his many dear friends and acquaintances. As a result, much of his writer's life is documented in letters, collected here and organized in chronological chunks. His wife Elaine has ordered each section with a biographical list of events of the period at the front and explanatory notes for some letters.

One 1951 letter, written upon the completion of *The Log from the Sea of Cortez*, says, "I finished my book a week ago. Just short of a thousand pages—265,000 words. Much the longest and surely the most difficult work I have ever done. . . . Anyway it is done and not quite all a relief. I miss it." Such a message needs no editor's illumination. Neither will the new reader need explanation. The author's lifelong interest in the tales of King Arthur is also documented here (and annotated in the Middle Ages chapter). Yet Steinbeck's clean writing makes this long chronicle of his life at once intriguing and accessible. Although there are no pictures, the margins are generous, and the spacing between letters makes the text easy to look at. The new reader will need help connecting the right letters in this collection with the books Steinbeck wrote. There is an index.

Related reads: Fiction titles by John Steinbeck include *Cannery Row, East of Eden, Tortilla Flat, The Wayward Bus, Cup of Gold, The Pastures of Heaven, To a God Unknown, Tortilla Flat, In Dubious Battle, Saint Katy the Virgin, The Long Valley, Burning Bright, Sweet Thursday,* and *The Short Reign of Pippin IV*. Nonfiction titles include

Bombs Away: The Story of a Bomber Team; A Russian Journal (with pictures by Robert Capa); *Once There Was a War; America and Americans;* and *Journal of a Novel: The East of Eden Letters.* Collections include *The Portable Steinbeck; The Short Novels of John Steinbeck;* and *Steinbeck: A Life in Letters.* Other works are *The Forgotten Village* (documentary) and *Viva Zapata!* (screenplay) See also a new collection of Steinbeck essays, *America and Americans and Selected Nonfiction,* edited by Susan Shillinglaw and Jackson J. Benson.

James Thurber (1894–1961) Collection

James Thurber was born in Columbus, Ohio, on December 8, 1894. Although blinded in one eye by an arrow during a childhood game of William Tell, he wrote well, showed exceptional artistic talent, and achieved academic and social success, even becoming his high school class president. He was less successful at Ohio State University, where military drills dissuaded him from regular participation, though he did write regularly for the school newspaper. His writing was something less than an instant success, but his university days eventually provided anecdotes for a best seller in *My Life and Hard Times,* and the university gave him an honorary doctorate and named a theater after him (posthumously).

The family moved around a lot, and Thurber commuted by trolley, contemplating life in the South Pacific. But his need for oculist and dentist attentions discouraged his pursuit of this as a career plan, so he settled for journalism, reporting and eventually writing a column for the *Columbus Dispatch.* In 1922 he married Althea Adams, with whom he had one daughter, Rosemary, in 1931. He went to France in 1927, where he worked for the *Chicago Tribune.* He and Althea were divorced in 1935. Two months later, he married editor Helen Wismer.

Upon his return to the States in 1929, Thurber had met E. B. White, who introduced him to the fledgling magazine, *The New Yorker,* which hired him as managing editor, from which position he progressed to writer. In 1929 White and Thurber had shared the writing and illustration of Thurber's first book, *Is Sex Necessary,* a parody of modern pieces on the topic of sex. At White's urging, Thurber began to submit drawings to *The New Yorker.* Actually, it was White (their offices were side-by-side) who in 1930 dug some discarded drawings out of the trash and submitted them. Later, Dorothy Parker would write of Thurber's characters in *The Seal in the Bedroom:* "They seem to fall into three classes—the playful, the defeated, and the ferocious." *The Owl in the Attic and Other Perplexities* (1931) was Thurber's first collection of essays from the magazine. The childhood memoir *My Life and Hard Times* (1933) is considered his masterpiece. From 1930 to 1947, his drawings, mostly ink, were well-represented in *The New Yorker* and on six of its covers; in advertising campaigns; and in his own books, including *Men Can Take It* and *Men, Women and Dogs*. Then his sight in one eye began to fail. Surgeries didn't help, so *The New Yorker* flipped his old cartoons and he wrote new captions to them. The good eye began to compensate for the lost one, resulting in legal blindness in 1951, when Thurber was in his forties.

Helen Wismer became his partner in all things, his business manager, his companion, and his nurse. She is credited with his continued success and publications on many topics, including some 30 books, children's books, two collections of fables, a play, and memoirs. Having a photographic memory, he would compose in his head for hours until his wife or a secretary appeared to take dictation.

McCarthyism hit the country and Thurber's mind. His behavior became erratic, making him less welcome at parties and increasingly more difficult to live with. Alcohol abuse was blamed. Then a diagnosis of a toxic thyroid was made, which also explained his irascible moods. Still he wrote, profusely. The theatrical review of his works, *A Thurber Carnival*, in which he played himself, was directed by Burgess Meredith in 1960. *Lanterns and Lances* was published in 1961.

In October 1961, while attending a Noel Coward play, he collapsed and was rushed to a hospital, where a large tumor was removed from his brain. He was never to recover. On November 2, 1961, he died of respiratory failure. His ashes were buried at Greenlawn Cemetery in Ohio. His wife Helen continued to edit and publish his works and collections of his letters. In 1994, *People Have More Fun Than Anybody*, a compilation by Michael J. Rosen of his previously uncollected works, was published for the centennial of his birth. He is unquestionably among the paramount humorists of our time. "A word to the wise is not sufficient if it doesn't make sense."

 Thurber, James. *The Thurber Letters: The Wit, Wisdom and Surprising Life of James Thurber*. Edited by Harrison Kinney. Simon & Schuster, 2003. 816pp.

> With the permission of Thurber's daughter Rosemary, this collection includes love letters Thurber wrote that have never before been published, as well as some illustrations not seen by the public before. The lucid language is guaranteed to give the new reader or learner of English an over-the-shoulder peek at the innermost thoughts of this man of genius.

 Kinney, Harrison. *James Thurber: His Life and Times*. Henry Holt, 1995. 1,238pp.

> Supported by Thurber letters and excerpts from his essays, this biography gives as full a picture as can be had of the peculiar life of one of America's greatest satirists. See, for example, the way in which Thurber

directed his frustration about his own disability at his ever-supportive wife, Helen. The language flows freely and will help the new reader understand the world in which Thurber lived. It is a great commentary on America as well as the subject author. Readers will meet other luminaries such as E. B. White, making them more accessible, too. This book is long, but the passages may be parceled out for discussion one-by-one.

Note: See also the Kinney-edited book of letters, annotated above.

 Thurber, James. *My Life and Hard Times.* **Introduction by J. K. Hutchins. Afterword by Russell Baker. Perennial, 1999 (1933). 128pp.**

"I suppose that the high-water mark of my youth in Columbus, Ohio, was the night the bed fell on my father." (But you see, it didn't fall on his father; it was little James who was in trouble. That fact did not change the story his mother had prophesied.) That is the first line of this memoir containing 10 essays: "The Night the Bed Fell," "The Car We Had to Push," "The Day the Dam Broke," "The Night the Ghost Got In," "More Alarms at Night," "A Sequence of Servants," "The Dog That Bit People," "University Days," "Draft Board Nights," and "A Note at the End." Meet here some of the strangest family members ever collected under one roof. Thurber tells about them all, kinky habits, strange beliefs, and all. These easy to follow, highly humorous tellings of absurd events are written in simple English, appropriate for first and second language speakers. About 25 Thurber illustrations support these tales.

 Thurber, James. *Fables for Our Time and Famous Poems Illustrated.* **Perennial Library, 1990 (1939). 128pp.**

Aesop, Ben Franklin, Poor Richard's Almanac, and Little Red Riding Hood are but a few of the victims in these more than 30 scathing parodies in which Thurber pokes fun at sacred American icons; they are illustrated by the author. ESL students will appreciate the absurdities; all readers will enjoy the trickery. For support readers may want to read the ancient *Aesop's Fables* retold by Ann McGovern and then Arnold Lobel's modern *Fables*.

J. R. R. Tolkien (1892–1973) Collection

The much disputed and denied claims were first made by a British newspaper. On a lark, a reader survey had determined that *Lord of the Rings* was the finest book of the last hundred years. Then other British newspapers and American ones joined the fray, with like findings. And this was when the author had been dead some 20 years. Born to English subjects Arthur and Mabel Tolkien in Bloemfontein, Orange Free State (part of what is now South Africa) on January 3, 1892, John Ronald Reuel Tolkien soon had a younger brother, Hilary. The next year their mother took the lads back to England to await the arrival of their father, who had to get an improved position before relocation. Instead he died of flu complications. Mother and babes then moved to Sarehole, a magical place that eventually became the home of the hobbits. J. R. R. thrived and won a scholarship to King Edward VI School in Birmingham, but he soon lost his mother. According to the wishes of his devout Catholic mother, Father Morgan of the Birmingham Oratory had been engaged to look after the lads, which he did, with positive results. During this time, J. R. R. revealed such a strong interest in language that he began to invent one of his own.

In 1915 Tolkien graduated from Oxford Exeter College with a degree in English language and literature. Then he joined the British Army. While home on leave in 1916, he married Edith Bratt, also an orphan, and promptly went to war. He returned home suffering from trench fever. The first of his four children, John Francis Reuel, was born in 1917. Tolkien then worked on the *New English Dictionary* staff and eventually became a professor of English, focusing on the relationship of Old English to Old Norse, Old German, and Gothic. In 1926, he met C. S. Lewis, who was to become a lifelong friend and powerful literary influence.

In 1937 he published *The Hobbit*, begun as a children's book and later converted into an adult story. In 1954–1955, the *Lord of the Rings* trilogy was published (for adults). Success was immediate in Britain and America. During the 1960s he collaborated on the French to English translation of the Jerusalem Bible and continued to write short stories. In 1968, the Tolkiens moved to the rural town of Poole, not far from Bournemouth. In 1971, after 55 years of marriage, Edith died. In 1972, Queen Elizabeth bestowed the Order of the British Empire on Tolkien. On September 2, 1973, Tolkien died of pneumonia and a gastric ulcer. But his work lives on. In 1977, *Simarillion* was edited and completed by his son Christopher; in 1998, New Zealander Peter Jackson directed a live action adaptation of *Lord of the Rings*; in 1999 New Line Cinema cast *The Lord of the Rings* trilogy; in 2001 *The Fellowship of the Ring* opened worldwide; in 2002 and 2003 *The Two Towers* and *The Return of the King,* respectively, were released. (All three are available on DVD.).

 Tolkien, J. R. R. *The Father Christmas Letters.* **Edited by Baillie Tolkien. Houghton Mifflin, 1976. 48.**

Starting in 1920, J. R. R. Tolkien began writing letters to his children. Actually, the letters are now attributed to Tolkien, but were actually signed by Father Christmas and were posted at the North Pole. Many were illustrated by the author, too. They are loaded with news tidbits about the North Pole, the elves, the Goblin War, and other stories most children missed out on during the years the Tolkien family was growing up. Polar

Bear, key helper to Father Christmas, discovered in Goblin caves a Goblin alphabet. It is reproduced here with the alphabetical translation and a message written by Polar Bear in this odd font. The book was also produced in pull-out form, with reproductions of the letters in envelopes, but this format may be difficult to find. Perhaps this book will inspire readers to write to the young people in their lives.

 Coren, Michael. *J. R. R. Tolkien: The Man Who Created* Lord of the Rings. Scholastic, 2001. 135pp.

Interspersed photographs of J. R. R. Tolkien, places he loved, and people who were his friends and confidants give spark to this insightful story about the orphan who grew up and invented a fairytale life for hundreds of characters, to the delight of thousands. Indeed, this story begins with a report of the results of a survey by a British newspaper referenced in the introduction to this collection.

Here is the tale, chronologically told, of an unassuming man whose life appears driven by hard knocks, an affirming wife (also an orphan), and gifted friends, not the least of whom was C. S. Lewis. Not surprisingly, this is the story of a spiritual quest, through which Tolkien became a devout Catholic and evolved from a position as Oxford professor to writer of the adventures of strange little folk such as Frodo Baggins, who are obliged to take up the gauntlet of truth and discovery just as life seemed to be settling down.

An extensive index, a brief bibliography, and a list of sources will assist anyone wanting to write yet another chapter. The language is very easy to follow. Chapters begin with black-and-white letter illuminations that at times are very hard to read. That aside, the print is clear and the story simply told. Here is a good book for the homeschooler library. Aspiring authors of all faiths and no faith at all will be encouraged by the survival of this unambitious storyteller, who simply followed his dreams.

 Hammond, Wayne G., and Christina Scull. *J.R.R. Tolkien: Artist & Illustrator*. Houghton Mifflin, 1995. 208pp.

With a boundless supply of large and small images, black ink and colored images, idea sketches and full renderings, and works in progress, page upon page of this handsome volume gives the reader a rare chance to visit J. R. R. Tolkien, the artist. Scenes inside Hobbit homes, calligraphic samplers, and illuminated manuscript pages reveal an intense connection between the artist and the writer.

Here is a chance to learn how the artist's ideas evolved and changed, each sketch changing the story and giving new meaning. Story illustrations, book covers, and decorations reveal the mind of a man who appears to have enjoyed going to his imaginary places as much as his readers did. The pages are about 15 inches high and deserve to be turned slowly, each in turn, for a very long time before the reading starts. The small print has lots of space between the lines. The language is not simple or couched in supportive context, except for the pictures and their captions. It is, however, a book that can be opened almost anywhere and enjoyed by almost anyone. Tutors may find that reading passages near pictures of interest to the student will foster an interest in reading the book from which the art is derived. An appendix on calligraphy, an extensive bibliography, and an index that is several pages long promise to support the person who is doing a research paper on Tolkien, his art, or his writing.

 Tolkien, J. R. R. "The Trolls." Excerpted from "The Hobbit" in *The Random House Book of Fantasy Stories*, 271–289. Edited by Mike Ashley. Illustrated by Douglas Carrell. Random House, 1997. 403pp.

Ashley's anthology of 27 stories includes excerpts from three longer works and represents many authors, including J. R. R. Tolkien. This book is out of print and unavailable from the publisher, but it remains a stronghold in fantasy circles and can be found in public libraries, SF and fantasy specialty bookstores, and online. Occasional illustrations; and large, easy on the eyes print; and a range of story lengths starting under two pages make these great bed-time or read-aloud texts.

 Tolkien, J.R.R. *The Lord of the Rings*. Illustrated by Alan Lee. Houghton Mifflin, 1991 (1954). 1,198pp.

Illustrated with 50 paintings by Alan Lee, this is doubtless among the most significant editions of Tolkien's saga to date. That said, one must remember that Tolkien himself was his own first illustrator. The One Ring, crafted by the Dark Lord Sauron and then taken from him, falls by chance into the hands of Bilbo Baggins, a hobbit, who in turn passes the magic ring to Frodo, his cousin. According to a charm, it is extremely powerful: "One Ring to rule them all, One Ring to find them, One Ring to bring them all and in the darkness bind them." The unassuming Frodo must now leave his beloved hobbit to go on a quest though Middle Earth to safeguard the world from Sauron's evil intentions.

This is one of the all-time fantasies, complete with strange names and invented places. It cannot be read quickly. For those who find the size of the book daunting, there are myriad editions of the various parts. Some are elaborately illustrated, increasing the number of pages, and some are solid print, limiting comprehension and pleasure. New editions are published every year, so libraries will have a variety from which to choose.

For those who would like to know the whole story without the thousand-page commitment, the BBC audio dramatization will serve very well. Even if the listener cannot keep up with every detail, the audio recording provides a world of listening pleasure and background knowledge for future reading. This Alan Lee illustrated edition is the trilogy *The Lord of the Rings*. It has three parts: *The Fellowship of the Ring*, *The Two Towers*, and *The Return of the King*, first published in 1954, 1955, and 1956, respectively. It is the sequel to *The Hobbit*, published in 1937. *The Simarillion*, published posthumously in 1977, is the prequel to all of them.

Related reads: Other versions of Tolkien's work are

The Lord of the Rings. Illustrated by Alan Lee, Houghton Mifflin, 2002. 1,216pp. The text is the same as the book illustrated by Alan Lee, only in a three-volume boxed set.

The Lord of the Rings. Houghton Mifflin, 2001. 1,137pp. This edition has the movie tie-in art.

Audio version:

The Lord of the Rings. Blackstone Audio, 1987. 13 tapes, approximately 19 hours, Read by a BBC full cast.

Another Tolkien title supported by audio is *The Simarillion.*

Video version:

The Lord of the Rings VHS is available from Warner Home Video, 2001, with closed captioning. Although this animated interpretation is widely acclaimed entertainment, listening to a powerful reading gives you every word of Tolkien's imaginative work.

E. B. White (1899–1985) Collection

Elwyn Brooks (E. B.) White was born the youngest of three brothers and two sisters on July 11, 1899, in Mount Vernon, New York, to adoring parents, Samuel Tilly White and Jessie Hart White. His father was a successful, self-made piano manufacturer, who had worked his way up through the business. E. B.'s first story, "A Winter Walk," was published in *St. Nicholas Magazine* when he was 12 years old, and he continued to write from then on. Upon his graduation in 1917 from Mount Vernon High School, he was awarded scholarships amounting to $1,000. He graduated from Cornell University in 1921. Then he worked as a reporter for United Press, American Legion News Service, and the *Seattle Times.* His last formal job was when he went to work for *The New Yorker* magazine, where he met and established lifelong friendships with other upwardly mobile writers such as Dorothy Parker and James Thurber.

In 1929, he married Katherine Sergeant Angell, with whom he had one child. He published *A Subtreasury of American Humour* in 1941 while working on *The New Yorker*'s weekly magazine, and wrote a column called "One Man's Meat" for *Harper's* magazine. The *Harper's* columns became a critically acclaimed collection in 1942, which was in print for 55 years, but his book *Is Sex Necessary?*, which he wrote with James Thurber, was a popular success.

In 1939, he moved with his wife and son to a rural spot in North Brookline, Maine. Life among the farm animals gave him ideas for stories, assuaged his occasional bouts of depression, and relieved him of a regular work schedule. *Under the Wild Flag* (1946) was a collection of political essays. In 1959, he published his revision of William Strunk Jr.'s privately printed, out-of-print *The Elements of Style*; it remains in print. He also wrote children's books: *Stuart Little* (1945), *Charlotte's Web* (1952), and *The Trumpet of the Swan* (1970). They, too, remain in print and can be found in audio and video formats. It is for these that he is perhaps best remembered. He died on October 1, 1985, of Alzheimer's disease. He had written more than 17 books of prose and poetry, had won the Laura Ingalls Wilder Award and an ALA Notable Children's Book Award, and was elected to the American Academy of Arts and Letters.

 White, E. B. *Charlotte's Web*. 50th Anniversary Edition. Illustrated by Garth Williams. Afterword by Peter F. Neumeyer. HarperCollins, 2002 (1952). 224pp.

When Fern's father headed out to kill the runt piglet born the night before, Fern raced after him and persuaded him to give the little animal to her instead. That was her entrée into the world of barn animals that eventually led to her friendship with Charlotte, a compassionate, literate little spider, who cared about the forgotten and unloved. Even Templeton the rat found a way to help, when a matter of life and death demanded it. This Newbery Honor book is about individual differences, friendship, thoughtfulness, and the cycle of life, with a message about literacy that drifts subliminally across the pages. This story appeals to people of all ages. Though Fern is a little girl, Charlotte is a mature spider. It is guaranteed to grip the heartstrings, deliver peals of laughter, and leave behind thoughts about life and values.

Audio version: *Charlotte's Web.* Listening Library, 1991. 3 cassettes, 3.5 hours. Read by E. B. White.

Related read: *Stuart Little* is a spoof on bigotry. A couple adopts Stuart, a mouse, because their son wants a little brother. Because he is a different species, Stuart is confronted by an unwelcoming sibling, a lecherous family cat, and mousenappers hired to get the little mouse out of the picture. Stuart Little is featured in a TriStar home video of the Columbia movie of the same name.

 White, E. B. *The Second Tree from the Corner*. Perennial Library, Harper & Row, 1984 (1954). 239pp.

Two open letters in this collection of essays, short stories, letters, and other previously published pieces will be of particular interest to the reader of other people's correspondence. The first is to The American Society for the Prevention of Cruelty to Animals; the other is to the IRS. Though the name E. B. White may conjure either thoughts of his academic literary guide *Elements of Style* or the timeless spider tale *Charlotte's Web*, the reader may also delight in these diverse offerings. Many very short fiction and nonfiction passages in this book, including automobiles, advice columns, health, wealth, family relations, animal behavior, and humor, provide great bedtime reading and discussion starters.

White, E. B. *Trumpet of the Swan.* **HarperTrophy, 2000 (1970). 272pp.**

Unable to trumpet like a natural swan, Louis can speak through a trumpet his father stole for him from a music store. And then, with the help of young boy, Sam, he learns to read and write. He also wins the love of his life, Serena, who is trapped in a pond. He negotiates to leave behind some of his children so that Serena may join him. Through this whimsical story, the reader will learn a great deal about swans, bird flight, and perspective. Here is an integrated curriculum device for literature and science.

Audio version: *Trumpet of the Swan.* Listening Library, 1992. 4 cassettes, 4.3 hours. Read by E. B. White.

Thornton Wilder (1897–1975) Collection

Thornton Niven Wilder and his stillborn twin brother were born on April 17, 1897, to socially responsible, newspaper owner-editor Amos Parker Wilder and the highly literate poet Isabella Niven Wilder, who took an active role in whatever community she was in and even ran for public office, becoming the first female to be elected to office in Hamden, Connecticut. Thornton had an older brother, Amos, and three younger sisters. All of the members of his family were gifted. Isabella infused a love of literature in all her children, and Thornton began writing at a very young age. Their father, on the other hand, provided them with broadening experiences, such as summer farm work, and selected their schools. Amos was appointed U.S. consul general to Hong Kong and Shanghai, so the family lived briefly in Hong Kong and then China, but Thornton went to school in California, attended Oberlin University in Ohio, received his bachelor's degree at Yale, and his master's degree in French at Princeton University in 1926.

That same year, his play *The Trumpet Shall Sound* was produced at the Laboratory Theatre in New York. His novel *The Cabala* was also published in that year. In 1927 *The Bridge at San Luis Rey* was published and won a Pulitzer prize. *The Angel That Troubled the Waters*, a collection of short plays, was published in 1928. Then came *The Woman of Andros* (1930); *The Long Christmas Dinner and Other Plays* (1931); *Lucrece* (1932), a translation of Obey's play *Le Vici de Lucrece;* the novel *Heaven's My Destination* (1935); *A Doll's House* (1937) on Broadway; *Our Town* (1938); and *The Skin of Our Teeth* (1942), a Pulitzer winner, followed by other plays and poetry, including *Someone from Assisi* (1962) and *Hello Dolly* (1964). Thornton Wilder died in his sleep, at home in Hamden, Connecticut, on December 7, 1975.

Wilder, Thornton. *Our Town.* **Perennial, 1998 (1938). 128pp.**

Grover's Corners and its inhabitants go through the simple, every-day experiences of small town folk in three different periods. The play is presented on a nearly barren stage with minimal lighting. Through its simplicity, it earned a Pulitzer prize. This play is often used for school performances and would lend itself to readers theatre presentations. The text is uncluttered and easy to follow, with adult themes such as death.

Note: The unabridged audio version of *Our Town* is available online for digital download.

 Wilder, Thornton. *The Bridge of San Luis Rey.* **HarperCollins, 1998 (1927). 148pp.**

In 1714, a rope bridge near Lima, Peru, breaks, dropping five people to their deaths. The only witness, Franciscan Brother Juniper, seeks out their stories in an attempt to discover whether the event was a fluke or fate. Each life has its own twists of intrigue and wonder, yet it is Wilder's search for the meaning of life that will give the reader much to ponder. The language in this novel is simple. The characters move, almost without options, toward their appointment with destiny on that bridge. For support, the audio reading by Sam Waterston will grip the imagination of readers at all levels. Wilder is a Pulitzer Prize recipient. Great discussion starter about fate/fatalism, values, spirituality, and freedom of choice.

Audio version: *The Bridge of San Luis Rey.* HighBridge Audio, 1997. 3 cassettes, approximately 3.5 hours. Read by Sam Waterston.

Related reads: Other Wilder titles include *La Cabalan; The Woman of Andros; Heaven's My Destination; The Ides of March; The Eighth Day; Theophilus North; Our Town* (a play); *The Skin of Our Teeth* (a play); and *The Merchant of Yonkers,* which became *The Matchmaker,* which became *Hello, Dolly!*

Virginia Woolf (1882–1941) Collection

E. M. Forster said of Virginia Woolf, "[She] gave acute pleasure in new ways, and pushed the light of the language a little further against the darkness." Her primary effort went into her novels, according to her husband, Leonard Woolf, although she kept extensive diaries, which have been published and are readily available at libraries. In the middle of a long work, when she needed a rest or got an idea, she would draft out a short story or essay and then drop it in a drawer. Later, when approached by an editor for a short work, she would go into the drawer, pull out one of the forgotten stories or essays, and polish it up. She mixed fiction and nonfiction efforts together.

A Room of One's Own is very easy to follow, having been first prepared as a speech. *The Years* is a collection of anecdotes, almost like drops in a diary. The significant body of work she has left can be found in libraries, but rarely all of it in any one place.

The impact of Virginia Woolf revisits each generation. The film *Who's Afraid of Virginia Woolf?*, starring Liz Taylor and Richard Burton, was a major work in its own right. *The Hours*, a literary response by Michael Cunningham to her books *The Years* and *Mrs. Dalloway*, is now a critically acclaimed motion picture.

 Felder, Deborah G. "37 Virginia Woolf." In *The 100 Most Influential Women of All Time: A Ranking Past and Present*, 129–132. A Citadel Press Book, 1996. 374pp.

When Virginia Woolf's father died, she moved with her brother and sister to Bloomsbury, where they became central to the formation of the Bloomsbury Group made up of artists, writers, and critics.

Each of these short biographies contains a picture and three-page history focusing on significant contributions. The index also refers to significant social movements and events. The book has both a bibliography and an index that includes those honored and the runners-up.

 Woolf, Virginia. *The Diary of Virginia Woolf*. 5 v. Edited by Anne Olivier Bell, with an introduction by Quentin Bell. Hogarth, 1984 (Harcourt Brace Jovanovich, 1977).

These volumes are largely out of print or are unavailable indefinitely, but they can be found in some general collection libraries, college libraries, and literary bookstores. Any volume for any year (which may show up at a swap-meet or in a used bookstore) promises hours of interesting readings in short passages. When opened, they foreshadow the fictional characters and essays that have become Woolf's published work. Modern readers will not grasp every allusion to current events of the 1920s and 1930s but can still gain significant insights into this author's troubled and remarkable life.

 Webb, Ruth. *Virginia Woolf*. <u>The British Library Writers' Lives.</u> Oxford University Press, 2000. 128pp.

On January 25, 1882, Adeline Virginia Stephen was born to Leslie and Julia Prinsep Duckworth Stephen, a relatively affluent couple, both of whom had been widowed and brought to their union three Duckworth children and one daughter, Laura Stephen. Virginia was the couple's third child of four, and soon became her father's favorite. Leslie was the editor of the *Dictionary of National Biography*. People of letters, among them Henry James, frequented the Stephen home, no doubt providing an influence on the future author. Contributions to the *Hyde Park Gate News*, a weekly family journal produced by the Stephen children, showed the literary promise of Virginia. In 1912, she married a former classmate of her brother, Leonard Woolf, and in 1917 the couple began a small publishing business. However, chronic headaches and other maladies encroached on Virginia's otherwise successful life.

This elegantly presented book has wide margins and lots of space between the lines of type, and delivers images of Virginia Woolf at all ages, along with portraits of her family members and loved ones, copies of her hand-written drafts, and transcripts of the letters she wrote just prior to her suicide. In one note, written to her husband, Leonard, just hours before she stepped or jumped into the river, she wrote: "I feel certain that I am going mad again: . . . I begin to hear voices, and cant concentrate. . . . You have given me the greatest possible happiness. You have been in every way all that anyone could be. I don't think two people could have been happier till this terrible disease came."

A year-by-year chronology from 1882 to 1941 documents the events in the lives of many of the fascinating members of the growing community surrounding Virginia Stephen Woolf. There is a short list of further reading suggestions. There is an extensive index referencing Bloomsbury and the Bloomsbury Group 19 times, and such notables as Quentin Bell, Arnold Bennett, Violet Dickinson, T. S. Eliot, Thomas Hardy, George Bernard Shaw, Ethel Smyth, H. G. Wells, and W. B. Yeats. Woolf's mental illness is referenced 16 times, and her suicide 9 times. If one could read only one book about this author, this is it. It is an excellent choice for reading aloud and topic discussions of feminism, authors, mental illness, and letter writing.

 Woolf, Virginia. *Flush, a Biography by Virginia Woolf.* **Harcourt, Brace, 1933. 185pp.**

For treasure hunters, this little gem of a book is named after Elizabeth Barrett's cocker spaniel, Flush. Although it is definitely about the adventures and tribulations of the little animal, who bore witness to his invalid mistress's life on Wimpole Street and her romance (which led to elopement) with the poet Robert Browning, it is also a lighthearted rendering of the Browning's life in Italy. Perhaps Woolf's lightest work, this book is hard to find, but know what it is when you see it. Woolf's language is never simplistic, but this famous story line of a great love story is easy to follow. For support, start with *The Brownings: Letters and Poetry*, edited by Christopher Ricks.

 Woolf, Virginia. *Jacob's Room.* **A Harvest/HBJ Book, 1950 (1922). 176pp.**

The episodes of Jacob Flanders' life flitter across the pages, never quite demanding a place or a solution to the things that might have mattered. His old volunteer Latin tutor, who wanted to be a suitor to Jacob's mother, sees him from time to time over the decades, but never quite connects, never quite speaks to Jacob. And so it goes with near-connects. The momentum is constant. Things happen.

This is considered one of Woolf's experimental triumphs. The simple, clear language is easy to get through, though some sentences are four or five lines long. The pages are solid print. Readers who just want to get a taste of this classic author may prefer listening to part of the book on tape before trying to read it. A tutor might play passages for discussion topics.

Audio version: *Jacob's Room.* Blackstone Audiobooks, 1997. 5 cassettes, 7 hours. Read by Nadia May.

 Woolf, Virginia. *Mrs. Dalloway.* **A Harvest Book, 1997 (1925). 211pp.**

Though it takes place in only one day, as Mrs. Clarissa Dalloway prepares to host a dinner party, this illumination of the complex cerebral world of Mrs. Dalloway through elaborate flashes reveals her relationships with friend Sally Seton—now Lady Rossetter—and admirer Peter Walsh. In the pre–World War I world before she married Richard, Clarissa's life had meaning. It does now also, of course, but things are different. Mrs. Dalloway is the only connection with the "rational" world of shell-shocked Septimus Smith, a man whose melancholia drives him to suicide before day's end. Almost as a window into her own tormented soul, Woolf allows Mrs. Dalloway to know and understand far more than the people closest to her can reckon. This book also gives the reader a view of members of several classes that have far more to think about than appears essential or beneficial—mind clutter. Yet it is Mrs. Dalloway's stream of consciousness that delivers the text.

For support, readers are encouraged to read the *The Years* to get used to this style of delivery. This book was made into a movie starring Vanessa Redgrave.

 Woolf, Virginia. *A Room of One's Own.* **A Harvest/HBJ Book, 1957 (1929). 118pp.**

To speak about women's issues, most particularly the inequality between the sexes, Virginia Wolf prepared two essays for delivery to the Arts Society at Newnham and the Odtaa and Girton in October 1928. They have since been altered and expanded as presented here. The notion that a woman should have a right to a personal income sufficient to sustain her and a room with a door she can lock against all possible intruders was radical in 1928, as it remains in many places today. Listening to the audio recording while following along will support the new reader. Discussion topics supported by this book include gender equity, women's issues, and writing.

Audio version: *A Room of One's Own.* Books On Tape, 1979. 5 tapes, 5 hours. Read by Penelope Dellaporta.

 Woolf, Virginia. *The Years.* **Harcourt, Brace, 1937. 435pp.**

An extended family interacts, meets, understands who is who, interacts for years and then generations, without ever getting to know one another. No conversation goes uninterrupted. No thought is complete. *The Years* offers a stream of consciousness from one family link to another, without significance.

That said, this is not a boring book; it is a window into our self-consciousness and ourselves. Although it is not a simplistic style of writing, and there are 435 pages, this is not a difficult read. Neither is it compelling. It will not keep you awake at night, but it is an excellent bedtime book. For support, first try *Jacob's Room* (annotated above), another book using the same approach. This will support anthropology and sociology units on families, family values, and time.

Cunningham, Michael. *The Hours*. Farrar, Straus & Giroux, 1998. 230pp.

Starting out with the suicide of Virginia Woolf in 1941, Cunningham's interweaving of fictional characters and the historical figure of Virginia Woolf leads the reader into a mind game that exhibits an intricate understanding of the renowned author and her work. The reader should be likewise informed and inclined. This book is not for the uninitiated. Readers will want to read or listen to several Virginia Woolf works before launching into this one, even in recorded form.

There are three women: Virginia Woolf; her character Mrs. Dalloway of 1923 vintage; and Cunningham's own character, Laura Brown, who is a miserable 1949 wife who is reading the Woolf book *Mrs. Dalloway*. The title of the book is at once an obvious play on Woolf's title *The Years*, but was also the working title for *Mrs. Dalloway*. This is not a book to read in a rush. Neither is it one you can put down for a month or two between chapters. (Though one might well revisit the odd chapter now and again after reading the whole.) It is a mind game that makes Woolf fans insiders as the tangled web of events unfolds. The language is not at all difficult, but the complexities of plot make this a challenging read. For maximum enjoyment and ease of comprehension, read *Mrs. Dalloway* and *The Years* (annotated above) first. The audio edition is a gripping listen, and the video is all the star-studded cast promises, but reading this challenging book after the original Woolf books will make the reader truly appreciate how inspiring these tales can be.

Audio version: *The Hours.* Books On Tape, 1998. 4 cassettes, 6 hours. Read by Alexander Adams.

Video versions:

> *The Hours.* Paramount Pictures and Miramax Films, 2003. Starring Meryl Streep, Julianne Moore, Nicole Kidman, Ed Harris, Toni Collette, Claire Danes, and Jeff Daniels. Director: Stephen Daldry.

> *Virginia Woolf, Novelist, 1882–1941.* <u>Famous Author</u> series. Kultur International Films, 1999. 1 videocassette (VHS), 30 minutes. This documentary uses archival material, drawings, and paintings to present the life and times of Virginia Woolf.

King, James. *Virginia Woolf*. Norton, 1995. 699pp.

Ending with suicide, fraught with emotionally traumatizing experiences including years of sexual abuse starting at the age of six and the death of her mother when Woolf was 13, this biography views Woolf's lifelong obsession with death and her mental illness as conditions that forced themselves out in the form of literary works. James links the author's life—including her intimate relationships with her sister Vanessa and socialite Vita Sackville-West —and her work in a scholarly fashion. Though the text is not difficult from sentence to sentence, the length of this book is significant for any reader. Fortunately, there is an audio recording that allows the listener to get this monumental work in comfortably brief sections. Anyone interested in the work of Virginia Woolf will find this the next best thing to reading her many volumes of diaries and her published letters, and in a way easier. King has read it all and has drawn conclusions that the reader may consider at leisure.

Audio version: *Virginia Woolf.* Books On Tape, 1994. 17 cassettes, 25.5 hours. Read by Donada Peters.

 Woolf, Virginia. *A Haunted House and Other Short Stories.* **A Harvest Book, 1972 (1922). 148pp.**

Here are 18 short stories by Virginia Woolf, along with an introductory essay by her husband, Leonard Woolf, who edited the collection after she died. Leonard reports that some of the stories were published in magazines, while a few were doubtless still in very rough form. The last story, "A Summing Up" references Mrs. Dalloway (of a novel by that name) and takes a cerebral stroll through the heads of the women who are obliged to be present and silently attentive as their husbands talk. Virginia Woolf's fine language is not simple. The words are uncomplicated, but the storytelling is circular. Her sentences are long and seemingly fail to be going anywhere until the conclusion bumps the reader with the point. Yet even as these stories move past the half-century mark, they report human nature with such freshness that they might have been written yesterday. The short stories are a good way to introduce readers to Woolf's fiction. They would make good women's discussion group content. Reading them aloud to new readers will help the students hear excellent writing.

Related reads: Other short works by Woolf include *The Death of the Moth and Other Essays* and *The Captain's Death Bed and Other Essays.* Other fiction titles include *The Complete Shorter Fiction of Virginia Woolf, The Voyage Out, Night and Day, New Gardens, Monday or Tuesday, Three Guineas, Between the Acts,* and *Mrs. Dalloway's Party.* Nonfiction titles include *Roger Fry: A Biography; Contemporary Writers;* and *Women and Writing.*

Author/Title Index

Subject Index

Authors treated as subjects are included here. Works by authors are included in the author/title index only.

About the Author

LA VERGNE ROSOW has been using the classics to foster literacy among adults and children for about 20 years. She is the founder of the Beaumont Library Literacy Program in California. In the United States and Thailand, she has taught English as a second language and English as a foreign language in community colleges and universities and has led teacher education workshops and taught teachers at the university level. Recently she taught English, reading, and social studies in a middle school in Watts, California; TESL education at the University of Southern California; and Teaching English as a Foreign Language at Khon Kaen University in Thailand. She has also been a workplace education program designer and teacher for international corporations.

Currently she is a member of the English faculty and is director of the Teacher Preparation Academy at Los Angeles Valley College in Southern California and continues to provide distance education via the Internet to teachers in Thailand.

She has published the books *In Forsaken Hands: How Theory Empowers Literacy Learners* (1995) and *Light 'n Lively Reads for ESL, Adult, and Teen Readers: A Thematic Bibliography* (Libraries Unlimited, 1996). Her articles have appeared in language and literacy journals, among them the *Phi Delta Kappan, Educational Leadership, The Reading Teacher, TESOL Matters, Journal of Reading, California English, inside english,* and *Tech Trends.*